DATE		
FEB 28'83		
JAN 0 6 1988		
MAR 1 3 1989		

LIVING TO BE 100

LIVING TO BE 100

1200 Who Did
And How They Did It

OSBORN SEGERBERG, JR.

CHARLES SCRIBNER'S SONS · NEW YORK

Copyright © 1982 Osborn Segerberg, Jr.

Library of Congress Cataloging in Publication Data

Segerberg, Osborn.
    Living to be 100.

    Bibliography: p.
    Includes index.
    1. Centenarians—United States.   I. Title.
HQ1061.S42   305.2′6   81–14567
ISBN 0–684–17292–5   AACR2

1 3 5 7 9 11 13 15 17 19   F/C   20 18 16 14 12 10 8 6 4 2

Printed in the United States of America.

Acknowledgments

I wish to thank William Reichel, M.D., of Franklin Square Hospital in Baltimore for his guidance and help through different stages of this project, but I assume total responsibility for the editorial content. I thank Philip R. Lerner, statistician with the Social Security Administration, for his help and invaluable statistics on American centenarians. I wish to thank Dr. Erdman B. Palmore of the Duke University Center for the Study of Aging and Human Development for information about the center's longitudinal studies. I am grateful to Sara Harris and Raymond Harris, M.D., of the Center for the Study of Aging in Albany, N.Y., for helping me in preparation for my research. I thank Robert Frese of the Social Security Administration in Albany, N.Y., for informing me about social security history and developments. Thanks also to Juanette Jernigan, chief of the Social Security Administration editorial staff, for her assistance in providing access to some volumes of *America's Centenarians*.

I am thankful to centenarians Miss Lillian Boehmer; Mrs. Olive Bushnell; Mr. Frank Fingar; Mrs. Katherine Franzen and her daughter-in-law, Mrs. Rudolph Franzen; Arthur B. Grant, D.D.S.; Walter L. Pannell, M.D.; and Mr. Charlie Smith for granting me interviews.

I wish to thank Daniel S. Rogers, information officer at the Gerontology Research Center in Baltimore for his help. Thanks to Joan A. Kearney of the Associated Press for information on several centenarians; to Meyer Zitter, chief of the Population Division, and Dr. Jeffrey S. Passel, demographic statistician, both of the Bureau of the Census for their generous assistance; and to Wayne D. Rasmussen, chief of the Agricultural History Branch of the U.S. Department of Agriculture, for supplying information about the history of farming in the United States.

I thank especially Kate and Maggie Segerberg and also Jennifer Back, Nancy Della Rocco, and Maureen Wills for helping tabulate various items in the questionnaire. I thank my wife Nancy for pieces of her mind, valuable as always. And thanks to Louise B. Ketz at Scribners for suggestions that substantially improved the format and other aspects of the book.

I am grateful to the following:

Academic Press, Inc., and Dr. Nedra B. Belloc for permission to quote from Table III in "Relationship of Health Practices and Mortality" by Dr. Belloc

Albany Times-Union for permission to quote from the interview with Sister Josephine Scanlan

Encyclopaedia Britannica for permission to quote from René Dubos' "The Mysteries of Life"

Grandma Moses Properties Co., New York, for permission to use her photograph at age 100, and to quote from Grandma Moses, *My Life's History*, edited by Otto Kallir, New York: Harper and Row, 1952. Copyright 1952, Grandma Moses Properties Co.

W. W. Norton Company, Inc., for permission to quote from *Childhood and Society* by Erik H. Erikson

The Sciences for permission to quote from "Type A Behavior: A Progress Report" by Meyer Friedman in *The Sciences*, February 1980. © 1980 by the New York Academy of Sciences.

Contents

APPENDICES

Punishment or Glory?

On a sunny, late-September afternoon in Berkeley, Mrs. Constance Oerter sits on a low chair in the living room of her daughter's substantial home not far from the University of California campus. Mrs. Oerter apologizes to the caller for not rising as she shakes hands, explaining that the chair is too low to get up easily. A woman of apparent means, she lives in a private-care home in Oakland, but her daughter comes for her often. "I go riding and visit my daughter, but I don't go out much to clubs and such."

Mrs. Oerter points toward her daughter. "That is the only one left." Her husband, a court reporter for many years, is dead. So are her other three children and a brother. As for herself, "I've had marvelous health." She broke her hip five years ago, but it does not bother her. "No pain at all since it healed."

Mrs. Oerter was a teacher in the same school she attended as a child. "It was my one and only job. I taught three years, then married. I didn't work after I married." She is a sharp-witted woman, handling the conversation with ease. When the younger visitor asks if she had voted in a turn-of-the-century election, she responds pointedly that women didn't get the right to vote until after World War I.

Asked what she does with her time, her reply is blunt. "Well, I just kill it. I wait from one meal to the next."

A moment later she says, "Growing old is a terribly hard thing." She is asked to elaborate. "Because a person loses all his friends. They die and you're left alone." She says this without self-pity; it's just a statement of fact.

MORRIS ZONE IS a businessman who comes from a family of business people. He was born in a small town near Odessa in Russia and was

1

Charlotte
Bonner

educated in Hebrew religious schools. After he left school, Mr. Zone went to work in a tobacco factory that made cigarettes for the czar. That was the only way he wanted to serve the czar. A friendly examining physician gave him medicine that caused such a severe reaction that he was declared unfit for military service. When he came to America at the age of 28 and stepped off the boat in New York City, he kissed the ground.

While the garment industry eagerly sought immigrants as workers, Morris Zone regarded "tailor work" as a low occupation for a person with his background. He moved to Long Island to take a job in a rubber factory in Setauket. In a short time, he was promoted to supervisor. About a year after his arrival, his wife and three children left Russia to join him in America.

The family reunion quickly led to complications. His wife disliked her quiet, rural new home. She missed the gay, busy life she had led in Russia. She tried to persuade her husband to move the family to New York City and a more active life. When he refused and remained adamant, she deserted him and the children to take an apartment in Brooklyn. One week alone with the children was all he could take. He gave up his good job in Setauket and followed his wife to Brooklyn, reuniting the family.

Faced with the problem of how to earn a livelihood, Mr. Zone bought a job lot of rubber heels and made the rounds of shoe repair shops seeking buyers. He was the first jobber of rubber heels in New York City, and that innovative beginning grew into a prosperous rubber-supply business. He now supervises a staff of eight people and mainly concerns himself with sales. He has not taken a vacation in the eighteen years since his wife died. Each weekday he gets up at 5:30 to be at his office by 7:00. He leaves at 4:00 P.M. in order to beat the rush hour and get a seat on the subway.

He says his feet hurt when he stands too long, but that is the only concession he makes to his physical condition. His doctor says he is as healthy as a man of 40. He does not wear glasses, except to read, and can thread a needle without them. Dressed neatly in a trim business suit, he makes an attractive appearance. Mr. Zone likes the company of young women, and his daughter says he has a girl friend whom he calls Tootsie. He thinks this has helped to keep him young.

ALICE SUGGS lives at home with her husband in Nashville. She was born in Lincoln County, Tennessee, the daughter of a freed slave. She had no formal education but was taught by an aunt who was instructed by "her master, who was a school teacher."

Mrs. Suggs's life has been one of hard work and upward mobility.

She was raised on a farm and married a farm worker, a sharecropper of cotton. She did everything on the farm that a man did—except the plowing. She didn't do that because she thought it wasn't ladylike for a woman to be seen plowing with her dress tail "flopping in the breeze."

She and her husband eventually were able to buy a farm, and, in addition to her farm labor, Mrs. Suggs found the time and energy to bear and rear fourteen children. Twelve are still living, scattered around the country. A daughter works at MeHarry Hospital in Nashville; a son is a dentist in Shelbyville.

Three years ago, Mrs. Suggs fell while hanging wash and broke a leg. She is in a wheelchair, "just remembering and watching TV."

CHARLOTTE BONNER is confined to a wheelchair at the Oak Forest Infirmary near Chicago. Her wheelchair is self-propelled, and in it she zips around the infirmary for social calls. Her face appears to have developed the wrinkles and folds that readily accommodate smiling and merriment. Her exuberance and the good humor she produces in others make her popular with patients and staff members. One nurse says Mrs. Bonner remains happy because she accepts life. She does not whine or bewail the fact that she is in a wheelchair, her activities limited.

Although she was born in Chicago and spent most of her time there, her life has had an international flavor. Her father sent her to France to be educated in a convent. She says that "the nuns kept us so busy studying that we had no time for mischief."

Later, she married three times. "I tried three different nationalities for a husband—Brazilian, French, and Scotch."

"Well," she is asked, "what nationality would you tell girls to marry nowadays?"

She waves a hand, exclaiming merrily, "Try 'em all!"

FRANCISCO GUERRA looks the kind of life he has lived. His close-cropped hair is black, except on the sides, where it is white. His lean body looks hard and sinewy, not an excess ounce of flesh on it. His skin, broiled for years under the Southwest sun, is like leather—but malleable enough for smiling eyes and mouth.

Leather was Mr. Guerra's business for many years. He roamed through Texas and into Mexico for the Finnigan Hide Company to procure and classify animal hides. Earlier, he worked with a railroad gang that laid track from San Antonio west to the Rio Grande. He decided to stop at Eagle Pass, where he married the wife with whom he now lives. They had five children. Four are dead.

"I have never been sick a day in my life," he says. "I feel good."

Why? How has he been able to do it?

"I have lived so long because there is a Chief up there," says Francisco Guerra. "Maybe it's punishment, maybe it's glory. I am happy."

THESE PEOPLE share one commonality: All are American centenarians. Why did *they* live so long and not some of their nearly identical fellows?

If one seeks the reason for their longevity from the centenarians themselves, there is a profusion of answers. A good number say they don't know, but even more say they don't know and then go on to provide reasons. William Fullingim thinks he has been able to live so long because "I kept looking ahead and never looked back"; whereas Mary Kimball says, "I kept healthy remembering the past, the good times I had." Florence Shields "made a vow as a girl never to drink anything alcoholic, and I never have. I think that's the secret. I'm sure I wouldn't have lasted as long if I drank." Barney Richards thinks that what keeps him going is brandy, of which he drinks a goodly amount, taking it with water.

"I think," says Leslie Carpenter, "because I eat a lot of fat pork. I love fat pork." Joe Shortridge says his mother told him he would stay healthy if he ate plenty of salt and he "followed her advice ever since I was small." Vincenzina Castelluzzo believes the secret lies in drinking black coffee loaded with sugar. She drinks demitasse after demitasse with several heaping teaspoonfuls of sugar day and night.

Several centenarians say they never thought about living to be 100 years old. A few say they didn't want to live to be so old. And then there is George Crowder. "One day, when I was ten years old, I was picking strawberries on a farm near my home. A little girl, also about ten, was picking strawberries in the row next to me. We got acquainted. When the day was over, I grabbed her by the hand—her name was Mary—and I said, 'Mary, let's make a vow to live to be a hundred years old.' So we made the vow, and here I am."

"Did you marry Mary?" Mr. Crowder is asked.

"No, I didn't. I never even saw her after that. But I'd love to know whether she kept her part of the vow."

WHEN CONSIDERING a large group of centenarians, one is confronted with the range and bewildering variety of human life itself. Despite the confusion and contradictions, this report will try to answer the question put to Francisco Guerra. How *did* these American centenarians manage to live so long?

Bishop
Brantley

CHAPTER 1
Schema

This inquiry grew out of an earlier book, *The Immortality Factor*, a report on aging. For that book, I culled material from a great amount of scientific research, presenting my selections as evenhandedly and as objectively as I could. In retrospect, I began to see that while this fair treatment conformed to wire-service and network-news standards, the reader was left to make a difficult personal evaluation of competing scientific theories and explanations. However, in my own estimation, the implications of one particular research effort grew in importance. This was the Duke (University) Longitudinal Study of Aging, a sophisticated and detailed investigation of 268 subjects during the course of twenty to twenty-four years (see Appendix 3). The subjects were examined periodically for 788 physical, psychological, and social qualities. From this array of qualities, Duke researchers found that just a few key factors could predict longevity, separate long-livers from short-livers. These predictors were more than one-third more accurate in pinpointing years of life remaining than the life-expectancy averages of actuarial tables.

The factors for long life in order of importance at that time* were (1) work satisfaction—a person's feeling of general usefulness and ability to perform a meaningful social role; (2) happiness—a person's general satisfaction with his life situation; (3) good physical functioning; and (4) nonsmoking.

Contemplation of these findings only magnified their contradiction to the conventional way of thinking about aging and longevity: that the aging process is solely biological or physical. This narrower view

* The somewhat changed order in the Appendix is for the completed study.

of longevity has encouraged simpler strategies in order to achieve it; people have been bombarded with diets, for example, as the secret to long lives.

As for the other popular expression of conventional wisdom, that longevity is genetic and therefore the way to achieve it is to pick long-lived parents, the Duke study found *no* correlation between the ages of subjects and the ages of their parents. When I asked the study's chief scientist, Erdman Palmore, about this, he wrote: "My interpretation of this finding is that the main effects of genetics on longevity occur at ages before sixty (when our subjects entered our study). But for those who have survived sixty years, any residual genetic effects are washed out by the overwhelming weight of sixty years of environmental influence."

The first two factors cited in the Duke findings have both psychological and social components, areas ignored in the biological interpretation of longevity. The Duke model for longevity is a much more complex one than we have been accustomed to accept. Finding enjoyable work that one takes pride in and living in such a way that one has a happy personal life are far more difficult to do than popping pills or even running around a track every day. The model does not rule out biology, does not ignore the importance of having a good physical constitution and maintaining health. Rather, the model suggests that longevity is the product of the entire spectrum of one's life, and that limiting factors can originate in many areas even if the end result always is the cessation of biological function. The Duke findings imply that any person who wants to live to a ripe old age must consider the three arenas of human life—the physical, the psychological, and the social. All three interrelated spheres are necessary, none sufficient by itself, to account for longevity.

A way of cross-checking this model occurred to me. That was to match it against an entirely different group of experts on successful aging—not people who had studied it, but people who had done it: American centenarians. Just as Elisabeth Kübler-Ross enlisted dying patients as instructors on the final approach to death, why not turn to the same kind of authorities on extreme longevity? Of course, while centenarians had *de facto* credentials as experts on the subject, they might be unable to fathom the causes of their own longevity or unable to communicate the reasons with credibility.

Nevertheless, if significant numbers of centenarians did give evidence that corresponded with scientific research done on younger cohorts, that coincidence would be persuasive. This is the basic strategy of the inquiry: to measure the statements of centenarians under the lens of scientific findings; to triangulate informal, subjective evidence based on personal experience and intuition with rigorous, objective evidence gained by scientific researchers.*

THE INSTRUMENT for the inquiry is the ten-page questionnaire shown as Appendix 2. Essentially, the questionnaire examines attitudes and behaviors by asking 69 questions that subdivide into 350 items. The questions and their subdivisions are based on the research summarized in Sections II and III of the Appendices. The studies in these sections are given in the order of approximate importance that I initially attached to them, before starting the inquiry. Section IV summarizes research added after a substantial number of the questionnaires were filled out. Section V presents numerical lists and tables associated with the inquiry. The back of the book, then, is for the reader who wishes to examine in detail the scientific and statistical basis of the report.

While statistics do provide structure for the report, they omit the crucial element in an accomplishment as complex and rare as living 100 years. This remarkable longevity is always achieved by an *individual*. Each one is a pioneer, an experimenter, in an area that science does not fully comprehend. There is no scientific formula for living 100 years. Instead, each centenarian had to make individual decisions and find personal solutions while advancing through the maze of living. As much as possible this report focuses on individual human beings and their stories in order to aid understanding what they did and how they did it.

Once the fact is accepted that this cohort of centenarians is not a group in any ordinary sense, that the single qualifying commonality of living a century was achieved by individuals in isolation from one another, then one can begin to weigh the importance of other commonalities as they are ascertained by statistics. If significant numbers of centenarians have adopted a certain attitude or behavior, its pertinence to their longevity is worth considering. The numbers of practitioners serve as measures of the prevalence of certain patterns of living. The report shifts between aggregates and individuals, each kind of information complementing the other. From time to time, pertinent scientific findings are juxtaposed to allow direct comparison between research and what the centenarians are doing.

The questionnaire is divided into seven sections. The first section is devoted to general information common to all the subjects and the

---

* The Bibliography of Selected Readings section of this book lists valuable sources of information relevant to the inquiry.

last section to individual experiences and characteristics. The second, third, and fourth sections explore the three spheres of activity suggested by the Duke Study—social, psychological, and biological.

Other research supports the three-sphere concept. An influential study of aging conducted by the National Institute of Mental Health (NIMH) examined 47 men for more than 600 characteristics (Appendix 4). These traits were grouped in the areas of medicine and physiology, psychological and psychiatric, and social psychological—again the three spheres. When the panel was reexamined eleven years later, 24 of the original subjects had died, 23 survived. Of all the characteristics tested for, just two of them by themselves could indicate correctly in 80 percent of the cases whether the man was a survivor or nonsurvivor. These telltale indicators were "organization of behavior" and nonsmoking. Survivors scored higher in both categories. "Organization of behavior" measures the amount of planning and complexity of daily activities. It is a social-psychological factor. Nonsmoking is a physical behavior.

The three-sphere profile gets support from studies in medicine, beginning with Hippocrates. The father of modern medicine, wrote René Dubos in *Mirage of Health*, believed that "health depends upon a state of equilibrium among the various internal factors which govern the operations of the body and the mind; this equilibrium in turn is reached only when man lives in harmony with his external environment." The newest medical specialty—family practice—is based upon the same tripod. The family practitioner or team of practitioners treats the patient's body but attaches equal importance to his psychological state and his social relationships—especially the strongest relationships, with family members.

In between, there has been the documentation of psychosomatic medicine. Arnold Hutschnecker, a pioneer in psychosomatic medicine (Appendix 10), says, "Body and mind are one." Concurrent with this has been the development of stress research, begun by Hans Selye in 1936. Stress is the body's response to any demand made upon it, the adjustment or adaptation necessary for continued existence. If the challenge is too great, then illness appears. In the 1960s, Thomas Holmes and Richard Rahe devised a way to quantify life events according to their stress value. The death of a spouse they rated as the most stressful event in a person's life. Other highly stressful events are death of a close family member, divorce, marital separation, and a jail term.

It can be seen that the stress sequence begins with an environmental change. The science of ecology shows that the individual's life is governed by and its survival is dependent upon its environment and relationships with other living things. Society is the most important part of the human being's environment, and so it usually is a social change to which a person must adjust. The severity of the challenge can be lessened or heightened by the person's perception of it. The psychological perception determines the physiological response. The suggested common pathway is: social—psychological—physical.

This isn't always the case, however. Physical therapist Josephine Rathbone (Appendix 19) shows that the nervous and muscular systems are so interrelated that physical abuse can produce psychological repercussions such as nervous tension. And, of course, injurious or lethal physical interventions can take place directly.

Anthropologist Vernon Reynolds summed up the three-sphere model at the conclusion of his book *The Biology of Human Action*: "The structure that we have built is of a man whose body and mind are inseparable and both locked within society."

Sections V and VI of the questionnaire are entitled "Order/Discipline" and "Freedom/Independence." This second profile is based not only on longevity studies, but research on the fundamental properties of life. Since centenarians are supreme exemplars of life in our species, they should show a correspondence to these properties.

The decision to include this profile was prompted by the finding in the NIMH longitudinal study that the chief indicator of survival is organization of behavior. I had puzzled over the meaning of this finding for a long time. The concepts "amount of planning" and "the complexity of daily activities" seemed vague, and I could not see why they made such a great contribution to living longer. The mystery continued until I remembered the book *What Is Life?*, by Erwin Schrödinger.

Schrödinger won the Nobel Prize in physics in 1933 for his work on wave mechanics. Later, he turned from his towering vision of inanimate matter to the more difficult realm of living things. *What Is Life?* is a treatise on order and disorder. The natural tendency in the inanimate world is for things to go into disorder and to continue this process until they attain a maximum state of entropy, or disorder, called equilibrium. Living organisms, on the other hand, avoid this rush to decay. An organism maintains itself by, and Schrödinger used this arresting metaphor, "continually sucking orderliness from its environment." The organism does so through metabolism and through disposing its disorder by waste heat. Schrödinger referred to a living being's "astonishing gift of concentrating a 'stream of order' on itself and thus escaping the decay into atomic chaos."

As soon as this fundamental vision of life is transferred to the level of daily human activity, the importance of "organization of behavior" becomes clear. The people who had the higher degrees of orderliness in their lives were the survivors. Indeed, survival in old age can be seen as a struggle to maintain order and to avoid decay and disorder. The death of a spouse and other losses were seen by Holmes and Rahe as stress-producing events; but the death of a husband or wife or the loss of friends and close relatives also can be seen as breaking down the social order of an aged person who may no longer be able to find substitutes. Retirement can mean a drastic change from the regular routine pursued for many years. Bodily ailments not only signify physical decay but can end activities that have brought enjoyment and productivity for a lifetime. In this regard, goals can be seen to orient a person toward the future, causing him to act purposefully in the present. Forced relinquishment of goals along with the other changes threaten both the continuity and stability of a person's life. Unless the individual can furnish replacements and renew the orderliness in the megametabolism of daily living, the disorder mounts to the level that Schrödinger said is death.

Order does not exist in isolation but is associated with another fundamental attribute of life. René Dubos observed in his essay "The Mysteries of Life" in the 15th edition of *Encyclopaedia Britannica* (1974):

> One of the major trends of evolution has thus been the emergence of more and more complex ecosystems, exhibiting high degrees of integration. But, paradoxically, an opposite trend can also be detected as one ascends the evolutionary scale—namely, a trend toward freedom or at least toward increasing independence of the individual organism within the constraints of the ecosystem. Freedom becomes more and more apparent as one proceeds from the protoplasmic jelly of biological beginnings to warm blooded animals roaming in the wild, and finally to man.

If one examines brains on the ascending scale of living systems, one finds the same phenomenon: increasing complexity (or organization) *and* plasticity (or freedom). Nervous systems are absent in the lowest animal phyla, unicelled protozoa and multicelled but loosely organized sponges. Nervous systems are first found in coelenterates—coral, sea anemones, starfish, and jellyfish. The nerve nets are associated with the superior locomotive apparatus of these animals, which need to know more quickly what kinds of environments their improved mobility is getting them into. The nervous system begins coalescing into a primitive ganglion in flatworms and into ganglionic brains in insects. These ganglionic brains are powerful mental instruments, but there is a structural problem. The brain is wrapped around the intestines and there is no room for expansion. The bee's brain has about three hundred thousand cells, compared to the estimated ten billion neurons in the human brain. It was only with the internal skeleton in vertebrates that the brain could attain its maximum development, and the progression of that development can be observed from fishes to amphibians to reptiles to mammals. The first two classes have no cerebral cortex. In reptiles, the cerebral periphery is just one layer thick. In mammals, the cerebral cortex is multilayered and is responsible for the sophisticated mental activity absent in other classes and phyla.

Another kind of progress is observed. Virtually all three hundred thousand cells in the bee's brain are programmed at birth with the instinctual patterns that will form the bee's behavior. It is difficult, if not impossible, for the bee to learn something new, but that's not necessary for the survival of the bee and its colony. The inherited instincts are enough. As one moves from the brains of rats to dogs to chimpanzees to human beings, one finds that more and more of the cerebral cortex is unassigned at birth. This means ever greater potentials at each level to learn from experience or, to put it another way, to have freedom from the tyranny of programmed instincts. Most of the human cerebral cortex at birth consists of unassigned areas that will become organized by the individual's experiences and reactions to life. With our highly organized brains, freedom is an unavoidable part of life.

It may be noticed that what appear to be the same questions or items are repeated in different parts of the questionnaire. In certain cases, similar items fit into different patterns. For instance, the extent of a person's relationships reveal a great deal about the social sphere of his life in one context. In another, the relationships reflect that life's stability and structure. The relationships can indicate how much independence the person retains. That an individual is still working can give information about his or her socioeconomic status, psychological state, state of health, orderliness of life, and states of psychological and physical independence.

THAT'S THE FRAMEWORK. The raw material comes principally from interviews conducted by representatives of the Social Security Administration (SSA) and published in thirteen volumes from December 1963 to 1972. It still is customary for the president of the United States to send a congratulatory message when an American celebrates his one hundredth birthday. But there was a time when the occasion was also marked by a visit from an SSA field agent. Local newspapers

Henry Terhune

were notified in advance of the event, and their coverage invited. The centenarians had to give their consent for the interviews (the name of any individual on the social security rolls may not be revealed without his or her consent).

In the early 1960s, the SSA made an effort to standardize the interviews and collected them as part of a public-relations program. The initial group of interviews was published in four volumes. They were followed by one volume a year, except for the "class of '68," which required two volumes.

These interviews may be a high point of civility in our society. Here are emissaries from a huge bureaucracy taking time to call upon individuals who, from any utilitarian viewpoint, are marginal if not worthless citizens. Yet these meetings rarely are perfunctory. About a quarter of them are illustrated with photographs. Often enough, the social security agent is in the picture with the centenarian. Not always, but typically, the centenarian smiles with pleasure, shows recognition of being feted on an auspicious occasion, acts the cynosure. The much younger government employee exudes goodwill, regards the ancient with a kind of proprietary solicitude, and conveys pride at having a role in the event. Across the gulf of years, generations, experiences, and circumstances, each person in the frozen moment expresses a sense of participating in an event of significance. This feeling of significance comes through in some interviews, but the exact meaning remains elusive and never is articulated.

These cordial encounters were taking place during the years when our television screens and newspapers were filled with images of confrontations by other Americans, their faces contorted with the emotions generated by the struggle for civil rights and against the war in Vietnam.

Beginning in 1973, the Social Security Administration was given a greatly expanded role in disability and welfare programs. There no longer was time or personnel available for frills. Among the casualties was the series *America's Centenarians*. The volumes that were published have become virtual esoterica. Only about 1,000 to 1,200 copies of each volume were issued. They were distributed free of charge to SSA offices around the country, to a few major libraries, and other interested parties. But the volumes sent through the SSA system have disappeared. An official at the Albany, New York, office said the set probably had been thrown out when the unit moved to a new federal building. The SSA office at Manhattan's World Trade Center did not have the volumes, and an official there said that if *his* office did not have them, he couldn't think of a center in the United States that would. I asked SSA headquarters in Baltimore if it would

Agnes Rogers

canvass its offices so that I might have a set on extended loan. Headquarters could produce only four of the thirteen volumes.

I solicited about two dozen used-book dealers, including specialists in Americana and genealogy. No one had ever heard of *America's Centenarians.* I enlisted four out-of-print book-search services. I never heard from three of them, no luck from the fourth. This left the libraries. The New York State Library was missing only one volume, which was on microfilm, but the machine was out of order at the time. I was able to get that volume at the Albany State University library, a microfilm reproduction just above the legibility level. I did locate a partial set in private ownership, but I inferred the owner did not want to let the volumes out of his possession.

I had the feeling of retrieving people who were disappearing into oblivion. To be fair, however, if the volumes were held in little value, it is because they are no more than raw data. The random interviews lack coherence. In order to draw meaning, this extensive testimony had to be screened from an informed point of view, the data codified and the material edited for pertinence and interest. Then the culled and transposed information had to be organized in a way that would make it accessible to understanding its significance. This is what *Living to Be 100* tries to do.

There are 1,135 interviews in the thirteen SSA volumes. One interview was repeated in a succeeding volume. Seven interviews are with people who came to the United States late in their lives. These centenarians are excluded from this report because it could be argued that their longevity stems from their experience in other societies. As research sociologist Charles L. Rose says in "Critiques of Longevity Studies": "Longevity predictors will vary . . . from country to country because of regional and cultural differences." Studies of aged people in Abkhasia are not necessarily valid for Americans. Rose also notes that just as environments change with geography, so do they change with time. The experience of American centenarians born in the 1860s and 1870s is not identical with that of younger Americans. But while not identical, part of the centenarians' era has been shared, and this is as close as contemporary Americans can get to the centenarian experience.

To the 1,127 social security interviews were added interviews by the author, press and wire-service articles, and a few obituaries. The result is 1,200 centenarians, the subjects of this report.

The cohort is composed of 637 men and 563 women, divided as follows:*

---

* See Appendix 21 for greater detail on all statistics given in this section.

Eustacia
Quesada

Race	Male	Female	Total
White	529½	524	1,053½
Black	79½	31	110½
Hispanic	16½	3	19½
American Indian	5½	4	9½
Asian	6	1	7

The earliest birth year is 1838, the latest 1880. Ninety-two of the centenarians were born before 1860. Most of them (859) were born in the 1860s, and the peak year is 1868, when 216 were born. One hundred forty-four were born in 1869 and 98 in 1870, the next two highest years. Sixty-nine centenarians were born in the years after 1871, the last birth year for the social security interviews.

Two hundred twenty-two of the centenarians—18½ percent—were born in foreign countries and emigrated to the United States. One hundred thirty of the foreign-born were males, ninety-two were females. They came from thirty countries, including China, India, Japan, and Korea. Two were born on the high seas. Germany supplied the largest contingent—40. Next in order were Italy with 27; Canada, 25; Sweden, 19; England, 17; Norway, 12; Poland and Russia, 9 each; and Austria and Ireland, 7 each.

Eighty-five percent—1,022—of the subjects were 100 years old. Some of them were interviewed a few weeks or months before their one hundredth birthday. In every case that could be checked, with just one or two exceptions, these people lived past their hundredth birthday. All were accepted on the assumption that one or two months short of the requisite 1,200 months is of negligible consequence. Eighty-four were 101 years old, 38 were 102, 13 were 103, 12 were 104, and 8 were 105. Nineteen were between 106 and 113 years old. This is about the oldest age that will be accepted by scientists and statisticians, since none of these ages can be validated by birth certificates. One subject was believed to be 118 years old, one was 121 years old, another was 122 years old, and the redoubtable Charlie Smith died in 1979 in his 138th year—an age that the SSA accepted as authentic.

Most of the centenarians were married at one time, some for very long periods of time; 153 of them were married two or more times. Nine hundred and seventy-two of them were widowed, 118 still were married, 10 were divorced, 8 separated. Sixty-nine of them had never married and there was no data for 23. Only 5 of the centenarians who married stayed in the wedded state for less than ten years. At the other extreme, 2 had been married for 80 years. Two hundred

Augustus
Stewart

thirty-two were married for fifty years or longer; that is two-thirds of those for whom exact data is known. One hundred sixteen remarried once, 24 remarried twice, 8 remarried three times, and 1 centenarian remarried 9 times. One subject remarried on his hundredth birthday; another married close to it, but whether this was a first or subsequent marriage is not clear. Forty-two centenarians remarried when they were 65 years or older, 21 of these remarriages taking place after the age of 80.

Two hundred five of the subjects never had children. The most common family size was 2 children (156 centenarians), closely followed by 1 child (151). Next was 4 children (123), closely followed by 3 children (119). One-third of the group had 5 or more children. One man had 21 children, 2 of them out of wedlock (and he was the only centenarian to make such an admission). Two other centenarians had greater numbers of children: One man said he had more than 40 children, and another had 38 children evenly divided between two wives. The numbers of progeny swelled through the third and fourth generations, and the man who sired 38 children believed he had 235 grandchildren and great-grandchildren. The number of centenarians with descendants in the fifth generation drops sharply. Of the 945 centenarians who had children (there were no data for 50), 504 of them had great-grandchildren, but only 206 had great-great-grandchildren. And only 4 centenarians were living contemporaries with the sixth generation—great-great-great-grandchildren.

Few of these centenarians were famous. Only three earned international recognition: Grandma Moses, the primitive artist; Edward E. Kleinschmidt, inventor of the teletype; and Eleanor Robson Belmont, a great stage star in the United States and London during the first decade of this century who later married millionaire business leader and horseman August Belmont, and still later became the founder of the Opera Guild and savior of the Metropolitan Opera Company. Nellie Tayloe Ross was the first woman to become a governor, succeeding her husband, who died in office, in Wyoming. President Franklin D. Roosevelt subsequently appointed her the first woman director of the United States Mint. Charlie Smith's death was reported nationally because of his reputed antiquity. One man was a congressman, for one term. And Robert Adger Bowen wrote a novel that was on the best-seller list for six weeks before World War I. Mr. Bowen said that after the war, his analysis of Communist literature for the Justice Department was the basis of a recommendation to Congress by Attorney General A. Mitchell Palmer that the United States withhold recognition of the Soviet Union (the United States did not grant diplomatic recognition until 1933). While Mr. Bowen had a claim to fame, he did not win the recognition he may have deserved.

I personally am a nonbeliever in astrology, but for the fun of it I tabulated birth months and zodiac signs. March and January were nearly tied for the greatest number of births, and February was close behind. August was in fourth place, December fifth. Approximately 31 percent of the births came in the first three months of the year, about 25 percent above average. Pisces was the most popular zodiac sign with 11 percent of the centenarians (the average would be 8.33 percent). Only two other signs were close: Capricorn with 10.3 percent and Aquarius with 9.6 percent. The numbers of male and female births were almost evenly divided in Capricorn and Aquarius, but women substantially outnumbered men in Pisces. No less than 13.2 percent of the women were born under this sign, 55 percent above the average.

Now to compare the 1,200 subjects of this report with the total number of centenarians in the United States. Perhaps the most startling fact about American centenarians is that we don't know precisely how many there are, and it is only just now that we have a reliable ballpark figure. One part of the problem is that births went unregistered in the United States for most of the nineteenth century. New York was the first state to begin registering births, in 1880, but all states did not issue birth certificates until 1920. The other part of the problem is that as people live to be very old their ages tend to be exaggerated. "No single subject is more obscured by vanity, deceit, falsehood and deliberate fraud than the extremes of human longevity," states the *Guinness Book of World Records*. "Extreme claims are generally made on behalf of the very aged rather than by them." The tendency to exaggerate is more pronounced where traditions are passed on by word of mouth.

Guinness is interested in the record lifespan, and the longest one it accepted as authentic in its 1980 edition is that of a Japanese man, Shigechiyo Izumi, who celebrated his 114 birthday in 1979. In second place was an American, Mrs. Delina Filkins of Herkimer County, New York. She lived 113 years and 214 days and died in 1928. In third place is a French-Canadian bootmaker, Pierre Jourbet, who died in 1814. He lived 113 years and 124 days. Alex Comfort, a gerontologist as well as a sexologist, regarded Jourbet as the longest-living human being of record. In the 1964 book *The Process of Ageing*, Comfort wrote: "Birth certificates were introduced into Britain in 1837, so that now any age up to almost 130 years should be authenticable. There is no such certified record over 109 years—though in one instance absence of a birth certificate made an age between 111 and 115 highly probable."

Another reason *Guinness* editors doubt claims of extreme longevity beyond these accepted ages is statistical improbability. The record book says actuaries have figured the odds are that only one person of 2.1 billion could live to the age of 115. An editor wrote that a person's being more than a decade older than anybody else in a population as large as the United States is "statistical nonsense of a very high order." Statistician Philip Lerner of the SSA does not accept an age beyond 114 years. In November 1979, Robert L. Ringler of the National Institute on Aging told Congress that the intrinsic human lifespan is thought to be between 110 and 120 years.

The census of 1880 reported 4,016 American centenarians. The population of the United States in that year was about 50 million. In 1950, when the population was 150 million, the census reported 4,475 centenarians. During the intervening decades the figure hovered around 4,000, dropping as low as 3,504 in 1900. The 1960 census reported 10,369 centenarians; in 1970 the figure shot up to 106,441. Census Bureau statisticians suspected the last figure was radically wrong. A recheck of six enumeration districts in Maricopa County, Arizona, showed that a number of forms were filled out in such a way as to mislead the processing computer to register a birth year in the 1860s. Census Bureau statisticians Jacob S. Siegel and Jeffrey S. Passel believe the 106,441 figure is off by 95 percent, and their preferred estimate of centenarians in 1970 is 4,800. The 1980 form was changed to obviate the computing error, but the number of centenarians in 1980 still is expected to be overstated. The ages are volunteered and unverified; there is no way to check up on or correct the tendency to exaggerate for this age group.

This tendency disappears when age is reported by younger people. If anything, people in middle age are inclined to understate their age for social and business reasons. Most Americans have supplied their birth dates to the SSA long before they come close to the century mark. Congress passed the Social Security Act in 1935. It went into effect in 1937, and the first benefits were paid in 1940. At first the law covered only workers in commerce and industry, but over the years the coverage has been broadened to include most occupations, survivors of beneficiaries, and dependents (including parents), so that today most Americans are registered with the SSA.

Philip Lerner, an SSA statistician, has taken a special interest in centenarians on the administration's rolls, and through his efforts we now have a good estimate of the number of centenarians in the United States. As of June 1979 there were 13,216 centenarians on social security rolls (see Appendix 20). That's an increase of 1,294 over June 1978 and more than twice the 6,200 centenarians who were social security beneficiaries in 1970. Lerner believes the 13,216 figure is quite close to the total number of American centenarians. Seventy-two percent of this overall total are female, 28 percent male. Female superiority in survival can be traced through the stages of life. One hundred and six males are born for every 100 females. After age 21 or 22 in the United States, the female population exceeds the male population. In the age-65-and-older category, women outnumber men three to two. And the ratio increases to better than seven to three by age 100.

In the group of centenarians used for this inquiry, men outnumber women 637 to 563. The reason is that many more men than women were covered by social security in the earlier stages of the program. The percentages of black centenarians and members of other races in the sample correspond closely to the percentages in social security records.

In 1979, when the approximate number of centenarians was 13,216, the entire population of the United States was about 219.5 million. That is one centenarian for every 16,610 Americans.

Because the nation's population has swelled enormously during the years since these centenarians were born, a better way to judge their feat of survival would be to compare their numbers with their original birth group. Approximately 1,524,000 Americans were born in 1879. Of that total, 4,548 survived in 1979; that is one in 335.

Unquestionably, a substantial number of those 4,548 centenarians were born in foreign countries and thus did not come from the original American cohort. About 28.5 million immigrants came to the United States between 1877 and 1930, supplying foreign-born centenarians for all of the important birth years of this report. The breakdown for foreign-born cannot be extracted from social security records, but we know that of the sizeable sample for this inquiry 18½ percent were born outside the United States. Reducing the social security total of 4,548 centenarians by 18½ percent, we get one centenarian for every 411 Americans born a century earlier. Given the state of the art, those are the ballpark odds—410 to one—for these 100-year-olds. The chances of reaching 105 years are one in 2,904. And the odds against the achievement of the 228 centenarians 110 years or older are one in 27,823.

In November 1979 the House Select Committee on Aging assembled eight centenarians, ranging in age from 100 to 112, to talk to congressmen about longevity. *Science* magazine reported that sociologist

Mattie Taylor

Belle Boone Beard told the committee that centenarians show that "one is never too old to live alone, to dance, to hold public office, to handle their own finances, to drive an automobile or even get married." On the other hand, Jacob Brody, the chief of epidemiology at the National Institute on Aging, said that the centenarians who appeared at the hearing "are the peppies." He said there are plenty of lonely old ladies in nursing homes doing nothing. Constance Holden, the author of the *Science* article, observed that some of the "peppies" dozed through most of the proceedings and all of them needed help in addressing themselves to questions. The incident is mentioned in order to make clear the attitude of this report toward its subjects. Disparagement seems a strange and unjustified attitude and will have no place here. Something positive might be said about the fact that the centenarians were able to come from various parts of the country to attend at all—since 99¾ percent of their contemporaries lay immobilized underground.

This report takes the attitude that living 100 years is a difficult feat worthy of appreciation, yet this is not a book in praise of centenarians. The report is not about centenarians *per se*. To reemphasize the point: This report is about how they got that way, how they managed to live 100 years, and what they did or did not do that could have contributed to their longevity.

This book does not look, especially, for record setters. A person who has lived to an exceptional age, even among centenarians, will be noted, but there will be no caste system based on increments of longevity. All centenarians will be regarded as equals whether one dies at 100 years and one week or lives a decade longer. For the purposes of this report, living a century qualifies them all as successful agers. Each one merits consideration.

Other ground rules and caveats. I am not a scientist, but a journalist with some experience working with polls at NBC and CBS. I have tried to maintain a reporter's attitude, to keep an open mind in order to learn from the evidence presented by the subjects. I have not set out to prove something or anything, nor am I a disciple of any particular theory of aging or longevity.

The present tense is used in reporting the interviews in order to preserve the context in which statements were made and feelings and attitudes expressed. For most of us the future is opaque, although it becomes transparent after it moves into the past. The past tense imparts an omniscience that didn't exist at the moment of these interviews. The past tense diminishes the contingency of life, an element that centenarians are more conscious of than most people. When the centenarians spoke their words and thoughts, it was now for them.

The fact that most of them are dead is irrelevant to this inquiry. In the long run, as the philosophical economist John Maynard Keynes said, we are all dead.

Some other things to remember about these centenarians: Unlike most experts in our society, centenarians did not know they were authorities on longevity until after the fact; life conferred their credentials upon them. They are not theorists on the subject; all they know is their own individual experience. As they are not ideologues, neither are they proselytizers. They are not "selling" a product or philosophy. They are not represented by public relations firms nor subsidized by cereal companies. They did not seek to tell their stories; they were sought out.

The interviews with centenarians were supposed to be based on twenty-two questions recommended to the field agents by SSA headquarters (Appendix 1). This format was not always followed, nor were all centenarians equal to the task. I judged that 90 of the interviews—more than 7 percent—were incomplete. Another 133, or 11 percent, were partially incomplete.

There are other limitations to the SSA interviews. Understandably, the field agents scrupulously respected privacy. Sex was a forbidden subject, and no question was addressed to diet, smoking or drinking habits, or the subject's health history. Nevertheless, a fair amount of information about the latter three categories was volunteered or came up naturally during the discussions.

The field agents were not trained as gerontologists, but they were experienced interviewers and investigators. Their reports were usually brief and informal, but their observations were straightforward and uninhibited. The interviews do not compare to the precise, well-thought-out, exhaustive questioning done for scientific studies. The SSA interviews were conducted by hundreds of men and women in one-shot meetings, not by a few researchers who had a good idea of what they were looking for. Also, the questions were not put in such a way that gradations of answers could readily be quantified, as in scientific and public-opinion surveys.

The cohort of 1,200 centenarians compares with 47 subjects in the NIMH longitudinal study, 268 in the Duke longitudinal study, and 800 in the Baltimore Longitudinal Study of Aging (Appendix 8). A typical *New York Times*/CBS News poll is based on 1,468 telephone interviews. *The Hite Report* was based on 3,019 questionnaires returned out of some 100,000 that were mailed out on request. The Belloc-Breslow Health Studies (Appendix 16) were based on questionnaires returned by 6,928 adults in Alameda County, California. *The Redbook Report on Female Sexuality* was based on 100,000 returned questionnaires, but the authors of the report say: "The time and cost of processing all of the questionnaires would have been prohibitive, and would not have produced data that were any more reliable; in effect, we created a sample that was as representative of the original 100,000 as the pollster's sample is of the larger American population. We worked on a basic sample of 2,278 replies and a larger random sample of over 18,000, which we used when we needed more cases for special comparisons."

As this statement indicates, public-opinion surveys are carefully weighted to be representative of the entire American population. A *New York Times*/CBS News poll could boast that "one can say with 95 percent certainty that the results based on the entire sample differ by no more than 3 percentage points in either direction from what would have been obtained by interviewing all adult Americans." The statement adds that certain other errors crop up in the practical process of taking such a poll.

The centenarians were not selected with such demographics in mind, but that hardly matters. The public-opinion surveys, and even the 100,000 *Redbook* questionnaires, add up to only a tiny fraction of 1 percent of the populations they represent. The 1,200 centenarians amount to 9 percent of the population of living centenarians, a gigantic proportion in comparison to any other national survey.

The Hite, *Redbook*, and Belloc-Breslow reports are based solely on returned questionnaires. The statements in them must be taken on faith. Public-opinion surveys are based on disembodied voices at the other end of telephone lines. The Duke, NIMH, and Baltimore studies all examined and interviewed their subjects in person, but only the centenarians were interviewed in their places of residence, where the settings and circumstances of their lives were observed firsthand. Many of the statements made by the subjects could be corroborated visually. If the interviews were not rigorously carried out, they often are revealing through the naturalness of the interactions and spontaneity of the interviewer's reactions. The fact that a great number of people conducted the interviews has a benefit as well. When their reports show convergences, we can be sure that they do not reflect some preconceived mind-set toward the inquiry, and we can entertain confidence that the repetitions are something more than coincidence.

COMMUNICATION OBVIOUSLY IS a key part of any report. In this report there is the information that the centenarian imparts, the information that the SSA agent reports, and the author's judgment of the combined data. Even though the social security interview reports usually are brief, a surprising amount of information can be gleaned from them. We do not communicate by words alone, of course. The centenarian's appearance, his or her setting and circumstances, and former and present occupations can reveal much about the person. When one SSA representative couldn't locate his subject because he was working in a field, while another centenarian was bedridden in a nursing home, we have important indications of states of health.

While some interviews were brief, about one-quarter of the reports are illustrated with photographs—good, as the saying goes, for another thousand words. A trim, dapper man, nattily dressed and standing beside his new automobile bespeaks one level of competence. A person seated in a wheelchair conveys a quite different physical situation. The face of one pioneer farm-woman looks like weathered driftwood. The face of another emits the durable strength that her story confirms. Settings are as revealing as if they had been concocted by a short-story writer. The thousand-plus scenes visited by the field agents all over America are snapshots that tell stories.

Further information comes from the impressions and assessments of the SSA representatives. Their appraisals, while straightforward, may have been colored in some instances by the discrepancy between their expectation and the reality they found. One agent recorded his change in attitude at some length:

"I had many misgivings when I set out to interview Albert P. Davis, who is the only centenarian beneficiary in our service area. In the one and a half years I have been a field representative, I have interviewed hundreds of people in their homes. These interviews are sometimes depressing. This is not surprising, since most field calls are made because of the person's inability to come to the office.

"When I came into Mr. Davis's room, he rose to greet me. This was my first surprise. I introduced myself, and told him why I wanted to talk to him. Mr. Davis graciously agreed to answer my questions.

"I asked him first of his earliest memory. Mr. Davis smiled, and reached into his papers. He presented an article, entitled 'Second Childhood,' to me. I read the article and had my second shock. Anyone who reads it will get some idea of the formidable mental powers of Mr. Davis. His conversation is as well organized as his writing. He never gropes for a word, but always seems to find the one that perfectly expresses his thoughts. His sense of humor is keen. I never had to raise my voice or repeat myself."

As mentioned earlier, some items are repeated in the questionnaire. Discrepancies of varying degrees have appeared in some of the totals. These variances have different explanations, which will be cited for the specific cases as they appear. There are four general reasons.

William Williams

Photo courtesy of Tulsa Tribune

Waldo Putnam

1. Human errors in tabulating that fall under the *New York Times/CBS* News poll caveat "a margin of additional error resulting from the various practical difficulties in taking any survey."
2. A compiler tends to become more sensitized as he fills out a questionnaire. Consequently, he intensifies his scrutiny of the subject under study, so that toward the end he may be more likely to perceive a characteristic overlooked earlier.
3. Two items may seem to be the same, but their wording actually is slightly different, eliciting somewhat different aspects of the same topic. In certain cases, the discrepancies in wording may have been unintentional, but they produced welcome results in delineating nuances of information.
4. Even if items are worded identically, their setting in different contexts influences the assessed appropriateness of the response. There is nothing mysterious about this. An item becomes more or less obvious depending upon what one is looking for. It is a well-known psychological phenomenon that a person often notices something he expects to see but is less likely to see something he is not looking for.

THIS LEADS to the matter of subjective difference. Centenarians are aged. They look like old people, although often several decades younger than their chronological age. It is natural to generalize and believe they are the same as all old people. But most "old" people die in their sixties and seventies. The survivors usually die in their eighties, and all but a very few of the remainder die in their nineties. Centenarians are old but different.

Similarly, we look around us and see our fellow human beings with physical appearances approximating our own. In most ways we act on the premise that we are alike. We can agree when the traffic light is red and stop our cars, agree that two and two equals four, agree that today is a certain day in a certain week in a certain year. We tend to believe that we think alike even if there are some differences of opinions, religious beliefs, and so forth. And to a great extent, we do think alike. If the way we think is compared to that of any other species, then human thinking could be called stereotypic.

And, of course, the members of no other species possess anything close to the human cerebral cortex that makes possible our higher level of consciousness, ability to learn, analyze, think in terms of words and numbers, commit abstract thoughts to memory, and wonder about God and the universe. Because of its specific priority of perceptions and way of thinking, each species truly lives in a different world. This specificity is genetically ordained. The human brain is built from the genetic blueprint and designed to serve, supervise, and operate the human body.

But, as stated earlier, the human brain also has the greatest plasticity. Most cortical areas are unassigned at birth; one way or another, those areas will become organized by experience. This virtually unrestricted potential is—genetically—intended by nature. This marvelous strategy enables us to produce not only workers and drones, but also farmers and engineers, generals and pacifists, poets and scientists, and on and on. Commenting on Vernon Reynolds's *The Biology of Human Action*, cited earlier, anthropologist Ashley Montagu said: "As Reynolds shows, people are—to a great extent—the makers of their own nature. They are not the creatures, but the creators of their destiny." Neurobiologist Steven Rose explains it more clinically in *The Conscious Brain*: "Specificity may lay down the equivalent of identical twins, but plasticity distinguishes them, makes each the sum of his own unique experiences."

The practical meaning of each person's being the product of his individual experiences is that the only interior reality we can know for certain—except, possibly, with the most patient investigation—is our own. The subjective viewpoint, as we all know, is powerful. So much so that it persuades each of us that reality is just as we perceive it—and that everyone else perceives it as we do. Scientists long ago realized the fallacy in this assumption and discarded reliance on the subjective point of view as the way to find and establish truth. Scientists agreed to accept only objective evidence that could be seen by all and win concurrence from everyone (or at least a great many people): nothing less than open experiments that could be repeated, the results publicly retested. Subjective evidence—flashes of inspiration, brilliant insights, depth of feeling—that could not be objectively verified was left to mystics, religious leaders, and creative writers.

The subjective viewpoint has been distrusted for so long that we have all but forgotten that it is valid in one area: as it pertains to the person who holds it. That person knows how he or she feels better than anyone else. Many of us have heard or read about a person who does not feel well and goes to a physician for an examination. The doctor can find nothing medically wrong, and a short time later the person dies suddenly. Such cases are anecdotal. As it happens, however, the Duke Longitudinal Study of Aging in addition to giving thorough physical examinations asked the subjects how they rated their health. The individual's self-health rating emerges as a creditable predictor of longevity. Even more illuminating is a study by Eric Pfeiffer using two subgroups from the Duke panel (Appendix 13). He compared the twenty males and seventeen females who were considered the most successful agers with the twenty men and seventeen women who died earliest, the least successful agers. He sought to find the most significant physical, psychological, and social differences between the individuals in the two groups. He found that self-perception of health change was the second most important indicator in both groups, and that the subject's own perception of health change was superior to the physical examination in indicating how long that subject would live. In short, this scientific study shows that if the values as well as the limitations of the subjective viewpoint are respected, that viewpoint can provide useful information.

FINALLY, AND BRIEFLY, let me add some amplification of the inquiry's method and format. The questionnaires were filled in serially, the information transferred to the appropriate categories from a close reading of the raw interviews. The hope and expectation were that patterns would emerge—and with ever greater definition—as the codified evidence accumulated.

This in fact is what did happen. Some similarities became obvious almost at once, while some patterns were not detected until more than half of the interviews had been processed. The sequence of findings forms the report's outline in general, although all details do not unfold in a strictly chronological manner. To have presented them in such a random and disorganized fashion would not have been helpful to understanding, so related subjects have been grouped together and totals of the finished survey included with each grouping. But, in general, patterns associated with the centenarians' longevity are reported in the order of discovery, much as, during the process of development, images begin to appear on an exposed photographic negative.

CHAPTER 2

Order

The first pattern to emerge clearly from the questionnaire was orderliness. Like an election landslide, substantial entries in the "Order" category of the questionnaire showed up early and never deviated. A pattern of orderliness is discernible in the lives of more than 96 percent of the subjects.

At the same time, it became obvious that a high percentage of these people had lived and worked on farms. This discovery should have come as no surprise, because the farm was the main American home and workplace in the nineteenth century. In 1870 the total population of the United States was 38.6 million, and the farm population was 18.4 million. Farmers made up more than half of the work force. In 1880 the U.S. population was 50.2 million, with a farm population of 23 million, and 49 percent of the nation's workers were farmers. The farm population today is about 4 percent of the total population, with farmers somewhat below the 4 percent level in the labor force.

Seven hundred forty-six centenarians—62 percent—were associated with farms (see Appendix 25). For these people, farm life is second on the list of salient characteristics associated with longevity (Appendix 23). One hundred five centenarians spent their entire lives on farms, while another 229 spent most or part of their lives farming. Ten percent of these 334 farmers were women. There were 68 field workers, 108 farm wives, and 236 centenarians who had spent the first part of their lives on farms.

Farming imposes order. The long hours and heavy work load that certainly existed before mechanization enforced their own discipline upon the toiler. Just as time must be budgeted during the day, work has to be organized to mesh with the requirements of the seasons.

35

Nora Swart

Grandma Moses, who spent most of her life as a farm wife, said that "on a farm the days are nearly all the same, nothing changes but the seasons." The demands of the soil tied the farmer and his family to one location, and except for trips to church, school, and town for supplies, the farm was their world. While the nature of the work was ever-changing with seasonal cycles, the work itself was never-ending, in that there was no natural conclusion to it as in man-made projects. Nor was there an artificial termination, the retirement both decreed and desired in other occupations. Continuity characterizes the farmer's entire adult life. This stability of time and place extended to the family social fabric. All members beyond earliest childhood were functioning parts of an economic unit engaged in survival.

Mrs. Nora Swart exemplifies the many-faceted orderliness of farm life. She was born in Henry County, Indiana, and at age 9 moved to a farm in the next county. She went to school for eight years in a building that once stood across the road from the farm on which she now lives in Elwood, Indiana. When she was 17 years old, she married the boy on the next farm. They were married at her home in the morning, then had a family dinner and went to church in the afternoon. They didn't know about honeymoons.

"I have only moved twice since I was nine years old." The first move, after marriage, was to the home of her husband's widowed mother. Later, she and her husband moved to their own farm, where she has lived for about seventy-five years. In addition to being the mother of one boy and five girls, Mrs. Swart milked cows, made butter, canned beef, and did a variety of other farm chores. Her husband died when she was about 70 years old and she went on farming. She earned her social security benefits in her mid-80s, from the sale of chickens, eggs, sheep, and wool. She kept chickens on her farm until she was 93 years old and sheep until she was 98. She says she would go to the back door of her farmhouse and call, "Come on, girls," and the sheep would come up from the pasture.

Mrs. Swart has fourteen grandchildren, forty-seven great-grand-children and fourteen great-great-grandchildren. She has voted since woman's suffrage and still goes to the polls on election days. Although she underwent a cancer operation eight years ago and her eyesight is failing, she says she feels fine. Her daughters live in the area and take her places and do errands for her. But Mrs. Swart still lives alone on the farm, still cooks her meals, and "I still bake pies when I don't get too lazy."

Salvatore Tarascio also scored highly in the "Order" category, without pursuing farm work. He is a relatively small man, about five-and-a-half-feet tall, trim, neatly dressed in a suit, white shirt, and tie with a tie clasp. His mostly white hair is close cropped and he looks, in the words of the social security man who visited him, "much younger than his age. He is well nourished with no wrinkles [and] with lean, ruddy, outdoor, cold-weather complexion."

Mr. Tarascio was born near Syracuse in Sicily in 1870. He married at age 26, and at 33 came to Winsted, Connecticut, where he lives still. He was a freelance photographer, and six years after his arrival he was licensed by the state of Connecticut as a cinematographer. In 1909 he showed the first motion pictures in Winsted, an event remembered fifty years later in the local newspaper. His principal occupation for the past seventy years has been electrical work.

"My health is very good, thank God. I do not use glasses or hearing aids. As you can see, I can hear and see you without difficulty. My principal devotion has been to my family, my work, and whoever needed help that I could do something for. I am a serene man. I keep busy. Keep regular habits. Three lean meals per day with a glass of wine for dinner and supper. I'm in bed before 10 P.M. and up at 5 A.M. in the morning, busy with my work. I still rewind motors. I also have molds which I use to make religious art work." He adds that "social security is a good thing, but I never received enough to retire on. I have continued to work and my children have helped me."

A widower, Mr. Tarascio lives with the oldest of his five children and her husband. He has seven grandchildren and ten great-grand-children. He attends church every Sunday, is always happy to talk to people, likes TV. He is most proud of a dedication his linguist nephew wrote in the Spanish translation of a book: "Dedicated on

Sherman Evans

his approaching century to Salvatore Tarascio, my uncle, who by example, taught me that the glad will to work is its own reward."

A MORE SPECIFIC examination of the subsections and items will fill in the details of the "Order" category (Appendices 22, Section V, and 26D). The item that scored the highest rating is "organized lifetime activities/goals," a judgment of whether unifying threads of order were visible throughout a centenarian's lifetime. This kind of organization was apparent in 95 percent of the cases. Moreover, even at their advanced ages, 52 percent of the centenarians could be said to lead organized daily lives.

The high ratings are consistent with the findings of the NIMH study that organization of behavior—a high measure of planning and complexity of daily activities—is a prime indicator of longevity. This organization of life really is a synthesis of the other subdivisions in the "Order" category.

The first of these subdivisions, judging its importance from the quantity of scores, is "Work." Eighty-nine percent of these centenarians worked hard during their lives and 87 percent worked a long time. Further corroboration of this finding is supplied by another item under the "Work" heading: "had easy life." It could be positively asserted that only ten centenarians had lived easy lives. Whatever other attractions are associated with a life of ease, living a very long time isn't one of them.

An assessment of the characteristics associated with longevity in each of the lives found that hard work, work, and keeping busy or active are prominent factors for 70 percent of the centenarians (Appendix 23), by far the strongest pattern in the cohort. Twenty-seven percent of the subjects attributed their long lives to the same trio (Appendix 24), second only to an aggregate of moral and religious reasons.

That work is a dominant centenarian theme can be judged in another way: by how long these people worked. With a retirement age of 65, the average work life today is about 45 years. Of the 775 centenarians for whom there are exact or good approximate estimates, 2 percent of them worked less than 50 years while 7 percent worked 90 years or more—double the contemporary work life (Appendix 26A). More than 92 percent worked more than 60 years, nearly three-quarters worked more than 70 years, and about two in five worked more than 80 years.

Joseph Labarge of Cleveland had one of the longest work lives— just short of a century. This is the social security report on him in full:

In November 1959 (he was born in March 1857), when the social

security representative visited Mr. Labarge, he was sharpening his
ice skates, but confessed that he had not skied for the past five or six
years. He was, however, still working as a caretaker of an office
building in downtown Cleveland.

"I was born Joseph Ross," he said. "But after my folks died, I was
put out with some people in St. Joseph, Michigan, called Labarge.
They gave me their name.

"I began working at the age of six or seven, forking out cast iron
skulls from a charcoal furnace."

At 16, Mr. Labarge ran away from home. He sailed on the Great
Lakes for a time, saved enough money to buy a boat, then sold the
boat and used the profits to take a trip around the world.

When he returned from his travels, he stevedored, worked for the
White Motor Co., and then opened a garage which he operated for
eight years. At one time, he was chauffeur for the father of Elsie
Janis, sweetheart of the World War I Expeditionary Force. He also
worked on the construction of the Cleveland water intake tunnels.

On his one hundredth birthday, he went for a ride in a helicopter.
He continued working until just before his death on February 2,
1962—only a month short of his one hundred and fifth birthday.

Part of the reason that these work lives are so long is that, as in Mr.
Labarge's case, children in the nineteenth century began working at a
very early age. Alexis de Tocqueville, the French republican and astute
observer of American life in the 1830s, commented: "In America there
is, strictly speaking, no adolescence: at the close of boyhood the man
appears and begins to trace out his own path." In another passage in
Democracy in America, de Tocqueville says that "nowhere are young
women surrendered so early or so completely to their own guidance."

For members of both sexes in this survey, work usually started at
an unbelievably young age—unbelievable, that is, to a contemporary
reader until constant repetition blots out doubt. Extra responsibilities
and duties often fell to the oldest child. When Berthe Vette's father
lost his health, her mother took over his chores and responsibilities
while Mrs. Vette, the oldest of eight children, became a housekeeper
and surrogate mother. In retrospect, she believes the responsibilities
she was forced to take were too much for her to handle at her age.
At the time, she resented the curtailment of her time at school. By
the age of 16, despite a great desire for education, she could no
longer continue at school.

Charles Hall's father died when Charles was 10, leaving five children and no insurance. Charles liked school and was a champion
speller, but he also was the oldest child. He left school, went to work,
and through his efforts helped to keep the family together.

Dennis Garvin never saw his mother or father. "My mother died when I was born and an aunt took me to raise. My aunt died when I was eight years old and after that I made it by myself. It was 'root pig or die.' "

The record for working at the earliest age appears to belong to Joseph Cook. This is the lead paragraph in his social security interview: "Mr. Cook was born in Waterville, Kansas, and herding milk cows at the age of four. His father would put him on his horse, then if he had to get off his horse, the only way possible to remount was to let the horse graze and climb up his neck."

In most cases, the boys started out with farm work or household chores such as taking care of the firewood, while the girls began with housework and looking after younger siblings.

The other reason for the long work lives, of course, is that the centenarians quit working very late in life. Of the 482 centenarians whose ages at retirement are known, fewer than 1 percent retired before age 60 and only 3½ percent were retired by age 65 (Appendix 26B). Fifty-five percent of them retired after age 85, three out of eight during the tenth decade.

Two hundred nineteen centenarians still were working at the time they were interviewed (Appendix 26C). A centenarian was considered to be working if he or she was still pursuing a lifelong occupation and if those efforts were making an important contribution to the home economy. Forty-one centenarians gardened to the extent that they supplied an appreciable amount of the household food, and five to the extent that they earned money for their produce. One hundred and five centenarians engaged in housework, by far the most common occupation. Most of those doing the housework were women, but there were some men as well. If a centenarian lived alone and did all the housework, that was considered a full-time occupation. In other cases, the centenarians did sufficient work to allow other members of the household to work full time outside the home. Many more centenarians did chores and gardened but were not considered to be still working because their efforts did not make substantial economic contributions.

Of the 219 centenarians considered to be working, seventy were earning a financial income: ten were making money at farming; six from sewing or altering clothes; five from gardening; five as bankers; four as janitors; three were running stores; three were working for companies; two were heads of their businesses; there were two shoemakers and artists; and one judge, lawyer, physician, lecturer, priest, minister, rabbi, bridge columnist, longshoreman, commercial fisherman, funeral director, and surveyor, among others.

Nineteen centenarians, in addition to the seventy earning money,

were listed as gainfully employed even though not technically working. In almost all cases, the income was from rentals of rooms, farms,
or other properties.

"Still working" is a narrow definition of a centenarian's usefulness.
A more accurate measure is indicated by the item "performs useful
role(s)." Forty-two percent of the centenarians still were carrying
out one or more useful roles. Usually these activities were confined
to the home—doing household chores, cooking, gardening, taking
care of the yard, cutting firewood. In some cases, the centenarians
were making useful contributions to their communities, and 2 percent
of them were performing a useful role for society at large.

One person in this last group is Chief William Red Fox. His work
load of public relations, meetings, talks, and traveling would tax the
stamina of a man half his age. Red Fox is atypical, indeed singular,
but his story is given in some detail to show what a centenarian is
capable of doing.

Chief Red Fox was born June 11, 1870, in a teepee at Thunder
Butte in the Dakota Territory (now South Dakota), a full-blooded
Oglala Sioux. His first recollection is of a day in May 1876 when
about four thousand Indians left the Pine Ridge Reservation in
Dakota for the Big Horn in Montana on a buffalo hunt. Still a
youngster, he was tied to two long stakes, which were bound together,
attached to a horse, and dragged along the ground. It was a rough ride.

June 25, 1876, a Sunday, was the date of Custer's last stand. That
is the first historical event remembered by the chief, although the
social security report does not make clear whether he was actually
present at the Little Bighorn River. Red Fox says that "the Indian
mind was untrained but unstained."

His first schooling was on the reservation at Fort Yates in what is
now North Dakota. In his teens he was sent to the Carlisle Indian
School in Pennsylvania, graduating from high school when he was
19, in 1889. The next year he was back at Fort Yates as an inter-
preter at a salary of $45 a month. He entered the United States Navy
in 1898, serving during the Spanish-American War and the Boxer
Rebellion until 1902. His post was on a troop-transport vessel and
he did not see combat.

Chief William Red Fox spent a good part of his career as a Wild
West performer. He traveled with the 101 Ranch Wild West show
out of Oklahoma and was a personal friend of Oklahoma's most
famous son, Will Rogers. Both the chief and Rogers were trick ropers
and twirlers before the Oklahoman went on to become the nation's
droll sage of common sense. Red Fox spent about fifteen years with
the Buffalo Bill Circus and experienced his most exciting event

Arthur
Hargrave

with that outfit. "It was when I hit King Edward [VII] on the head with a rubber tomahawk when I was playing in a Wild West circus in London in 1904. Of course, the king was in on the stunt in advance so he was not unaware of what the action would be. The king liked Buffalo Bill and he also liked me. He said, 'Call me Eddie.' "

Later, these talents brought Red Fox roles in more than a hundred motion pictures, usually westerns, including *The Covered Wagon*. In 1937 he began working for the Boy Scouts, and in 1945, when he was 75 years old, he began his favorite occupation—touring public schools and "teaching the truth about Indian life." He wore Indian dress, demonstrated Indian dances, and talked with the schoolchildren about history and Indian lore.

At age 75, he also expanded his income by signing with the Rath Packing Company. His picture in Indian headdress appeared on packages of meat products marketed under the brand name "Rath's Black Hawk." At 95, he switched to Wilson and Company, Inc., as a public relations representative. "In this work," the social security interviewer relates, "he travels about eleven months of the year making personal appearances, talks to civic clubs, and makes radio and television broadcasts. He travels alone by air. A company representative usually meets him when he arrives at the city designated on his itinerary, and the representative assists with arrangements and introductions. His May schedule takes him to Atlanta, Birmingham, Chattanooga, and Danville, Virginia. In June he will travel to High Point and Wilson, North Carolina, and to Miami and Jacksonville, Florida. In July his itinerary will take him to New Orleans, Pensacola, Roanoke, and Shreveport. He plans to spend the month of August in Industry, California."

When he is on the road, he gets up at 5:30 every morning and takes a cold shower. When he is not on the road, he stays with his son, Billy Red Fox, in Corpus Christi, Texas. But even during his time off the chief does not always stay put. The year before his interview he took two of his five grandchildren on a trip to Hawaii during their Christmas vacation. Chief Red Fox says he has traveled to all the continents and visited most of the countries of the world. He has been to every important city in the fifty states. He has known every president of the United States from Grover Cleveland to Richard Nixon (the incumbent at the time of the interview), and stayed overnight at the White House on several occasions. Woodrow Wilson was his favorite president, but Teddy Roosevelt his favorite man.

Despite what would seem to be the chief's all-consuming schedule for the Wilson packing company, he found time recently to write a book entitled *How Empty Is Our Wilderness?* He expects it to be published soon and is looking forward to an autograph party. He still has one big unfulfilled ambition, and it exemplifies the mainstream continuity of his life. He wants to "get the Bureau of Indian Affairs abolished for my people. They are too restrictive in their bureaucratic ways."

A photograph of Chief Red Fox shows black eyebrows and slightly wavy black hair with some silver strands on top and more on the side. His forehead is about as wrinkled as one would expect of a man in his seventies. He does not wear eyeglasses. A half-smoked cigar protrudes from his mouth. He says, "I smoke eighteen cigars a day, but I don't inhale so they don't hurt me." The social security agent says that the chief's hearing is keen, but his eyesight is failing. His mind is quick, his memory is good, and he has a·fine sense of humor.

"I never intend to retire," says Chief William Red Fox, "but I have left instructions to be buried in Corpus Christi in full Indian regalia when I die."

NEXT IN IMPORTANCE in the "Order" category, after "Organized lifetime activities" and "Work," is the subsection "Stability," meaning the continuities in a person's life. A surprising number of these 100-year-olds spent most or all of their lives in a single location—78 percent—and nearly half of these stationary people never left that one place for their entire lives.

In 45 percent of the cases, the same location means an area no larger than a county or possibly two adjoining counties. Another 45 percent never roamed beyond one town for most or all of their lives. Although these people felt no need to move, the geography around them changed drastically in America's metamorphosis from a rural country of twenty-three million people in 1850 to an urbanized nation of more than two hundred million people in the 1970s.

Chicago, for example, was a town of less than 30,000 residents when Charlotte Bonner was born there in 1850. Mrs. Bonner, introduced earlier, is the cheerful lady residing in a nursing home in a Chicago suburb. At age 106, she recalled that she was born at State and Monroe streets in the heart of Chicago. "It would look mighty funny now," she commented, "with the two cows, the pigs and the hundred chickens my father kept there." The honeymoon of Mrs. Bonner's first marriage, in October 1871, was, as the social security report put it, "marred" by a fire. Mrs. Jeanie Woodis says: "I remember the great Chicago fire; sat on the steps and watched it. The first burn was within a block from us." Peter Wing was 13 years old at the time. The only thing that saved the Wing family's possessions "was the fact that they lived on the west side of the Chicago River.

He recalls walking to the Clark Street bridge with his mother and watching the fire across the river. Later, when there was fear that the fire would jump the river, his uncle removed their belongings from their home to a safer location. He recalls the excitement of watching the fire department racing their horses through the streets to the fire, and the drays, overloaded with household goods, racing the opposite direction with many objects falling from the wagons as they sped by."

Chicago rebuilt quickly and continued to grow in size and wealth. Before the fire, Marshall Field's department store already was doing a $12-million annual business. The store reopened less than four weeks after the fire in a remodeled cow barn and within a decade had doubled its sales, on its way to becoming the largest single department store in the world.

Mrs. Jennie Rea was born in 1868 to Thomas and Mary Hobbs. The Hobbses were founders and leading citizens of Joliet, Illinois; they had extensive holdings in Chicago, about thirty miles from Joliet. "I grew up in the days of gaslights. Gas was used for street and home lighting. Girls in my family grew up in a rather formal atmosphere. We were required to dress for dinner, learn handiwork, such as fine needlepoint, crochet, and embroidery. We did no common housework because employees did the heavy labor and all housework. Ladies did not open doors in those days."

Mrs. Rea is one of the very few centenarians born to wealth. She lived in a house with twenty bedrooms beside a "crick" and lake. "Father had a boathouse for the family and for guests and furnished boats for the pleasure of our frequent visitors." The earliest times she can remember were when "my father took me walking across the span over a nearby stream each Sunday, and I looked at the beautiful swan."

Miss Hobbs, as she was then, divided her life between Joliet and Chicago. Transportation was by buggy, surrey, and streetcar, and a good train operated between Joliet and Chicago. "My family was among the first customers of Marshall Field's, and I still maintain an open account at their store in Chicago."

In 1893, Mrs. Rea remembers, there opened in Jackson Park the World's Columbian Exposition of "arts, industries, manufactures, and the products of the soil, mine, and sea." Albert Uthe, a country bumpkin, came to see the exposition at the age of 30. "The first historical event of any consequence that Mr. Uthe could remember was the Chicago World's Fair of 1893. Apparently, Mr. Uthe had recently arrived from Sioux City, Iowa, and this was his first contact with an urban community of considerable size. The contrast between the wonders of the exposition and the simple, rustic life that he lived made a deep impression on Mr. Uthe." Said he: "I just couldn't get over all the wonderful things that were in that fair." Attracted by the marvels of Chicago, Mr. Uthe stayed the rest of his life.

Eighty-eight centenarians not only lived in one area and in one town, but spent the great part of their lives in a single house. Seven of those centenarians lived their entire lives in just one home. Miss Lulu Shields was visited in the house in which she was born at Church Hill, Mississippi, a river town fifteen miles north of Natchez. She lives alone in the house. When she was asked the standard question "Where were you born?," Miss Shields answered, "In this house." Indicating the other side of the room, she added, "Right in that bed there."

The importance of the "Stability" subsection is attested to by its quantity of high-scoring items—eight of the top eighteen in the "Order" category (see also Appendix 26D). Four of the items scored higher than 60 percent. In addition to "living in same place a long time," the items are "continuous place in family," 72 percent; "continuity in work," 70 percent; and "continuity in interests," 62 percent.

The sustained interest for the majority of these centenarians was churchgoing and religion. Mrs. Daisy Sharp, for example, recalls that on her third birthday she stood before a Sunday school gathering in Camden, Indiana, and faultlessly recited the Lord's Prayer. "I remember that the pastor had to help me up and down from the platform and that some of the boys and girls were giggling, but I got through it all right." The most enjoyable part of her day at age 100 is when her nurse reads to her from the Bible. She also looks forward to the regular visits of her pastor.

This thread of central interest provides a symmetry to many of these 100-year lives: The first preoccupation of early life remains at the end—when all the other concerns of their long lives have faded with advancing age—as a final consolation. Mrs. India Pickering's earliest memory is of the time she hid under a quilt that her mother was piecing together. Mrs. Pickering led an active life until 95, when she fell and broke her leg. Failing eyesight at 99 forced her to give up her last useful activity, quilting.

David Austin of Union, New Jersey, excelled in weekly spelling bees in school. Mr. Austin told the social security agent that on one occasion he was the only one of eleven boys on his team able to spell the word *shekel*. The agent dutifully reports in an aside, "During the interview Mr. Austin was very pleased with himself when the field representative could not spell the word but he could." How does Mr. Austin spend a part of each day at age 100? He works on word puzzles in the *Newark Evening News*.

Fred Shade's earliest memory is "chewing tobacco." As a 5-year-old he would pick cigar butts off the street, peel off some of the leaves, and chew them. The social security interview concludes this way:

Q. Do you have any outside activities—church, hobbies?

A. No, can't chase women anymore but would like to.

Q. Do you have any ambition you have not yet realized?

A. I think of things away back rather than ahead. All I think of ahead is chewing tobacco. If I had my legs, could go to work. I chew two boxes of Day's Work [tobacco] a month. Can't sit here and do nothing.

The item "traveled extensively" was included under "Stability" on the premise that it is difficult for the traveling life to be a stable one (see Appendix 22, Questionnaire Totals, number 50). This assumption is supported by the fact that only 4 percent of the centenarians' lives were characterized by "traveled extensively." Yet Charles Faith shows how, with self-discipline, being constantly on the move can be compatible with a stable life. He was a traveling salesman for most of his career. He told the social security representative, the reason for his continued good health is that he never drank, smoked, or "monkeyed around with females, except my wife, of course."

IN FOURTH PLACE behind the subdivisions "Organized lifetime activities," "Work," and "Living in one place a long time" is "Strong family fabric." This social structure could be seen in the lives of three-quarters of the centenarians. Three in five centenarians still were living with another family member (see Appendix 35). The usual arrangement was to be living with a child, most often a daughter. Even when centenarians lived alone or in nursing homes, however, children often resided nearby and provided loving support. In addition to the 461 centenarians who lived with children, another 373 saw their children regularly—again, about 75 percent of those for whom information was available. One hundred centenarians were living at home with their spouses. Three married couples managed to continue living together in nursing homes, and one pair resided in a hospital. In many cases, where there were no more relatives left, the oldtimers were supported by a social structure of friends and neighbors.

These family relationships are not simply one way, with the centenarians on the receiving end. A component of the "Usefulness" subsection shows that the centenarians were "important to one or many people," and by an almost identical 74 percent. The other people derived benefits from the centenarians and wanted to have them around. Most of this social interaction and support takes place within the home. Twenty percent of the centenarians still go to regularly scheduled meetings or get-togethers. Usually this means church.

Next in importance, in the "Regularity" subsection, is the item "still working or regular routine of activities," characterizing five of eight of the subjects. Two other items under "Regularity"—"arising and retiring at the same times" and "eating three meals a day"—are not addressed in most interviews. Therefore the figures of 11 percent and 15 percent undoubtedly are small fractions of the true numbers (see Appendix 22: Questionnaire Totals, number 48).

Typical is the statement of Sarah Ann Page of Cambridge, Massachusetts—and noteworthy because the "early to bed, early to rise" regimen is not the result of life on a farm. "I never was out sporting around all night long. You don't last long doing that. Oh, I can stay up late, mind you. I watch television 'til nine o'clock sometimes or if I have company in I may stay up to ten. But I believe in going to bed early and getting up early."

Twenty-four centenarians attribute their longevity to rising early and going to bed early. Another twenty-one centenarians believe they lived so long because they didn't carouse or run around, while seventeen subjects feel that the regularity in their lives contributed to their century of existence.

Lawrence Cutting of Lowell, Massachusetts, is one who believes his long life stems from his routine—regular work, meals, and sleep, and no bad habits. He worked in business for fifty-three years, fifty-two of them with the same wholesale firm that he eventually bought. In retirement he lives with his widowed daughter, helps her around the house, and works in the yard. He mows the lawn in the summertime and shovels snow in the winter. He takes a walk up the street every day and has an hour's nap in the afternoon. He loves to read and reads a good deal of the time. Aside from working in the yard and taking a walk, he has no outside activities. All his life he usually went to bed before nine o'clock and rarely went out at night. "I've been in Lowell seventy-six years," he says, "and haven't been to a dozen shows."

Sarah Mettlen, living with her 70-year-old son in Frankfort, Indiana, sleeps from 10 P.M. to 9 A.M. and from noon until 3 P.M. At 3 P.M. she has a cola. But on the day the social security representative visited her, they talked until after 4 P.M. and she accused him of cheating her out of her mid-afternoon drink. It was too late to take it after four o'clock because it would spoil her supper. She also expressed irritation at the Chicago White Sox for playing so many night games, because she had to go to sleep before she could hear the resolution of the games. The interviewer's closing comment shows that being routine is not the same as being dull: "All in all, it was a most delightful hour's chat, and I considered it one of the rewards of my job."

John White

Photo courtesy of Eugene Register Guard

If there is a paragon of regularity, it has to be Lee Chau of Hilo, Hawaii. Mr. Lee came to Hawaii from Canton, China, in 1889 at the age of 19. He went to night school and learned English, then became a cook at the Hilo Hotel. After that, and for more than sixty years, he owned and operated Kwon See Wo, one of the largest Chinese stores in Hilo. The business suffered when the store was struck by a tidal wave when he was 90 years old. Now he is on a different routine: "Except for occasional rheumatism attacks, he is in very good health—a condition he attributes to his rigid time schedule. He eats at 7 A.M., 11 A.M., and 5 P.M. and permits no interference with the set meals. He goes to sleep at exactly 8 P.M., and arises at 2 A.M. Then he meditates yoga style for two hours, exercises one hour, sleeps one hour, and is up at 6 A.M. to prepare breakfast."

"MODERATION" IS IN LAST PLACE in the "Order" subdivisions, but this could be from lack of information. For nearly half of the subjects, there are no direct references to or clues about the role of moderation in their lives. Yet when it is mentioned, this classification rates very high in the centenarians' own estimation of why they have lived so long. Four percent of the centenarians making attributions ascribe their longevity to moderation; nearly 15 percent believe their long lives are due to one particular aspect of moderation—no (or moderate) drinking and/or no smoking. In an objective assessment of salient characteristics associated with the subjects' longevity, "moderation" and "no smoking/drinking" combined are strong influences in one of six centenarians.

Many more men attached importance to their moderate and abstemious habits than did women. Among the forty centenarians who attribute their longevity to moderation, only seven are women, a ratio of five men to one woman. Of the 138 centenarians who believe they were able to live so long because of abstention from alcohol and/or smoking, only thirty-one are women, a ratio of three and a half to one. One explanation for the disproportion could be that the centenarian women saw no difference in their behavior in these respects from other members of their sex, whereas centenarian men knew that they had departed from more prevalent male ways.

The best evidence that the centenarians lived in moderation comes from their appearance. Most of them for whom information is available are of average weight or lean. Twenty-six centenarians—9 percent—could be described as overweight. Not one is obese or gaunt.

THE "ORDER" CATEGORY in the questionnaire has an alternate title: "Discipline." Among the definitions of *discipline* are (for the noun) "control gained by enforcing obedience" and (for the verb) "to punish or penalize for the sake of discipline." This kind of discipline is the supreme memory for Dan Leeman of Fairfield, Connecticut. "For years now I notice that I remember less and less. The earliest thing I remember occurred when I was a very small boy. I had a pet dog who was rather playful and full of energy. One day he jumped around an old woman neighbor who took a cane to him. I was young and, not knowing much better, said, 'You old witch—don't you hit my dog again.' Those were my famous last words. My father, hearing about the happening, took a horsewhip to me and laid them deep in my mind. It's strange how I remember that incident above all others."

That account stands alone in the severity of a beating administered by a parent. In fact, few more than half-a-dozen centenarians refer to whippings at home. It would be interesting to know if during a time of "spare the rod and spoil the child," the parents of these long-lived people indeed did spare the rod. But that determination is beyond the competence of this material. What we do find are a great many references to happy childhoods in loving homes. If the rod was not spared, perhaps the occasions of its application were accepted as the norm and thus not remarkable enough for remembrance.

There are more references to corporal punishment in school, where physical enforcement of discipline in school was widespread. There was some justification in teachers' taking stern measures: In all the one-room schoolhouses the teacher was the sole enforcer of order. This meant that young women might have to confront older male bullies and male teachers fistfight with ruffians who invaded the premises. Again, this corporal discipline in the schoolroom may have been noted more often than punishments at home, but it also was accepted in most cases. James Baxter, who attended a one-room, one-teacher school maintained by a sawmill for the workers' children near Greensboro, North Carolina, remembers his teacher, Miss Malinda Sewell, very well. "She wore me out with a switch many a time when I was bad." Mr. Baxter still regards Miss Sewell with affection. "She was a good teacher, but I was a poor learner."

There are other definitions for the word *discipline*: "to impose order upon" for the verb and "orderly or prescribed conduct or pattern of behavior" and "self-control" for the noun. It may be seen from this chapter that the discipline in these centenarians, rather than the product of coercive outside pressures, springs from the manner of living and kinds of activities they have chosen. It will become even more apparent in succeeding chapters that the discipline is imposed from within—it is self-discipline.

CHAPTER 3

Hard Work

"A fellow in Oklahoma claims the reason for living so long is hard work and hard labor. If that is the case, I will live for another hundred years because I have worked hard all my life." "I don't set down and sit there. I get up and keep moving." "If I had sat down and folded my arms, I wouldn't be here today. Better wear out than rust out." "My father used to say, 'You will rust out before you wear out.' " "Work as hard as you can as long as you can." "I worked like hell." "Hard work—I never made an easy dollar." "I was old but I was young because I had to work so hard." "Moderation and hard work." "Good habits and hard work." "Early to bed, early to rise, and a lot of good, hard work."

Work with the qualifier "hard" was given more than any other single reason by these centenarians for their longevity. Hard work is by far the most salient characteristic associated with the longevity of these people, evident in 55 percent of the cohort.

The importance of hard work became apparent right after the order pattern. As indicated, a good deal of this hard work took place on farms. The changeover from human power to horsepower was not effected extensively until about 1875. "My daddy gave me a hoe when I was five or six," said James Payne, a Kentucky sharecropper of tobacco, "then I went to the plow when I was about eight." The mechanization of American farming was not completed until after World War II. It may seem difficult to believe now, but horses and mules still outnumbered tractors on U.S. farms until 1954.

There's no way of judging, but possibly centenarians not only worked later and longer than most people—but harder, too. John

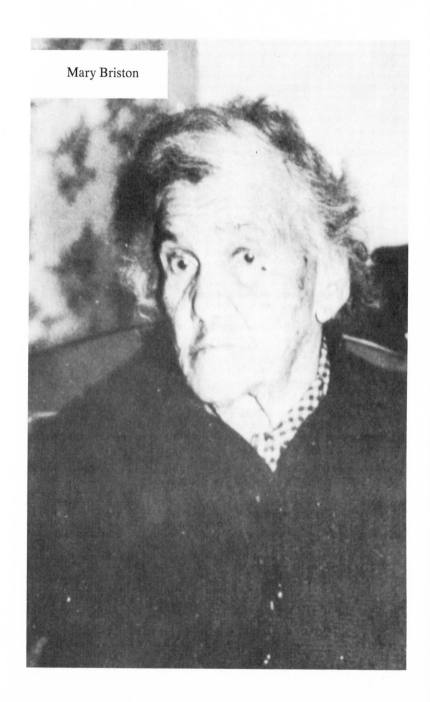

Mary Briston

Phillips as a boy drove a team of horses to help his father with the harvest and as a man drove a ten-horse threshing machine, as well as doing other kinds of arduous work. "I don't like to say it," Mr. Phillips says, "but you find men that won't do their part of the work. I never had trouble getting work, because I held down my end of the job."

Sexual equality was practiced on the farm. "It didn't make any difference to my father that I was a girl," says Mrs. Alice Palla, referring to her childhood days in Tulare County, California. "I still had to get out and help in the fields." Mrs. Anna Moten's first job in Haywood County, Tennessee, was "following my father as he split rails, so did I. In almost no time at all I quartered a rail as fast as he. I plowed and did all the boys' work at home as far back as I can remember. I've stripped sorghum, everything."

"My first job," says Mrs. Mary Briston, "was putting out cotton seed, and I was thirteen. They wanted to give me thirty-five cents a day because I was a child, but I told them I would do as much work as the grownups and wanted forty cents a day, and I got forty cents and did as much as the grownups." Mrs. Bell Coleman in Alabama still remembers with pride that she was able to pick more cotton—five hundred pounds a day—than the men who worked beside her and she often was assigned to the "lead row."

For Miss Lulu Shields, who lived all her life in one house in Church Hill, Mississippi, work at first was cause for shame. Like most southern whites, her life was changed radically by the hard times that followed the Civil War. "As she grew older, it became necessary that she work on the farm. In fact, her first job was hoeing cotton and corn on their farm. It was from this work that she learned a lesson that she never forgot. As a child she was forced to work. As she worked in the fields people passing in buggies could see her hoeing the cotton and corn. As she was ashamed to be seen, she tried to hide whenever people passed. One day as a man in a buggy was passing, she tried to hide to keep him from seeing her in the field working. Afterwards, a friend told her she should not have been ashamed because the man in the buggy had only one leg and would have gladly worked had he been able. Miss Shields said that that taught her never to be ashamed of work." Miss Shields tended her own cattle until her late nineties.

This is how the interview went with Mrs. Hattie Riggs at Ludlow, Kentucky:

"What was your first job?"

"I worked on a farm."

"What kind of work did you do most of your life?"

Lulu Shields

"Housework. I married at age twenty-three. Like most girls, I didn't like to work, but had to all my life at home."

"Why do you think that you have been able to live so long?"

"I had to work. I worked on the farm and got plenty of exercise."

"What do you do with your time?"

"I work. I have made twenty pair of pillow slips for my daughter during the past year. I like to listen to music."

"Do you do any work or household chores?"

"I cook supper for my daughter, son-in-law, and grandchild."

"Do you have any ambition you have not yet realized?"

"Yes. I would have loved to have learned a trade during my life, but never did. I never had a chance to learn one."

That interview took place in March 1968, when Mrs. Riggs was nearing her 100th birthday. She lived another nine and a half years. She was believed to be the oldest person in Kentucky when she died at age 109.

If equality on the farm were judged by work, then females were more equal. When Mrs. Minnie Brown was 15 in Kansas, she married a boy one year her senior. "His mother was dead, and he lived with other people, moving from farm to farm, working the cotton fields. After Mrs. Brown had her first child, she carried the child out into the field with her and picked cotton. She would stop working only when the child was hungry, and then only long enough to feed him. Her children, as they grew up, worked in the fields along with her and her husband." A daughter said that her mother could pick more cotton in one day than any of the children.

When Mrs. Helen Hasse was asked what kind of work she did most of her life, she replied: "Secretarial and bookkeeping until my marriage. Then, of course, I worked as a farmer's wife from five o'clock in the morning until sometimes twelve at night—that was the hardest work of all." Mrs. Dora Failing, mother of six children: "We had a farm after I was married and I was kept pretty busy. There were three hundred acres and we had hired hands. At nine in the morning we would take out a lunch to them. At noon they all came in for a hot meal. In the evening they had to be served another hot meal and another light meal before they went to bed. What with raising the children, cooking, washing and keeping the house clean, I had my hands full."

"When asked why she thought she had been able to live so long, Mrs. [Fannie] Helms replied, 'Why, I don't know—probably because I have worked hard all my life.' She said that she had always lived on a farm and when her children were small she did all the cooking, canning, washing, and ironing, made the children's clothes, knit their socks, and milked the cows. As soon as the children were old enough, they milked the cows, but after they were grown and went away from home, she milked the cows again."

HARD PHYSICAL WORK is not restricted to farming; it is a prime part of other occupations in which the centenarians were engaged. Because many of the centenarians worked at several occupations during their lifetimes, a total of 2,800 jobs is listed for the group (see Appendix 25). At least five out of eight of these occupations required hard labor.

One hundred and eight women were farm wives; for another 360 women, being a housewife was the primary occupation. Even in a nonfarm environment, doing all the housework, washing, ironing, cooking, cleaning, and making clothes—as well as raising children— was hard work and time consuming. A woman's work, it was said, was never done.

In third place on the list of occupations is mill or factory worker, the only other occupation with more than a hundred representatives. Fourth is schoolteacher. The reason for the high place of this occupation is that it was common for girls to teach for a few years before they married.

These are the rest of the top twenty occupations: domestic/housework, sawmill/logging, laborer/railroad-track worker, store clerk/salesman, seamstress/dressmaker, grocery or general-store operator, carpenter, public-office holder, rancher/cowboy, company worker, cook, serviceman, miner, handyman/odd jobs, janitor, president of company.

Perry Bradford spent most of his life in western North Carolina and eastern Tennessee. "Mr. Bradford is a robust six feet, two hundred twenty-five pounds, and is very active for his age." When he was asked about his first job, he replied: "Rowing people across the run at Chestoria, North Carolina. I guess I was about sixteen when I left home and got the job. I got paid seventy-five cents a day. That was pretty good money, but I never saw too much of it. I had to take the money up at the local store in trade and trade the store goods for my room and board." As for the work he did most of his life, "Well, I've done several things. I worked as a carpenter, worked on the railroad, and worked in the iron mines at Ambryville. All the time I worked on public works I also operated a farm. For a while I farmed two farms."

Oscar Swisher was making barrel staves at the age of 11. "And only a few years later, in West Virginia, he aided his father in cutting and skidding timber with the aid of oxen. What was then plain hard work is now relived with joy as Mr. Swisher relates how they struggled to move their steam-powered sawmill up and down the hills. The heavy boiler was positioned in various places beside a stream to locate it as near as possible to the standing timber. The 'portable' mill took the sweat and shouting of a great crew of men and the tugging of ten yoke of oxen and a pair of horses to get it from one site to the next. In those days the government, buying timber for a construction project, wanted what today would be impossible: thirty-foot lengths of hard wood no less than twelve inches by twelve inches. The Swishers found, felled, sawed and delivered it."

Henry Hunt went to work for the D. L. Fair Lumber Company in Louisville, Mississippi when he was 18 years old. His job was loading railroad ties, and he did this same kind of work for sixty years. Each tie, he estimated, weighed about two hundred pounds and he hefted each one by himself. Mr. Hunt believes he loaded about a hundred and fifty million ties by the time he was 78 years old, when he was forced to leave the job. "They told me I was gettin' too old and would have to quit, but those that told me are all dead now. I outlived them." He continued to work at another job and later did yard work for various people. "I've never been sick a day in my life," says Mr. Hunt. "Work never hurt nobody."

Similar sentiments were expressed by Ed Wisbey. "I have built two-story houses by myself from bottom to top. People told me I was going to kill myself by working so hard, but I look around today and most of those people are gone and I am still going." "Still going" means helping his daughter to package items in her candle-manufacturing business, drying dishes, and hoeing weeds in the garden.

The report on Henry Bean of Samson, Alabama, begins: "The interviewer, accompanied by Harry N. Scott, district manager, arrived at the Sellers Farm at 2:00 P.M. on Thursday, September 24, 1959. We learned that the beneficiary was clearing woods adjoining the Sellers's family's church cemetery about five miles from their home.

"We located the cemetery and found Henry with an axe in his hands at work clearing a blackjack oak grove adjacent to the cemetery. As we approached he told us to watch our step as he had killed seven rattlesnakes in that area the day before. Needless to say, we were very careful."

The report goes on: "His life has been nothing but hard work. His meals consist of corn bread and tap gravy (lard, flour, and water) for breakfast and corn bread and vegetables for other meals.

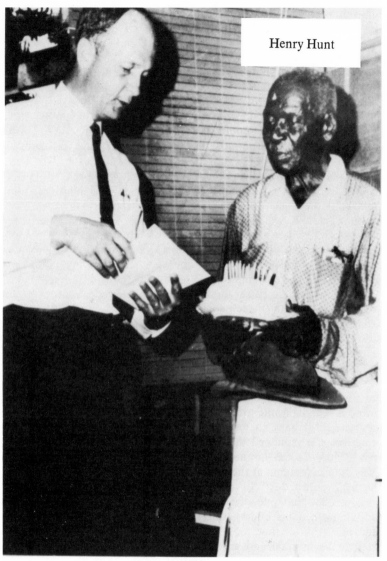

Henry Hunt

Photo courtesy of Winston County Journal

He does not eat any kind of meat and does not drink any alcoholic beverages. Many years ago he used to make whiskey for the white folks.

"As a slave, he helped clear land and split rails for fences. Since the Civil War he has worked on farms and cut timber for sawmills. During the last forty-five years he worked for the Sellers family for wages. Until a few years ago he was known as the best cotton picker in Geneva County. He could pick over seven hundred fifty pounds a day. Up until two years ago he could pick a hundred pounds of cotton before breakfast.

"He goes to the Baptist Church every Sunday and still works hard. Most of the work is tending to the cattle. He acts as veterinarian and helps look after sick cattle. He has a complete set of veterinary tools for this purpose.

"A few days ago a man asked him how he managed to live so long. He told the man about how hard he worked and how he didn't eat any meat or drink any whiskey. The man told him if it took that to live to be a hundred years old, he didn't want to live that long."

In reading some of these stories, one sometimes has to stop and remind oneself that these people are 100 years old. Such is the case with Henry Thomas of LeRoy, New York. "The amazing thing about Mr. Thomas," the interviewer writes, "was his youthful appearance. He was rather short, thin but very wiry, with a good firm handshake, and he attributed his good health and vigor to the fact that he exercised daily by cutting firewood. He had a huge shed with small pieces of stovewood which he estimated to be between forty and fifty cords. He goes one-half mile to the wood lot in an old car and cuts the wood and brings it back to the shed and cuts it into the stove size. His housekeeper explained that she had a little difficulty holding him at the house to keep his appointment to see the interviewer since he was kind of 'chafing at the bit' to get out to the wood lot since it was such a beautiful day."

"You see that pile of wood out there?" Otto Welge of Chester, Illinois, asked his interviewer. "Well, before I had my operation I helped cut all of that. . . . Now I just sit around because I just got out of the hospital and am not supposed to do much. But see that old ax over there? I'm gonna use that some. I'm going back into the woods. I love to chop trees; I love to swing the ax and feel the sweat break out."

Dr. Walter Pannell was a practicing physician when I visited his East Orange, New Jersey, office in November 1979. Patients arrived at the office during the course of our meeting. A trim man, he was deceptively young looking. His only concession to his extreme age

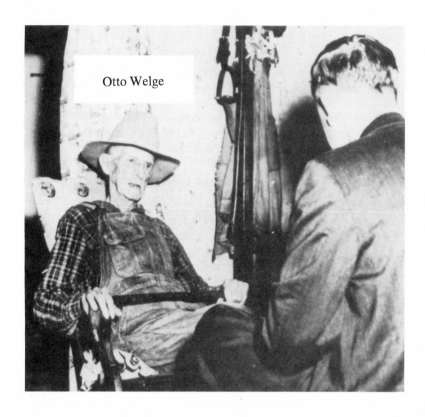

Otto Welge

was the use of a magnifying glass in addition to his eyeglasses to read small print. On the subject of strenuous physical activity, Dr. Pannell says, "If you work up a sweat, then you have gotten your exercise. If you don't sweat at all, you're in trouble. You have to perspire a little to be healthy, but from your own efforts." Dr. Pannell was an athlete in his younger days and still walks a quarter of a mile to and from his office each day.

Sports activities are rarely mentioned by these centenarians (nine men played baseball as youths and that's the bulk of the references), and exercise is usually cited in connection with work activities. Twenty-nine centenarians attributed their longevity to exercise and another ten of them to walking. Exercise took place apart from life-long physical activity for only sixteen centenarians.

One of them is Frank O. Jones, whose lifestyle is closer to that of most Americans today. Mr. Jones climaxed his teaching career as superintendent (for twenty-six years) of Northwest Junior High School in New Haven, Connecticut, a school that was renamed for him when he retired at the age of 70. Then he managed the nationally known Cary Teachers' Agency for another thirteen years. He also conducted Sunday school classes for half a century at the Wethersfield State Prison in Connecticut, and was affiliated with the Boy Scouts, YMCA, and Salvation Army for a similar period of time.

Despite the amount of time spent in these sedentary pursuits, there is another side to Mr. Jones's life. He played tackle on the Brown University football team (the team managed by John D. Rockefeller, Jr.). He sailed off the coast of Maine. He played tennis until he was 85 years old (the only reference to tennis among the 1,200 centenarians). He shoveled snow from his sidewalks and cut firewood until his late nineties. As an educator he strongly advocated sports and believed that schools should prepare students for living. Mr. Jones believes he was able to live beyond 100 years because of the spark given to him by his family early in life and because he kept physically fit, exercising daily.

In the past, the virtues of hard work have been praised in American society. But these virtues were other than the ones cited by the centenarians. Hard work has traditionally been lauded for molding character, building strong moral fiber, and as a means of getting from the bottom to the top with appropriate financial and social rewards—the work ethic. For the centenarians, it is, rather, the work therapy.

IT WAS ONLY in the early 1970s that Dr. Alexander Leaf of the Harvard Medical School, studying long-lived people in Soviet Abkhasia, made a connection between their hardy physical existence and a low incidence of fatal heart attacks. The Abkhasians were accustomed to tramping up and down mountainous terrain and did agrarian work very late in their lives. A Soviet gerontologist and heart specialist believed the old people did suffer heart attacks but were protected from the worst effects by a highly developed heart-lung system that was able to provide sufficient oxygen to the heart despite some arterial blockage. In other words, they could survive damage that would have been crippling or lethal in less strong cardiovascular systems.

In addition to strengthening the heart and the blood vessels, strenuous activity strengthens the musculature, builds endurance, burns calories, and reduces fat. It is only since about 1975, however, that scientific evidence has indicated that exercise protects against the paramount killer of Americans, heart disease (see Appendix 15 for a more detailed discussion). Even as late as December 1977, a report by the National Heart and Lung Institute Task Force on Arteriosclerosis stated: "Lack of exercise is generally regarded as a relatively minor independent factor in the development of atherosclerosis; it is believed to act primarily through other mechanisms—for example, altered caloric balance. Exercise may have a much more significant role in the overall feeling of well being and in rehabilitation."

At about that same time, however, Dr. Ralph Paffenbarger, Jr., a professor of epidemiology at the Stanford University School of Medicine, reported to a meeting of the American Heart Association that a study of nearly seventeen thousand Harvard alumni found there were fewer heart attacks among men who engaged regularly in strenuous sports activities than among men who were less active. There was a direct correspondence between physical exercise and heart attacks: the more calories expended in physical exertion (up to two thousand calories a week), the fewer heart attacks. The protection against heart attack was provided no matter how the calories were expended—by walking as well as jogging. But at each level of caloric expenditure, the more strenuous physical activity gave greater protection than less intense activities.

Earlier in 1977 Dr. Paffenbarger and colleagues reported on a study of nearly three thousand seven hundred San Francisco longshoremen covering a twenty-two-year period of their health records. The stevedores were divided into three groups, according to the energy required to do their work. Men doing low-energy jobs with about one-half the caloric demands of the highest category were comparable to office workers. Men in this group suffered more than five times more fatal heart attacks than did the longshoremen doing the physically strenuous work.

Beginning about 1975 increasing evidence began to show that when there are high levels of one form of blood cholesterol—what are known as high-density lipoproteins (HDLs)—the presence of atherosclerosis is relatively rare and the risk of heart attack is low. Then Peter Wood of the Stanford University Heart Disease Prevention Center compared the levels of blood lipoproteins of forty-five male runners with the levels in forty-five sedentary men. The physically active men had half again more HDL than the inactive men. A later study by G. Harley Hartung and colleagues found a close relationship between HDL levels and distances run per week. Runners who averaged 40 miles a week had 65 milligrams of HDL per deciliter of blood; men who ran an average of 11 miles a week had 58 milligrams; and the inactive men, 43 milligrams. The research reported: "Our data suggest it is primarily the jogging and running, rather than diet, that elevate HDL."

Lower than normal amounts of HDL in the blood are associated with lack of exercise, smoking, and obesity. William Castelli, director of the well-known Framingham study of cardiovascular disease, says that for every 5 milligrams the HDL level falls below the average value (45 milligrams for men, 55 for women) "your risk of heart attack increases by roughly 25 percent."

One of the major differences between the lifestyles of the American centenarians and contemporary Americans is the change in the nature of work. Reliance on the expenditure of human energy to get the job done has been replaced with power tools and powerful equipment run by fossil fuel and electrical energy. Productivity has been increased tremendously, and there would be no way to go back to widespread manual labor without a reduction in the standard of living.

But along with increasing productivity, a motivating goal of the past century has been the elimination of hard labor with the substitution of ease and convenience. This has occurred even in the most rugged occupations. John Boyd, who used a mule and a horse to skid logs out of forests of the Northwest, was asked to compare today's logging with what he did. "There's nothing to it now," he said.

Dr. Arthur B. Grant, a dentist for sixty years, grew up on a farm and after that worked as a railroad section-hand with pick and shovel. He told me: "In those days we *worked*. The young fellows today, if they had to work as hard as they did in my day, they'd lay right down." Very few Americans today experience the hard work for long periods of time common to so many of the centenarians.

As some of the scientific studies cited indicate, stenuous activity doesn't have to take place in the form of work in order to confer its benefits; it can be performed in sports activities or exercises. However, those pursuits are not the same as work in one crucial respect. For the centenarians, hard work was a necessity. Engaging in active sports and exercising are voluntary, an extravocational or leisure activity. Dr. Leaf in observing the Abkhasians noted this key difference. He referred to "the incredible amount of physical exertion necessary just to attend to the daily business of living." He also said, "Given the choice, most people will exert themselves as minimally as possible with daily existence."

It is ironic, after so many years of being sold on the benefits of washing machines, miracle detergents, and labor-saving devices in the home, for American women to read that Mrs. Nancy Kempton "believes she has lived so long because of years of hard, steady work about her home, especially washing clothes with a washboard."

Charlie Smith

CHAPTER 4

Trinity

Another strong influence on a great number of the centenarians appeared more gradually, conveyed through a variety of references to the trinity of God, religion, and the Bible.

Just more than one-half of the centenarians for whom data is available were associated with a religious life. Of these 556 centenarians, 523 attended church for a substantial part of their lives (see Appendix 34A for denominations). And 430 of them still were going to church at the time of their interviews or had stopped going only recently. Religion is number four and belief in God number five on the list of salient characteristics.

When one turns to a subjective evaluation by the centenarians themselves, the importance of this area of their lives is still more impressive. If one combines all these related attributions for longevity—God's will, doing right, leading a good clean life, being a good Christian or religious, trust in God, the Lord's blessing, serving God, treating people right, helping people, the Lord's reward for goodness, observing the Golden Rule, honoring parents, with God's help—the total (adjusted for overlaps) is 39 percent of the centenarians. This aggregate is nearly half again larger than the second-place hard work–keep busy–work pattern.

This is a sampler of the attributions: "The main thing is I tried to live as a side companion to the Lord." (This man's one unrealized ambition was to possess "plenty of money to be used to help people in distress.") "If people live a right life, try to do what is right, they live, but if they do what is wrong, they will not live long." "A gift of God." "I shall live every minute of every day striving to do as much good for as many as possible within the borrowed time." "Faith in

God—you have to have faith or there's no way." "By working hard, being a Christian, treating everybody right." "Live a good religious life and to love your neighbor. That's what I've done all my life. I've tried to keep the second commandment as well as the others." (This woman was referring not to Exodus 20 but to Matthew 22:39, wherein Jesus says the second great commandment is "Thou shalt love thy neighbor as thyself.") "If you live right, you preserve your own life. But you can't talk it—you must live it."

This last quotation is by a black man. And this is the response of another black man, Dennis Garvin, who as a boy of 8 was thrust upon the world alone to "root pig or die":

"When we asked Mr. Garvin why he thought he had lived so long he immediately grew serious.

" 'The Lord,' he replied with reverence. ' "Seek ye first the Kingdom of God," ' he quoted, and then, pausing briefly, continued, ' "Ask and ye shall receive." ' Then, after a further pause, he proclaimed what was in truth the essence of his conviction and faith: 'But you have to live it.' "

For most blacks, faith in God, religion, and the Bible were crucial instruments of survival. The triumvirate served as a guerdon in a society that if not always hostile, imposed disadvantages. Of the eighty-three blacks who responded to the question about their longevity, 75 percent attribute their survival to God and their moral behavior. The faith is implicit and absolute. "I've got nothing to do with it. It's God's command," said one man. "Because God said I could," said another. "It doesn't matter what you do—you live just as long as God put you here to live."

Often the faith takes the form of a compact with God, and the long life is His reward for living a good life, taking care of family, and, especially, obeying the fourth commandment. The fourth commandment says, "Honor thy father and thy mother: that thy days may be long upon the land which the Lord thy God giveth thee." This commandment is taken literally by a number of centenarians, and, since the believers have carried out their part of the covenant, they are not surprised when the Lord delivers on the second part.

Observance of this commandment is not made narrowly, however, but leads to a generalized behavior that can be seen to have a survival value in its own right. Honoring thy father and mother is equated with being an obedient child. Says Mrs. Rebecca Capers, whose parents were slaves in Georgia: "The Bible says if you are obedient, your days will be long. I guess that is my case. I try to be obedient." "I love church," she added, "but have only been able to go once this year due to weakness. I have gone to church since I was a barefoot girl—churchgoing is the most exciting thing I know of." Andrew Williams said he had been able to live so long because "I've been obedient to God and man—first to God, and then to man." When James Campbell in Arkansas City, Arkansas, was asked the question, he said, "The Boss Man upstairs says 'Be obedient' and I have. I've been whipped by whites and by colored folks, too. But can't nobody say I've been too sassy."

The fourth commandment also served as an introduction to the Golden Rule. James Williams was born a slave on a huge plantation near Louisville, Kentucky. There were about three thousand workers and seventeen hundred plows on the plantation. "Mr. John Becker owned the place and he was a good man," says Mr. Williams. "I loved Mrs. Becker—she was closer to me than my own mother. I didn't even know who my mother was until I was nine or ten years old." Even after the slaves were freed and the Civil War was ended, Mr. Williams remained. "I was a house servant and when Mrs. Becker wanted me she said, 'Baby, come over here.' I always walked over and put my head on her knee and she would give me some kind of food or ask me to take some water to the field hands. For the next thirty-three years I stayed with the Becker family and left only because Mrs. Becker died. She taught me everything I know, and nobody thought as much of me as she did."

In response to the question about his longevity, Mr. Williams replied: "When I was just a little baby, Mrs. Becker taught me that the good book says, 'Honor thy father and thy mother, that thy days may be long upon the land.' Mrs. Becker said that didn't mean to honor just the white folks or the Negroes, but to honor all those who were your elders. I've done that all my life."

Mrs. Anna Moten, who as a girl learned to be an expert rail splitter and sorghum stripper, linked her long life to divine inspiration and earthly teaching, with the Golden Rule as the instrument. The black woman attributed her longevity to "my mother, father, and God's blessings—I prayed for it and got answer for long life. My mother taught me to treat everybody right, whether they treated me right or not, and I figure God blessed me for it."

When the famous Charlie Smith was asked his formula for long life (this interview took place in 1961 when he reputedly was 119 years old), he said, "The Ten Commandments teach you and me and everybody else, you see, to honor thy father and thy mother, that your days shall be long on earth, which the Lord thy God give you. I ain't so perfect, but I do try to live nearer to the commandments."

The interviewer elaborates further: "Although he has never learned to read, Charlie has a remarkable familiarity with the Bible.

When asked his ideas about life or his conjecture as to why he has been able to live so long, he replies as often as not with a quotation from 'the Scriptures.' Asked if he went to church, Charlie said, 'I've joined everything a person can join but the church. You can live right without belonging to a church. The Lord will hear your prayer just as good anywhere as he will in the church. He heard Jonah's prayers, didn't he? And he wasn't in no church, was he? He heard Daniel—he was in no church, was he? He heard the three Hebrew children—they weren't in no church. God heard their prayers.'

"When he was asked how he thought a man should live, he said, 'You don't want no bad treatment, do you? Well, treat the other fellow the same way—and that's the Bible! If you hate who you walk and talk with, hate them and love your Maker who you ain't never seen, you see, the line of truth ain't even. That's Scripture!' "

A perfect statement of the Golden Rule and the philosophy behind it. From the centenarians' experience, the Golden Rule is not only a moral precept, it is also a practical rule for human beings to get along with one another. It reduces the friction in interpersonal relations, invites friendly behavior, and improves the chances for survival.

Harrie Edmonston of New Castle, Indiana, a white man, said that when he was a supervisor at Chrysler Corporation, he always tried to put himself in the shoes of the person he was supervising and treat that person as he himself would have liked to be treated. A unique management-labor policy? Well, Mr. Edmonston is a rarity—one of only three centenarian men to have worked in management for a large corporation.

Following a career in religion seems to confer a better-than-average chance of becoming a centenarian among the white-collar, non-physical occupations. There were a dozen Protestant ministers, two Roman Catholic priests, one rabbi, seven preachers, four church leaders, two nuns, a missionary, and three ministers' wives—a total of thirty-two—among the cohort of centenarians. This number compares with seventy-nine schoolteachers (but most taught for only a few years), thirty-eight public-office holders (again, many of them only for limited periods), twenty-two company presidents, twenty-one bankers, eighteen salesmen, sixteen bookkeepers/accountants, fourteen writers, ten physicians, eight educators, seven lawyers, and two newsmen.

Methodist Bishop Herbert Welch, D.D., L.L.D., was born in 1862 in Greenwich Village, New York City, and held pastorates in Brooklyn, Manhattan, and Vernon, Connecticut, as well as bishoprics in Boston, Pittsburgh, Japan, China, and Korea. His most exciting experiences include the big earthquake in Japan in 1923, bandit raids in China, and serving in Korea during the independence movement. He retired as senior bishop at the age of 74, then became president of Ohio Wesleyan College. After retirement from that post at 85, he organized the Methodist Committee for Overseas Relief and as president of that organization raised and distributed $7 million to needy people throughout the world. Bishop Welch still maintained a lecture schedule when the social security representative called on him in New York City in June 1962. The agent concludes his report: "His entire life has been, and still is, filled with service to his fellow men. He is active physically and mentally. Last month he lectured at the Columbia Medical School on the world situation. His subject was 'Have we grounds for hope?' It is his opinion we have!"

The experience of William Spybey is more typical. He grew up in the small town of Bremen, Ohio, and worked in his father's dry goods store. At the age of 15 in 1883 he joined a new Methodist church and helped organize its Sunday school. Within the next few years, "Mr. Spybey began to do preaching on his own, especially to itinerant day laborers who were building the C & O Railway from Cincinnati to Virginia. Sometimes he preached to as many as twelve hundred men. This started him on his career toward becoming a minister. Folks who had heard him preach asked him to conduct services in their homes. At the age of 18, he was elected by his Sunday school as a lay preacher.

"Mr. Spybey recalls that he always thought he was too small to be a preacher because all the preachers he had observed in his early years were large, robust men, and he was and is today very small in stature. After becoming a lay preacher, Mr. Spybey attended theological school in Evanston, Illinois, and also took courses at Northwestern University, finally becoming an ordained minister.

"Mr. Spybey served in churches in the Cincinnati area for many years. While serving in southern Ohio as a minister, he was very active in the W.C.T.U. and believes his efforts contributed much to drying up several counties including Miami County. These were dangerous times for active, well-known 'drys' and Mr. Spybey said he was once threatened with being shot if he continued his prohibition efforts by a local bootlegger. He was not deterred, however, and continued his prohibition work."

Despite these stirring times, the Reverend Spybey concluded his interview by saying, "I have run my race with quietude and that's about all there is to it."

In addition, there were several men who wanted to become preachers. Such a one is William C. Mize, who was interviewed in Ben

Lomond, Arkansas, on May 8, 1962. "Mr. Mize was born in Alabama. At the age of 5, he walked with other members of his family to Mississippi to live with an older sister. This was immediately after the end of the Civil War, and Bill recalls how he saw many 'Yankees' on the road to Mississippi. Some of the soldiers were kind and some would not even speak to the 'Rebel' displaced persons.

"In 1881, Bill Mize moved to Arkansas. He came to Ben Lomond in the fall of 1882 and built the house in which he still lives. When he first came to Arkansas he worked as a laborer on farms for other people, and he worked 'harder than seven thousand men.' He says that in those days he was known as 'one-eyed Bill' (he lost the sight in one eye when he was still a youth). He worked hard, mostly for others until 1911 (when he was 50 years old), when he scraped together enough capital to go into storekeeping for himself. He was in business selling groceries and general merchandise until about 1955. Mr. Mize says that after he got a little property, he became respectable and was no longer known as 'one-eyed Bill,' but Mr. Mize instead. He told all this with tongue in cheek.

"When asked if he has any unfulfilled ambitions, Bill said, 'I should have been a preacher. I always wanted to be.' Maybe Bill's lifelong ambition will finally be realized after all. On Sunday, May 20, at 11:00 A.M., in the Methodist church at Ben Lomond, Arkansas, Bill will deliver a talk to his friends entitled, 'What is Man, and Man Know Thyself.' After 101 years on this earth, Mr. Mize should certainly know his subject, and knowing Bill, it will certainly be worth the trip to hear him."

In another part of the report, the field representative wrote, "Mr. Mize derives most pleasure now from reading his Bible and listening to his radio."

Seventy centenarians noted that they still were reading the Bible or having it read to them. When Arthur Dial of Munford, Alabama, was asked the reason for his longevity, he responded: "I have tried to live the good life and do what the Bible says a man ought to do. I have worn out six Bibles in my life." Ingvald Pedersen and Anna Schwab said they read the Bible through every year. And retired farmer John King of Edmond, Oklahoma, had just finished reading the Bible for the 142nd time. "I like to read the New Testament," Mr. King said. For Drewery Moore of Salem, Virginia, the Bible was the instrument that enabled him to become literate. "Mr. Moore did not attend school; however, he learned to read and write through a self-teaching method by studying the Bible. He states he has spent a good part of his life reading and following the Bible. He is quite proud of the fact that last July, on his hundredth birthday, the Men's Bible Class from his church came to his home and conducted their class on his front porch as a tribute to him."

In our more sophisticated age, there may be a tendency to discount these professions of the importance of a religious life to longevity. In our more secular age, there may be an inability to value or understand the connection. The interview with Mrs. Flora Evelyn Whisenand in Martinsville, Indiana, may help illustrate the point.

The interviewer is impressed with the woman's decrepitude, but he is also piqued by the question Why her, what is the key to the mystery of her extreme longevity? One gets the impression that as much as the interviewer would like to discover the answer, he is not optimistic that he will be able to learn it from her, because of her frail condition. The field representative begins his report with an aside:

"(I interviewed Mrs. Whisenand at the Cherry Nursing Home in Martinsville. She has been confined to bed since 1958 [four years ago], because of the infirmities of her advanced age. It seemed to me that she is blind, although others did not mention it.)"

As well as can be ascertained, the others in the room are three visiting ladies, including at least two sisters-in-law, and two nurses. The atmosphere at times suggests the Mad Hatter's tea party with no one constrained to let the subject speak for herself.

"There were no children of this marriage, but Mrs. Whisenand 'did love children. She had a lot of patience with them.' So her sister-in-law, Mrs. Minnie Clark, remarked, and continued: 'She loved to work in the flower garden and vegetable garden and enjoyed every minute of it. Also, piecing quilts was her hobby. She was a likeable person and had a lot of friends.' She was like a mother to many young relatives and neighbors. One of the nurses described the tours around the countryside of Aunt Flora and Bonnie Clark, a niece by marriage. These two were very devoted to each other and spent many happy hours in their horse-and-buggy travels.

"The two practical nurses spoke of Aunt Flora with obvious affection, something not usual with those who care for the aged and infirm. Their fondness for her stems from her cheerfulness, her patient acceptance of her infirmities, and the fact that she never asks for anything. She rarely needs any medicine and has had no medical attention since she has lived in the home."

Mrs. Whisenand does get to say, "Nothing much ever happened to me. I was always a great home girl. I never worked out." Her whole life took place in the rural area around the villages of Centerton and Brooklyn with her husband, a farmer who worked part-time as a school-bus driver. The interviewer sums up his report:

"This old lady has no activities, no hobbies, and no real interest, I think. She was lying in her bed and seemed not to be listening or caring about our conversation as we made our way to her bed. There were three other ladies in this room, and they chattered throughout my visit, which created a considerable stir among them. They took exception to some of the comments of the nurses. The personal record of this patient indicates that she was a member of the Methodist church at Brooklyn. Mrs. Frank Clark explained that she had been reared in the Christian church at Brooklyn but had changed her membership later. The two had been members of the Rebecca Lodge at Brooklyn when it was active years ago.

"Q. Do you have any ambition you have not yet realized?

"When I asked Mrs. Whisenand this question, she responded: 'There was nothing I wanted to do that I couldn't. . . . I made several trips on the school bus with my husband, around Brooklyn.'

"Perhaps this, indeed, is the secret of her longevity. Born during the Civil War, married seventy years ago, living her entire life in a rural atmosphere, she nurtured flowers, crops and farm animals instead of the frustration and boredom born of forced retirement in our industrial society."

This summation and opinion about the woman's longevity is offered right after the question is put to Mrs. Whisenand herself:

"Q. Why do you think you have been able to live so long?

"A. She made no comment when I inquired if she had an explanation for her long life. The nurses and other ladies in the room volunteered that she came from a long-lived family. A cousin, John Fields, came striding into her room last summer, at the age of 97, for a visit from his home in Indianapolis. He has since died. Her brother, Calvin, died at the age of 99 two years ago. Mrs. Whisenand offered the following, which I presumed had some bearing in her mind on this point: 'Nothing has transpired in my life that I'm ashamed of.' "

Quite possibly this woman's life in a rural setting was a factor in her longevity. Quite likely, based on what was learned from the experience of other centenarians, her leading a busy life free from the frustration and boredom of retirement was a factor. Possibly, too, genetics played a role. But on this occasion, on a matter of obvious importance to her, the old woman does not let the others speak for her. Searching her mind for the crucial answer, she passes over the conventional physical and genetic reasons. She perceives that what has enabled her to go on living for so long was observing a moral life that allowed her to be at peace with herself.

CHAPTER 5
The Invisible People

Something that Mrs. Flora Whisenand said fits into another centenarian pattern. Making a trip on the school bus is not your everyday citation for the memorable experience of a lifetime. Mrs. Whisenand's interview was the 676th to be studied, and by this time the pattern was clearly discernible. But recognition came slowly and piecemeal because of the random appearance and unexpectedness of the clues.

The first hint came in the 131st interview, with Charles Steurer. He was born in Mount Vernon, New York, in 1867 and grew to young manhood during the period when Horatio Alger's rags-to-riches novels advised boys about *Struggling Upward* and to *Strive and Succeed.* The youngest of seven children, Mr. Steurer still remembers the thrill of getting his first ready-made clothes—an overcoat he bought at the age of 12 with money he saved from the three dollars a week he earned at a guitar factory. He became a cabinetmaker, then went into business for himself. As residents of the Westchester area, including the Rockefellers, responded to his craftsmanship and integrity, he prospered. At the age of 45 he incorporated his business and further enhanced his success. As a centenarian he is wealthy enough to indulge his interest in philanthropy.

Mr. Steurer is pictured seated beneath two paintings in his home. Every day he reads two newspapers, the Bible, and a book of poems. He has given thought to the poet's philosophy and to his own, for the interviewer states: "Happiness, he believes, is not something to be found anywhere; it is a state of mind. Unlike the poetic Browning, the practical Steurer believes that the grasp should never exceed the reach. Grasping for too much is a symptom of an incurable disease. Getting one thing means wanting another and contentment is never

Charles Steurer

Photo courtesy of County News Bureau, Westchester County, N.Y.

attained. Contentment and happiness have been attained by Mr. Steurer because, as he says repeatedly, 'I have the God-given gift of peace of mind.' "

Although Robert Browning's line from "Andrea Del Sarto" is misquoted, the philosophy of the poem is correctly inferred. Browning was saying that great art springs from great aspirations. Mr. Steurer rejects this as a personal philosophy. "The grasp should never exceed the reach" is not the statement of the usual self-made businessman. Nor is it the policy of today's commercial enterprise, with a credo of grow or die. Acquisitions do conglomerates make. Most Americans, immersed in debt, enjoy lifestyles and luxuries beyond their means.

But most startling of all, the statement goes counter to the conventional American success story presented in Alger fiction and enshrined in the legend of the untutored rail splitter who rose to become a great president. Each retelling of the cliché of the triumphant underdog resonates an empathetic string in the American psyche. The greatest hero is he or she who risks all, gives all, and wins all to become Number One. That may be the route to achievement and success—but not to contentment and happiness, says Charles Steurer.

One hundred forty-one interviews later, Mr. Steurer's philosophy surfaced in a quite different kind of centenarian. Albert Raff spent most of his life as a farmer. He started work early in life on his father's dairy farm, and by the time he was 7 or 8 years old he was milking cows in the morning before going to school. He only went to school during the winter months and never received much education. "What you learned in the winter," he says, "you forgot in the summer." He also worked in a rolling mill, and when he was asked why he had been able to live so long, he replied, "That's what I wonder. Maybe working seven years in the rolling mill sweated all the poison out of me."

At the end of the interview, Mr. Raff was asked if he had any unrealized ambitions. "I couldn't do them now anyhow, so I gave that all up. The way I was raised, if you couldn't do something, you might just as well forget about it."

Here is the same unblinking pragmatism. He realistically decides what is possible, what he is capable of doing, and eliminates the rest from his thoughts and desires.

The attitude was expressed in a somewhat different way by Robert Yarborough of Meridian, Mississippi. He say he worried about things as a young man but learned a long time ago to take things as they come. "If I can do anything about it, I'll do it. If I can't, I just forget it. Take things as they come and don't worry about them."

Frank Harlow "attributes his longevity to his optimistic attitude toward life—that right will prevail and it is senseless to worry, since everything one worries about does not happen."

"Doesn't worry" is a characteristic watched for closely in this investigation. Belle Boone Beard reported in a study of 100 centenarians (Appendix 5) that when asked the secret of their longevity, the most frequent answer from the subjects was "I don't worry." In this inquiry, the attitude was found in 10 percent of the centenarians, was judged to be a salient characteristic in 6½ percent, and was given as a reason for their longevity by about 5 percent of the group. From the examples of Robert Yarborough and Frank Harlow, it can be seen that this is derived from experience.

The streak of pragmatism in the centenarians is just as much in the American grain as Horatio Alger. Pragmatism is the name for a distinctly American school of philosophy given impulse by Charles Pierce and made popular by William James in the late nineteenth and early twentieth centuries. Pragmatism was an attempt to rescue philosophy from abstruse logic and make it a useful instrument for practical living. The American philosophers said that the way to test the truth of an idea is simply to observe its consequences in conduct and action.

Today, pragmatism means a practical approach to problems and affairs. Once this trait is looked for in these centenarians, it can be found manifested in a variety of ways. Without exception, the centenarians are not theorists. When they give reasons for their longevity, they are practical reasons, based on personal experiences and judgments from those experiences. One man—count him, one—expressed his concern for posterity, but many centenarians showed in words and actions how deeply they felt about the welfare of their own progeny. In other words, their thoughts were focused on the practical needs of the present and the immediate future.

Most of their significant memories are restricted to events that impinged upon their own lives. Even when they cite great historic occurrences such as the Civil War, the memories are about fathers and older brothers going off to fight and coming home. When World War I or World War II is named as the most significant historic event, one discovers that a son or grandson was fighting in those conflicts. Hard times are well remembered: in the South after the Civil War, in the Midwest during the Depression of 1893, and all over in the 1930s.

More than a few centenarians could not name one significant historic event in their lifetimes while they never failed to remember significant events from their personal lives. To some extent this may reflect the nature of memory itself. One man remarked that in old age one's memories are not so much of historic events as of little, personal things. Another reason is that these earlier Americans were not wired into the world the way we are today. But the reason most often given is that they were too busy hacking out a living for themselves and their families to pay attention to extraneous matters. As Mrs. Margaret Tinsley put it: "Life on the prairie and in a sodhouse was hard, so that historical events just never occurred."

More than sixty centenarians and their families showed their pragmatism by homesteading, a practical way for people of little means to acquire land. The Homestead Act of 1862 provided that any person who was head of a family or twenty-one years old and was a citizen of the United States or had filed intentions to become one was entitled to as many as 160 acres of public land. If he lived on the land and cultivated it for five years, the homestead was his with the payment of a few fees. Or he had the option, after six months, of buying the homestead outright. The land usually sold for $1.25 an acre, or $200 for the 160 acres.

The easy financial terms were only a small part of the actual price. The other requisites to make the deal work were hard labor over many years, endurance of all kinds of hardships, and the fortitude to live isolated in the wilderness among the Indians. Above all else, the centenarians and their families wanted the land. They never seemed to think the cost was too high. They were willing to do whatever was needed and in the process became tough, hardy people. Some of them gained prosperity as the worth of land and agriculture rose in the mid-twentieth century.

Most of the centenarians were not well off, though, and when another good deal offered by the government appeared late in their lives, they responded pragmatically. Social security legislation was passed by Congress in 1935, went into effect in 1937, and began paying retirees in 1940. About 95 percent of this group of centenarians was 65 years old or older in 1937 and therefore ineligible for benefits under the original law that provided future benefits only to workers under age 65 in commerce and industry. However, over the years coverage was broadened. In 1939 the age restriction of workers was eliminated; in 1950 farm and domestic workers and nonfarm self-employed became eligible; in 1954 self-employed farmers and professionals except for lawyers, doctors, and dentists were covered; two years later the law covered lawyers and dentists; and in 1965 physicians were included. Additional categories of dependents and survivors gradually were brought in. In October 1966 the Prouty Amendment affected the remaining members of the centenarian cohort still not receiving social security payments. This was a one-shot piece of legislation extending old-age benefits to all Americans who were 72 years old or older by January 1, 1968. By this time, most of the centenarians already were 100 years old or in their late nineties.

Of the 380 centenarians who talked about their initial reaction to social security in the early days, two-thirds of them never expected to receive payments or never thought about it. Usually this meant both, in the way that Albert Raff and Robert Yarborough put out of their minds matters they decided did not pertain to them. Sherman Parsons articulated the attitude: "I didn't pay much attention to it because I didn't think it would ever mean anything to me." The initial reaction of more than one-third of the group was that social security was a good thing. The two segments add up to more than

100 percent because forty-nine centenarians—13 percent—expressed both reactions: They pragmatically considered insurance for the aged a good program even though they realistically did not expect to share in the benefits.

For some centenarians, pragmatism is observable in that their interest in social security appeared and then increased in direct proportion with their expectation of receiving benefits. Farmer Charles Reuter kept himself informed about government programs. He was 85 years old when self-employed farmers were brought under social security, but he qualified by selling a few calves, chickens, and dairy products. Daniel Bowles was in semiretirement on his farm but managed to meet the minimum requirements for coverage in the same way.

Albert P. Davis was a photographer for sixty-six years. "When the social security law was first passed, I didn't think of it, as I was self-employed. Later, when I saw others collecting benefits, I began thinking about it.

"I had always been my own boss. In 1943 [at age eighty-four] I gave up my own business and went to work for another studio with the idea of getting social security coverage. I worked three years and then retired."

At least a dozen centenarians, some in their eighties, came out of retirement in order to get social security payments. "I never thought too much about it," said Illinois farmer Homer Cheeley, "till I began to get too old to earn my living." This occurred three months past his one hundredth birthday: That's when he first went to the district office to inquire about coverage.

The practical approach to affairs is evident in the reaction to the last public event to have an impact upon this group of centenarians— the program to put Americans on the moon. Thirteen centenarians expressed themselves on the effort. Three were in favor, ten opposed. Seven of the ten objected because they thought the money could be better spent on Earth.

Alvan Couch is one of the objectors. An avid reader of scientific literature, he still makes telescopes for young people and just completed a moonscope for a great-nephew. Speaking nine months before Neil Armstrong will set foot on the moon, Mr. Couch places the space program in a larger national context: "Another problem facing our people at the present time is their disregard for sound fiscal habits in their own individual lives. The extravagance of our present administration, the national debt we are building, is reflected with the individual citizen. People today borrow money and have no desire to pay it back. I have studied astronomy not only in college, but all through my life, and I have read reports from those scientists who are experts in this field that the moon is a desolate and wasted land and could not be considered for habitation. How much better it would be if we could use some of the billions of dollars that are going each year to our space program for the betterment of our people—the rehabilitation of our poverty-stricken citizens."

Ivan Musselman says, after the moonwalk: "That's the craziest piece of work men ever thought about. What good did it do? It caused the country a lot of debt. It's better to tend to the work to be done on Earth." He regarded with the same practicality the fact that he had no more ambitions. "Having no ambitions doesn't bring in money, but it also doesn't cause money to be spent."

The interview with Lew Broncheon reveals how unorthodox some centenarians can be on the subject of ambition. Mr. Broncheon was born at home in the back of his father's shoemaker shop in Lake County, north of Chicago, January 4, 1866. He did farm work at an early age and did not get much education, going to school only during the winter months. He received ten cents an hour for a ten-hour day on the farm. "I did help build the U.S. Steel Wire Mill Plant in Waukegan at the turn of the century. I got my social security coverage working as a janitor in several restaurants and taverns here in Wauconda. I also worked in noncovered employment as a watchman for the County of Lake and the State of Illinois and I was also Village Marshall here in Wauconda."

Near the end of the interview, the reader learns there was another, interesting part to Lew Broncheon's life. He says he believes he has been able to live so long because of the outdoor life he led as a young man—farming, trapping, hunting, and fishing. Then he adds: "I was a baseball pitcher and played semipro ball for years. I was a right-handed pitcher. I was fifty-three years old when I pitched my last game."

And it is not until the last two sentences of the answer to the final question, about unrealized ambitions, that one learns that baseball was the central pursuit of his life. "My main ambition in life was to be a big league baseball pitcher. I almost made it."

"I almost made it" is an astounding perception and assessment by objective standards. The gap between aiming to be a big leaguer and only becoming a semipro is so great that the person would be judged a failure by most people. But that is not the way Lew Broncheon sees it. Untroubled by negative thoughts about his past performance and achievements, Lew Broncheon is satisfied with his life. And, judged by the norm, his living one hundred years is an extraordinary achievement and his life a success.

Lew Broncheon

Mrs. Jennie Williams, a bright and intelligent woman who was a housewife most of her life, makes a direct connection between longevity and relinquishing ambition. She believes the reasons for her long life are "walking up a little bit" (exercise) and "forgetting ambition." Among the reasons Egbert Van Nostrand of Winsted, Connecticut, gives for his longevity is that "I have had no overwhelming ambition." Albert Uthe says, "I can't say that I've ever had any particular ambition that I have not realized." But he also says, "I've never had ambition for big things." On his one hundredth birthday, Donal McLaughlin, a successful New York City architect, told friends the secret of his longevity was never exerting himself with "too much work or ambition."

Grandma Moses was the most successful person in this cohort, judged by the extent of her fame and appreciation of her paintings. Yet ambition had nothing to do with her accomplishments. In her seventies, a widow, her usefulness as a farm mother coming to an end, she was asked by her daughter Anna to make a worsted painting (in which one makes an outline, then sews wool through the canvas instead of using paint). She made a number of these worsted paintings until her hands began to go lame from arthritis. She took a home remedy, using a drop of turpentine, for three months. The pain went away but the hardness in the joints remained. At this point, her sister Celestia advised her to take up painting, saying she could do that better and faster than worsteds. "So I did," writes Grandma Moses in *My Life's History*, "and painted for pleasure, to keep busy and to pass the time away, but I thought of it no more than of doing fancy work."

Nor did she aspire to fame. She placed a few paintings in the window of a drug store in nearby Hoosick Falls, New York, because her practical and utilitarian nature (she called it "Scotch thrift") required her to see, as long as she had made the paintings, if she could sell them for a few dollars. That was the extent of her hopes. "I also exhibited a few at the Cambridge Fair with some canned fruits and raspberry jam. I won first prize for my fruit and jam, but no pictures.

"And then one day, a Mr. Louis Caldor of New York City, an engineer and art collector, passing through the town of Hoosick Falls, saw and bought my paintings. He wanted to know who painted them, and they told him it was an old woman." At the age of 79 Grandma Moses was at the gateway to undreamed success and fame.

Compare these attitudes to this statement by psychotherapist Arnold A. Hutschnecker (see Appendix 10), a pioneer in psychosomatic medicine: "From birth and through the years of struggle

Grandma Moses
(1860–1961) at
the age of 100

toward maturity, each human being aspires toward some achievement, clear or clouded, conscious or unconscious. Toward this he strives through the entanglements of life, its success and defeats, until he reaches his mark—or until he becomes convinced that he can never reach it and life ceases to have meaning. Then he dies."

That statement was a conclusion drawn from Dr. Hutschnecker's experience in counseling many people who had reached life-or-death crises in their lives. It can be seen that goals are tricky things. While they beckon us on through life into the future and thus serve survival, attaining them can be as truncating as deciding they are unattainable, unless one can formulate new goals or substitute other values. If this is indeed the case, then there is a survival value in disengaging from goals—"forgetting ambition."

A less drastic course is to reduce the importance of goals and therefore their power over a person's life. Make goals more manageable, more serviceable, less dictating. It figures that if a person sets modest ambitions—"realistic" aspirations—then his chances of attainment are better than those of a person who seeks high goals. The lower the level of ambition, the less the competition, the less likely is a person to be frustrated or disappointed, the more likely that a person can be a success within his own frame of reference.

This may not be a consciously elaborated strategy for the centenarians, but there can be no doubt that "low aspirations, low expectations" characterize the lives of many of them. This counterstrategy —counter to the conventional thinking of most people—has the paradoxical effect of making many of the most outstandingly successful livers in American society invisible.

The reason for this curious effect stems from what we have been conditioned to believe success is and who the successful are. A successful person is exceptional, outstanding—he or she stands out from the crowd. Television, motion pictures, and the theater insinuate that the important people are the ones in stage center who orate, emote, or in some other way call attention to themselves.

In the familiar drawing-room play, the domestic says only "Yes, ma'am" or has no speaking lines. His or her function is to show that the lead character is wealthy. Another popular image of a domestic is a gross woman who does disagreeable manual chores "beneath" her employer. But being a domestic is the fifth most common occupation among the centenarians. Seventy-seven centenarians were domestics, only twenty-seven centenarians were wealthy.

While a Gary Cooper or a John Wayne is seen in sharp definition in the foreground, blurred in the background are the members of his posse: farmers (the number one occupation), clerks (number eight),

storekeepers (number ten) and other prosaic types (forty-one centenarians were carpenters, twenty-five cooks, twenty-four handymen,
eighteen teamsters, fifteen watchmen, seven blacksmiths, seven butch-
ers, six plumbers). We judge the star to be successful because he or
she gets not only attention, but also adulation and a lot of money.
But only four of the centenarians were in the acting profession, and
then only for small portions of their lives. Chief William Red Fox,
an American Indian woman, and a Chinese-born man played minor-
character or "extra" parts in the movies. Eleanor Robson was a
great stage star during the first decade of this century, but she left
the footlights forever soon after her thirtieth birthday to marry
millionaire August Belmont.

Being a housewife, once a highly respectable occupation and the
leading one for the centenarian women, seems to have evolved into a
vocation of such ill-repute that the people who profess it are somehow regarded as unqualified for something better or at least more
interesting. Decades of huckstering have implanted the notion that
housework is demeaning and dull. Working in a mill or factory, the
number three occupation for this group, is another low-status job. To
be sure, some centenarians filled positions with high social status, but
they were a small minority.

With few exceptions, these centenarians were not principal actors
in the events of their times, but rather witnesses to history. Some,
like Frank Moore, could write footnotes. During Mr. Moore's final
year at Shurtleff College at Alton, Illinois, "Susan B. Anthony was
scheduled to give a lecture there, and I was selected to meet her train.
I hired a horse and buggy and drove her the two miles to the college.
On the way, I naturally asked her if she really thought she would
succeed in her crusade for votes for women. I will never forget her
reaction. Her black eyes snapped and she furiously told me she
certainly would succeed. I always felt it was a shame she didn't live
long enough to get to vote."

A decade later in Mr. Moore's life, he met another famous person.
"One time in the 1890s, my wife and I were on what was then a fast
train from New York to Chicago, and when we went to the diner,
we found you could get an entire meal from 'soup to nuts' for a
dollar. I ordered oysters on the half shell from the menu, and the
waiter, with an embarrassed look, whispered that they were out. I
looked across the aisle at the large man busily eating oysters, and
then back at the waiter. He leaned over and whispered that the man
was President Cleveland and that he had gotten the last of the oysters.
Later, I had a chance to meet him."

A few centenarians were present at exactly the moment history was made. Enos Hartzell was a young man of 17 en route from West Virginia to his native Lehigh County, Pennsylvania, on July 2, 1881. As he was waiting in the Ohio & Potomac Railroad station during a stopover in Washington, D.C., Mr. Hartzell witnessed a shooting. The victim was President James Garfield. "Mr. Hartzell stated that the assassin hid behind one of the doors as the President entered the station and leaped from behind the door and shot President Garfield. This was one of the most exciting events he ever witnessed during his lifetime."

Mrs. Dora Failing, who worked so hard as a farm wife feeding the hired help five times a day, was another eyewitness to history. "I was at the Pan American Exposition in Buffalo, New York, September 6, 1901 when President McKinley was shot. I saw the Negro fellow grappling with the man who shot McKinley. President McKinley and his party had gone over to Niagara Falls to look around. When he came back and started shaking hands with people who had gathered, the assassin, with a gun concealed by a handkerchief around his hand, shot McKinley."

The centenarians' more customary intercourse with presidents was to hear one speak or to shake one's hand. Their usual roles were as visitors to the Centennial Exposition in Philadelphia, the St. Louis Exposition of 1904, or the World's Columbian Exposition in 1893; as spectators at circuses and county fairs; as witnesses to the Chicago fire of 1871 and the San Francisco earthquake of 1906; as attestors to the electrification of homes and the installation of telephones, to the passing of the horse and buggy and the coming of the auto.

So if this were a Greek drama, the centenarians would not be the main actors; they would be members of the chorus. As Greek drama evolved, the chorus moved to the background and a subordinate role until eventually it disappeared from the stage. But during the high period of Aeschylus, Sophocles, and Euripides, the chorus played an integral role in the drama, providing reactions to and commentary upon events unfolding in stage center, foretelling the inexorable course of the drama, and even warning the principal characters of their fates. The witnesses, the commentators, the mass shapers of history were, even without separate identities, the people.

This brings us back to the point of departure. Centenarians are superachievers in surviving, highly successful in gaining a duration of life that eludes most people. Successful people are outstanding— they literally stand out from a crowd. But this is where the analogy breaks down for centenarians. Most successful people know, or at least assume, they are important. Such a self-appraisal does not characterize centenarians. "I don't know what all this fuss is about,"

Estelle Pollatschek said jokingly at her one hundredth birthday party. "I'm not important. I never did anything worthwhile except to get old." Neither are centenarians physically distinguishable at a glance from other aged people. Nor do most centenarians stand out from the crowd in other accomplishments, our customary measure of successful people. Most centenarians are background people, functionaries, spear-carriers. They blend with the crowd and become invisible.

THE INTERVIEW WITH Mrs. Elizabeth Agler of Orlando, Florida, begins by stating that she lives with a retired daughter, is quite alert, has some trouble hearing, and has to squint a bit to see. The paragraph goes on to say that Mrs. Agler "was pleasingly modest. 'There is nothing exciting about my life,' she said; 'I can't see why anybody would want to write anything about me.' "

Mrs. Agler's self-effacing remark is in keeping with preceding statements made by centenarians, and this kind of answer eventually led to the revelation of still another aspect of the centenarian pattern under consideration.

The question "What was the most exciting event in your own life?" seems a natural to ask these very old people. They have lived exceptionally long lives that must be replete with experiences from times that have the enchantment of distance.

The most common answer to the question was "Getting married"—offered by twenty-one women and twenty men. Mrs. Jennie Ely's response, however, was less than emphatic. The social security representative reported that she couldn't recall anything "especially exciting, unless it was her marriage to Reverend Ely."

Mrs. Louda Copeland of Garland, Texas, changed her answer in mid-interview. This kind of correction happened occasionally because the centenarians took the questions seriously and wanted to be sure they had answered as honestly as possible. At first, Mrs. Copeland "guessed" the most exciting event in her life was when she married. "Later, after several other questions had been asked, she came back to this one and said she thought the answer given was wrong. 'I think the jet airplane flight two or three years ago was the most exciting event. I was going to Greenville, South Carolina—we flew real high—I don't remember but the speaker announced how high we were. We stopped in Atlanta, Georgia. I remember a man with a wheelchair met me at the plane. I didn't expect it. There really hasn't been too much excitement in my life. It was very quiet.' "

Nineteen centenarians replied that coming to the United States was the most exciting event in their lives. Several centenarians seemed to parry the question by saying the whole of their lives had been exciting, without naming anything in particular. But from time to time, some very specific answers appeared.

Daniel Walker of Miami, Florida, said that his most exciting experience was "when he got a job as a janitor in Mr. Thompson's barber shop on Flagler Street during World War II"—at the age of 75.

Cornelius Ramsey of Dothan, Alabama, "described the most exciting event in his life as if it were yesterday. This was the occasion of his only boat ride, on the mail boat from Wewahitcha to Panama City, Florida."

For Mrs. Anna Nix of Georgia, "the most exciting event in her life was a trip to Milledgeville, Georgia, with her employer to see her daughter."

Mrs. Ida Brooks remembered "going to the basement of a restaurant where she worked to get some potatoes and being knocked unconscious by a jar that slipped out of the hands of another employee and hit her on the head."

Sister Josephine Scanlan, living in retirement at the Convent of the Sacred Heart at Kenwood in Albany, New York, treasures this highlight from her life. It occurred in 1899 when she was 25 years old: "I remember as my favorite experience, when I was traveling as a very young religious, traveling from St. Louis to Kenwood, Albany. My superior told me not to get off the train until I reached Kenwood, Albany. I was to go straight there as my superior told me.

"When I reached Rochester, the conductor said 'All off the train.' But I stayed on the train because I was told to stay on until I reached Kenwood, Albany. The conductor said to me, 'Didn't you hear me, sister? I said all off.'

" 'Yes,' I told him, 'I heard you. But I was told by my superior not to get off the train.' He then took my grip and he pushed me off. I was standing on the platform and it was late in the evening. I didn't know a soul, and I didn't know we had a house in Rochester. I didn't know where to turn. I thought, what will I do tonight!

"All of a sudden, a gentleman appeared, a tall gentleman. 'Sister, where are you bound for?' he said to me. I told him Kenwood, Albany. He said, 'Follow me,' and he went down a flight of stairs and up a flight of stairs and onto a train on another track.

"I was so happy. I got on the train, turned to thank him, and he was gone. Now who was he? I think to this day he was St. Joseph. If he had been an ordinary man, he would have said something to me like 'You'll arrive in Albany in an hour or so,' but he said nothing and disappeared like lightning.

"It is the most pleasant experience of thinking that God took care of me when I was all alone, quite late in the evening and not knowing anyone."

A surprising number of centenarians could not think of a single exciting event. When Sarah Mettlen, the Chicago White Sox fan with a sense of humor, was asked the question, her reply was "Skip it."

Sometimes the social security interviewer would not accept the negative response, as in the case of George Gipson. Mr. Gipson came to Alabama as a young man and for more than half a century worked for a coal mining company. Almost all of those years were spent above ground in the "horselot" where he took care of two horses and ninety-eight mules until the age of 90. When asked about the most exciting event in his life, he said, "There wasn't any excitement—I have never been in jail." Thinking he had misunderstood, the government interviewer reworded the question and tried again. "There's not much to get excited about," Mr. Gipson explained, "when you spend all your life looking after mules on the farm and for the coal company."

William Johnson led a varied life, and the interviewer was so taken with his subject that it was difficult for the field representative to accept Mr. Johnson's evaluation of exciting events. The report begins this way:

"William Johnson is a small, slender man with flowing white locks. He has a very youthful appearance for a man who will reach his one hundredth birthday in December. There is scarcely a line in his face. He is neatly dressed and well-groomed and walked into the room more like a man of 60 than one of 100. He told me he was born on a turpentine farm in the seaport of Beaufort, North Carolina. His father was a Dutchman and his mother part Cherokee and part Sioux Indian. He showed me a portrait of his father and was proud of his father's very long hair. He said that when his father died, his hair was so long that he was able to tie it around his waist. His earliest recollection is of playing in the woods behind his home in Beaufort. He also remembers almost drowning when he was about three years of age. He had gone out in a boat with his father and an uncle and, in his childish way, he thought he could walk on the water and simply left the boat to walk ashore. This experience is probably the most exciting thing that ever happened to him in his life."

The interviewer adds that Mr. Johnson went to private school for seven or eight years, then was a fisherman for seven years off the shores of Beaufort, and wandered around the South before finally coming to New England where for a while he worked in an apothecary shop. "He helped grind herbs for medicinal purposes and made root beer and helped maintain the store." At age 65 he became a messenger for an insurance company, not retiring until he was 91 years old. He was a great reader; studied German, Spanish, and French; played the flute, drums, and bugle. "He marched in bands when a youth and in torchlight parades during presidential elections. He loved music and stated that the one ambition he never did realize was to be able to blow a cornet satisfactorily.

"In a life as long as Mr. Johnson's," the interviewer writes, "one would think that there had been many exciting events, but he is unable to recall any events he would call exciting. I tried to jog his memory and so did his daughter, but we could arouse no memories."

The unexpected response of denying that any exciting events took place occurred so often that I went back to the beginning to categorize the answers to the question. There was an interesting division of responses. Five hundred nine centenarians answered the question. One hundred nine of these said that their lives had been wholly or at times exciting. Four hundred said or indicated they had lived quiet lives with no exciting events.

A quiet life appears as a salient characteristic for one of every four of these centenarians, number three behind hard work and farm life.

These quiet lives did not just happen. Like not worrying and reducing desires to fit reality, a quiet life was deliberately pursued. When Martha Dees of Otter Creek, Florida, was asked the question, she replied: "I have never been excited in my life. My daddy told me never to be that way." The interviewer refused to accept this, for he writes: "I asked Mrs. Dees if she was excited when she married either the first or second time, and she replied, 'No, I just knew I was supposed to get married because I was a woman.'"

When Mrs. Copeland, the lady who decided that a recent airplane flight was more exciting than her marriage, was asked why she had been able to live so long, her answer was: "Cause I've lived a quiet simple life, I guess."

Mr. Johnson, who could not be coaxed or coerced into admitting to any exciting experience, believed he had been able to live long because he had worked so hard all his life. "Throughout the interview he referred to the fact he had been a very, very hard worker. He had driven double teams of horses, had hewn wood, carried coal, and had worked very hard. His daughter thinks it is because he has always remained calm in the face of adversity and any family strains. His calmness and patience are legendary in the family."

Sixteen centenarians attributed their longevity to living a quiet life, a number far down the list of attributions. But if one adds related characteristics and attitudes—doesn't worry, never gets excited

or upset, living one day at a time, calm or happy-go-lucky disposition, is content or has peace of mind, taking things as they come,
simple life, no fighting or never in trouble, and has no ambition—
one gets a cluster of attributions in fourth place behind the aggregates for religion, work, and moderation.

It might be argued that a calm or happy-go-lucky disposition is a
natural endowment, not a learned way to live. While this may be
true, the possessor of this trait valued its life-preserving quality and
therefore presumably had the sense to encourage its expression.

CHAPTER 6

Declarations of Independence

While the questionnaire item "Attitude toward social security" (56F) was useful in illuminating the practical nature of many centenarians, the item was more important in revealing their sense of independence. The following are some answers to the question asked by field representatives "What were your reactions when you first heard about the social security program?":

Neils Neilsen, a longtime fisherman of Gloucester, Massachusetts: "I didn't think much of social security when I first heard of it. I thought it was charity."

Noble Barfield, a black farmer living in Jasper, Florida: "I don't know. I believe in every man scratching out his own life. I don't believe in me scratching out yours for you, and I don't believe in you scratching out mine for me."

Mrs. Martha Dees, the poor white woman living in a shack at Otter Creek, Florida: "I thought it was nonsense, but after Frank and I started getting paid I didn't know what to think." This is the same Martha Dees whose father told her never to get excited. The social security agent didn't accept her position on that at first and questioned her further on it. He did the same thing on this subject: "When I questioned her about this she had what you might describe as a pioneer attitude of believing that the government owed people nothing but to leave them alone."

Louis Oliver of Corte Madera, California: "I thought it was a

Matilda Rogers

proposition to keep tabs on people. I didn't think much of it. Nobody did at that time."

James Williams, a black man of Tampa, Florida: "I didn't believe it—in Florida you have to work for what you get. Ain't nothing free down here."

Robert Wheeler of Marion, Kentucky, who still runs his farm and attends directors' meetings of the bank where he once was president: "When social security started, I was in business. I called my employees together and held an election to determine if the employees wanted coverage, and we voted not to come under. I later found that we had no choice. At that time I did not believe in the program, believing that everyone should make his own way in life." Taking care of oneself was a philosophy expressed by several other centenarians, and Alexander McCulley saw that social security had the effect of making people dependent upon the government.

Forty-two centenarians said they didn't like the idea of social security, didn't want it, or didn't think it would work. These people account for only 11 percent of those who express themselves on the subject. However, they become part of a sizeable bloc if they are joined with the two-thirds majority that never expected to get social security or never thought about it. While that response bespeaks the centenarians' realism or pragmatism, it represents their independent attitude as well. A number of them state explicitly that they never expected to receive benefits because they expected to take care of themselves; they never thought about social security because they were too busy working and taking care of themselves.

Mrs. Mary Kipp of Cincinnati is a case in point: "Mrs. Kipp's husband died about forty-eight years ago, and at that time she returned to work. The work that she obtained consisted of washing, ironing, and general housework in private homes. This continued until she went to work for Lunkenhiemer's Cafe in the kitchen where she remained until retirement at 77. In 1935 when the Social Security Act was passed, she was well over 65 and thus was not eligible to pay for it. She stated that the other women laughed at her because she was too old to receive social security checks. This did not disturb her at the time because she was working and was only interested in receiving her salary for the work she did. When people over 65 were covered by the 1939 amendments, Mrs. Kipp began building credits toward retirement."

The concept of social security was so alien to some of these people that they could not see how they were entitled to it. Joe Shortridge of Circleville, Ohio, began receiving benefits in his ninety-ninth year under the age-72 amendment. "He was quite surprised when he found out that he qualified for this, as he thought that 'you had to need it to get it.' The social security benefits are only a small part of his income." Laura Crews of Enid, Oklahoma, also came under the age-72 benefits, when she was 96 years old: "I didn't want to take it at all since I hadn't worked for it, but relatives persuaded me to apply for it, and it has come in handy."

Otto Welge, the old farmer who loved to swing an ax "and feel the sweat break out," told his social security visitor: "I raise some animals for slaughter and a few for sale, but not enough to really have income. I have a little land that I rent out now and get rental income from that, but by and large my social security is my income at this time. I never thought I would see the day when I was a young man that I would be living on something like this, but I sure am thankful for it now."

Mrs. Matilda Rogers came to Kansas in 1894 when she was 42 years old in a covered wagon with her husband and five children. For three years they lived in a sod house before building a frame one. She worked in the fields—plowing, shucking corn, and stacking hay. Her husband died when she was 77 years old but she continued farming. Mrs. Rogers was 107 years old at the time of her interview. "She still owns the farm on which the family settled when they came to Kansas. Her grandson now rents it and cares for the cattle which she owns. Her social security was earned on the income from these cattle. Her family says that she does not really understand what social security means or why she receives a check each month, but she knows how many acres of her farm are in crops and how many are pasture."

The social security question separates the independent and pragmatic attitudes. Five centenarians said social security gave them a sense of security, while thirty others said the old-age insurance made them feel independent.

Not only are the independent and practical attitudes separate, but they can be antagonistic. Isaac Jacobson, an attorney for many years in New York City and one of the most philosophic of the centenarians, articulates how the attitudes conflict, and how they can be reconciled. "Mr. Jacobson discussed his attitudes toward social security when the law was passed in August 1935. He said that he was opposed to it at that time since he was an independent thinker and didn't feel that the government should get involved in people's lives. Then he added, 'Now that I see how social security works, I think it is a fine thing. It actually fosters my independent thinking because it helps provide my financial needs. This is important because I feel that a person who lives within his income is truly rich.' "

Once the centenarians come to realize that the program does not threaten their independence but rather ensures it, their appreciation is doubly felt and strong expressions of gratitude are offered by all except a small minority. Mrs. Antonette Spagnoli showed at age 95 how quickly her understanding of the significance of a social security income could be transposed to action. "Her two children supported her until 1966 (when she was 95), when a neighbor told her about the special age-72 benefits. Since getting these benefits, she has made her children stop supporting her."

"They have to buy everything for me now," says Mrs. Rebecca Miller of New Paris, Indiana, "but I pay for it from my social security. I don't want anything that's not mine." The social security representative then comments: "Thus the benefits which she has been receiving for over twenty years have helped her maintain that spirit of independence and self-reliance which is the story of her entire life."

THE "FREEDOM/INDEPENDENCE" PATTERN is not as visible as the "Order/Discipline" pattern. Whereas 40 percent of the operative items in the "Order" category were checked, the figure is 30 percent for the items under "Freedom/Independence." Still, the "Freedom" pattern is well enough defined to make "Order-Freedom" the dominant profile, evident in 94 percent of the 1,200 centenarians.

The leading trait under "Freedom/Independence" (see Appendix 28) is a mental one—"curious, interested in immediate world about him/her"—found in 84 percent of the centenarians. It is the only high-scoring characteristic in the "Intellectual" subsection (see item 55C, Appendix 22). Along with this mental freedom and aliveness is the other freedom probably most valued by any of us—the ability to function well physically. Viewed as a sign of independence, five out of six of these centenarians could be said to have good physical functioning. Five of the top fifteen items are in the "Physical" subsection, one that offers an excellent scale for comparing the gradations of fitness that apply to us all. While 84 percent of the centenarians have good physical functioning, 72 percent still are mobile without any aids. This is followed by two extraordinary statistics—two-thirds of the centenarians are free from any disease and 42 percent get along without dependence upon the health establishment. Thirty percent still are capable of doing physical work. Finally, in the area where the toll of old age is most apparent, only one in four remains free of physical disability. But since we are dealing with 100-year-olds, perhaps the statistic should be presented the other way around: Remarkably, one-quarter of these ancient people survive without any kind of physical disability.

In third place is the important "family relationship." While "family relationship" in the "Order" category signifies stability and structure in the centenarians' lives, here it is a measure of their social independence. An examination of these centenarian lives shows the support of a loyal and loving family to be one of their most valuable resources, for many of them the equivalent of possessing and maintaining both jobs and homes. The familial-support services enable the centenarians to enjoy a quality of life and social interaction that would otherwise be difficult to achieve.

Their ability to maintain social independence (see Appendix 22, number 60) can be seen further in that 30 percent of them still have a variety of friends and about one in five still takes part in organized group activities. Perhaps the most noteworthy statistic in this index of social activity is that one centenarian in ten remains in a position to meet new people—thus preserving the potential to repair losses from the social attrition that accompanies advancing age.

"Freedom from stress or anxiety" is the fourth most common characteristic, identifiable in more than three-quarters of the group. All four items in the "Psychological" subsection are in the top fifteen, suggesting the importance of this area to longevity. Leading an "autonomous life," with freedom from dependence on various social and health services (excluding family and social security), is in eighth place, a description of five of eight of these centenarians. Another figure indicative of the character of these people is that nearly half of them still make the decisions in their lives. They retain this essential mechanism of independence despite the physical frailty that keeps most of them from earning a livelihood and forces them to rely on the services of relatives. And more than one-third of the centenarians are free of the emotional and intellectual rigidity that is commonly regarded as a primary characteristic of old age. When this flexibility was considered as "ability to accept change" in the "Psychological" category of the "Sociopsychobiological" profile (34M), it was recognized as a characteristic of nearly all the centenarians—93 percent. Centenarians do not show their age when judged by their adaptive potential.

Their independence is quite clear when judged by one of our most common measures—economic independence. Three-quarters of the centenarians are economically independent; not well off, but able to make ends meet. In addition, the "Socioeconomic" subsection in the

"Social Sphere" category (Appendix 22, item 20) shows that social security is the major factor in maintaining economic independence. Social security payments (item 20C) are the sole or main source of income for 75 percent of the centenarians. This measurement was made for most of the subjects during the 1960s and early 1970s, just before the oil-induced inflationary spiral took off. Nevertheless, market prices fueled by the Vietnam War already were exerting unrelenting pressures, always pulling ahead of pension income. Younger retired Americans were finding that social security income was inadequate to maintain their accustomed lifestyle. Of course, most of these hard-working centenarians from an earlier time had never had the opportunity to grow accustomed to a high style of living. But undoubtedly the main reason that so many of them were able to live solely or mainly on their social security checks was their pragmatic approach to life, by which they scaled down their needs and desires to correspond with what could be provided. In the economic area, that pragmatism translates to frugality and was aptly expressed by Isaac Jacobson when he said, "I feel that a person who lives within his income is truly rich."

In addition to the 75 percent of the centenarians who were economically independent, 21 percent lived in comfortable circumstances or were wealthy, revealing the odds against the long-term survival of a poor person—96 percent to 4 percent, or twenty-four to one. Even so, a poor person might take consolation from the fact that his odds still are better than those of a rich person. Only 2.4 percent of these centenarians were wealthy compared to the 4 percent who were poor.

Other criteria of independence were "living in one place alone" (13 percent) and "managing their own homes" (22 percent). Forty-three percent still were "able to perform useful roles" and 19 percent still were "working at their chosen vocations."

Occupations are an index to independence in another way: by the amount or degree of interpersonal freedom they permit. Item 29 in the questionnaire, "Work Arrangement," shows that 32 percent of the centenarians were their own bosses while 3 percent worked alone. The tabulated numbers add up to more than 1,200 because in some cases, where the choice of a single, preponderant characterization was not clear, multiple entries were made. Wherever possible this practice was avoided, in order to reflect as much as possible the emphases for the major part of these work lives. A farmer worked alone, but in some cases employed help and in any event is listed under the more descriptive "own boss." Whereas a traveling salesman may have been employed by a company, he spent most of his time unsupervised, working alone. Working for others would apply to domestics and those people with similar interpersonal or very small-scale arrangements. Housewives and farm wives are listed under this heading. However, an equally reasonable characterization would have been that they were their own bosses and ruled within their homes. Certainly the obedience of their children in carrying out prescribed domestic roles until age 21 justifies such an interpretation. If the 468 housewives and farm wives are transferred to "own boss," then that category increases to nearly 70 percent, dwarfing all others.

Such a result coincides with the findings of Flanders Dunbar, the director of psychosomatic research at Columbia University's College of Physicians and Surgeons during the 1930s and 1940s, who studied centenarians and nonagenarians. From her findings as summarized in Appendix 7:

> They have escaped conflict with authority, including seeking vocations where they are their own bosses. Also they don't want to boss others. They prefer small businesses to large corporations. If they are professionals and artists, they have their own offices or research projects or they associate with groups that have much in common.
>
> They value independence and try to apply principles of democracy as a basis for cooperative and productive living. When this is impossible, they are likely to start anew, unembarrassed by any sense of failure.
>
> They have worked long hours and hard, but usually managed not to punch a time clock.
>
> They are rarely interested in getting to the top.

The result also is consistent with the Jewett study (Appendix 6):

> Independence of choice in their vocations: they tended to be their own bosses, had more freedom than the organization man, retirement at 65 was not forced on them. They worked at farming and in the nursery business, the professions of law, medicine and architecture; they headed small businesses. The majority did not retire early.

The appropriateness of these job descriptions can be seen by turning to the list of occupations for this cohort of centenarians, Appendix 25.

The aspect of independence reveals still another virtue of farming in connection with longevity. Not only was the farmer his own boss living independently on his own land, but the self-sufficiency of the autonomous farm unit of the nineteenth and first part of the twentieth centuries almost cut the umbilical cord of any dependence upon the larger community. "We were very self-reliant," says Sidney Davis of Paxton, Illinois. "Had about all the things we needed right on the farm. Only a few things had to be bought at the store, like coffee, sugar, and salt."

The account of Mrs. Alice Darby of Uniontown, Pennsylvania, goes into greater detail. "She was raised on an old-fashioned American farm. The family was nearly one hundred percent self-sufficient. They raised all their own food, made their own clothes, candles, tools, and furniture. They even made their own sugar from sugar cane grown on the farm. The general store meant just coffee and those few things the family could not grow or make for themselves.

"Mrs. Darby remembers, 'We didn't have much time to play. Summertimes, we worked until it was too dark to see. Wintertimes, we did the chores, went to school for a few weeks, and in the evenings we knitted the clothes we wore.' She learned to knit when she was only five years old and she fondly recalls gentle moments in the long winter evenings when she, her mother, and sisters would sit around a candlestand knitting.

" 'My mother spun the wool, the only light we had was from home-made tallow candles, and we used turkey quills for knitting needles,' she said."

Today's industrialized farms are more productive, and utterly dependent—upon expensive equipment, upon oil to power the machinery, and upon chemicals to keep up and protect the productivity. Rather than being instructed in the values of independence, today's farmer is taught the necessity of interdependence.

If by the criteria and characteristics considered so far these centenarians commonly can pass for much younger people, there are a few items in the "Freedom/Independence" sphere that show where the oldtimers have lost their youthful quality and are vulnerable. Only thirteen centenarians still were driving an automobile. This loss of mobility affects a person's social, personal, and work life.

The other items revealing vulnerability also are in the "Social," "Work," and "Personal life" subsections, but aside from their assignment to these different areas the items are the same; they show that centenarians have lost their freedom of choice. Twenty-five centenarians—2 percent—could be said to be capable of embarking on some new social course or generating a new sphere of friends. Most of the centenarians were secure in the social matrices they had developed over the years, but judged not able to go beyond maintenance of the status quo to initiate some new social milieu. It is true that when centenarians entered nursing homes, they were notably successful in ingratiating themselves in their new environments. While such accomplishments testify to considerable social resilience, they were made as accommodations to forced moves.

Similarly, only sixteen centenarians were judged to have the potential to begin another line of work or to switch from what they were presently doing. And a mere ten centenarians were seen to be in a position to embark on new directions in their personal lives. They were where they were as a result of their actions over very long lifetimes: The momentum of all their years and all their experiences propelled them along their set courses. They were locked in.

Judged by its absence in these ancient beings, we may deduce that the quintessence of youth is the widest possible freedom of choice in all areas of life.

LET'S FLESH OUT the statistics and take a look at a number of centenarians who represent varying degrees of independence. Alice Darby, who as a young girl knitted by candlelight with her mother and sisters on a Pennsylvania farm, as a centenarian widow lives with her grandson and his family. "Mrs. Darby is no longer strong enough to go outside, but she still has an independent streak a mile wide. She has her own rooms, does her own cleaning, and keeps things neat as a pin. She prepares her own meals and she feels that breakfast is the most important meal of the day. 'I've just got to have my eggs and toast in the mornings,' she said."

Elias Estrovich lives with his daughter in Whitestone, Queens, in New York City. His family owned movie houses in several Russian cities before the Bolshevik revolution. He came to the United States in the 1920s and opened a Russian restaurant in Manhattan. When that failed during the Great Depression, he went into the woodworking business. "I felt myself like a boss. As long as you're your own boss, that makes you happy."

Mrs. Rebecca Miller, who was praised for the "spirit of independence and self-reliance which is the story of her entire life," is pictured as she is coming out of what she called a "new-fangled" voting machine. The automatic voting machines were installed in New Paris, Indiana, for the first time during the 1960 Kennedy-Nixon presidential election. Her spirit shines out of her eyes, out of her face. She is looking directly at the camera through rimless glasses. Her toothless mouth is opened wide, and a viewer of the photograph can imagine her cackling laugh of exuberance. Mrs. Miller leans on a cane but gets additional support from a man in shirtsleeves standing behind her and somewhat to the side.

Rebecca Miller

"By choice she lives alone in her substantial eight-room brick house, which is only about a mile and a half from her birthplace. Until about three years ago she did all the housework and took care of her large vegetable garden as well. After operations for two hip injuries in her ninety-eighth year she made a concession to her own self-reliance and consented to have a housekeeper come in during the day to do the household chores. Her meals are still prepared on her old, wood cook-stove, which she refuses to trade for a modern stove.

"An avid newspaper reader until a few years ago when her eyes grew weaker, she still is able to pick up a surprising amount of news with the aid of a magnifying glass.

"Perhaps Mrs. Miller's greatest strength outside of her own indomitable spirit are her two devoted sons, Everett, 64, and Orba, 77, her three grandchildren, and nine great-grandchildren all living nearby. It is quite evident that the close family ties have contributed much to the fullness of her life.

"Mrs. Miller says her health is good. She doesn't get sick but is weak at times. She eats very well. With the assistance of a wheelchair and a walker she has no difficulty getting around her home.

"A staunch Republican, she has voted in every election since woman suffrage."

This is the account in part of William Keller ("Don't call me Mister; my name is Bill") who lives deep in the Blue Ridge Mountains, close to the center of the feldspar and mica mining-industry in western North Carolina:

"Taking a rocky road which I hoped led to his home, I stopped to inquire. A good-natured old woman cackled from her porch in answer to my request for directions, 'Hit hain't but a mile.' 'Hit' wasn't, and although I drove right by his place into an open-pit feldspar mine, a little backtracking brought me to a cowshed and a lean-to, which, with a clump of locust trees, completely hid from view the unpainted shack which was Bill's home.

"I made my way up the steps of the porch, being careful not to break a leg, and Bill greeted me as I appeared at the doorway. I sat down with him in a room which served both as the living room and bedroom. Lying on the bed, but cordial to the stranger, was Mrs. Keller, a mere 81 years old. I learned that she had not been out of bed for five and a half years, but she had not forgotten the ability to laugh.

"Bill had a heavy set of fairly close-cropped black whiskers, with enough of his cheeks showing to indicate that he was no more wrinkled than an average person of 60. His long, graying hair dangled loosely over his neck and ears.

"Bill was talkative enough when the questions came. It was soon obvious by his responses that he had lived a very plain and simple life, characterized largely by hard work. When asked the earliest thing he remembered, his one-word answer was 'Farming.' Further inquiry revealed that he began working when he was six on the family farm in Alexander County, North Carolina, where he was born, and that most of his life has been spent in the mountains of Tennessee and North Carolina. 'I did coal mining a right smart of my life and public works the biggest end of my life—woodloading and such likes as that.' He disclosed that he never went to school and could not read or write. He was generally unfamiliar with great historical events, and it was apparent that the 'outside' world had passed him by.

"His reaction when he first heard about the social security program? 'I thought it was a fine job. I thought that the man who was doing that was purty sensible.' He thought it would mean payments to him 'if he lived.' Does he have other income? 'That's all I get. Me and the madam get sixty-four dollars. Not kept up like I ought to be kept up, but I squeeze through somehow.'

"What does Bill do with his time? 'I set around and make baskets and take care of sick wife, get up with her three, four, five times every night.' I saw the baskets he was making, of blue and yellow and red wire. He said that he made $1 or $2 a month. I bought one for $1.50, getting Bill off to a good start on this first day of July.

"Bill looks to be in good health. Mrs. Keller mentioned his asthma, and Bill said, 'My asthma don't stop me from going but sometimes I think it's a-going to.' He ascribes his longevity simply to 'the good will of God.' Bill has few outside activities, and he leaves his neighborhood only to go to town for 'rations' and the mail. Sometimes he gets a ride on a truck loaded with feldspar ore, and sometimes he makes the four miles round trip on foot. 'Can't afford a mailbox,' Bill says, to explain the absence of home delivery.

"Bill was pretty agile climbing down the steps to pose for a picture in front of his home. After a couple of shots, he suddenly thought that he would look good in his hunting outfit and hurried in to reappear quickly with a rifle, two powder horns, a bullet pouch. The rifle was of ancient design and handmade; it had been in his possession for sixty-seven years. Bill has been making his own bullets, and while he has not hunted for four or five years, he would still have no trouble picking off a squirrel. Bill said that he hadn't climbed a nearby mountain for five years. Apparently his wife's illness has kept him more tied down than is his wont. A pile of wood under the lean-to in his front yard indicated that Bill has not lost the physical vigor needed to chop all the wood he needs.

"Bill has been married twice but never had any children of his own. He and the 'madam' manage to get along in independent fashion. He owns his modest property, on which he pays annual taxes of 'five, six, seven dollars.' "

"Mrs. [Anna] Olinger was interviewed at her home on the edge of Kansas University campus at Lawrence, Kansas. She is a joy to talk to and appears much younger than her years.

"Mrs. Olinger attended Michigan State University, at a time when girls couldn't attend unless they had a relative on the faculty. She also attended Moody Bible Institute in Chicago. Her strongest ties with a university, however, are with Kansas University, and date back to 1911 (when she was 40 years old). Her husband, a Presbyterian minister, died in 1921. She had been very busy as a minister's wife until that time.

"In 1928 she started working for the Presbyterian Student Center at KU and remained there until 1940. She was the associate director of the center. She said, 'They told me a woman couldn't do that job, but I showed them.' She has remained closely associated with KU since that time. She still has students visit her and corresponds with many. She has a large Christmas correspondence list and still writes notes in each card she sends. Mrs. Olinger indicates there have been many changes in students over the years. Appearance seems to stand out most in her mind.

"Mrs. Olinger has two daughters, one son, two grandchildren, and three great-grandchildren. She considers herself to be in good health. She says, 'I'm the busiest woman in town.' She belongs to a literary club, DAR, DAC, and church. She still attends church in good weather and is very fond of taking rides in the car and going out to eat.

"She attributes her long life to being able to adjust to the times. She is relaxed and flexible. She has a great amount of empathy for people and an eagerness for life, saying, 'I can't wait to get up in the mornings.' "

Mrs. Mary Muckler of Dell Rapids, South Dakota, was widowed at the age of 53 when her husband was gored by a bull. She took over operation of their dairy for about a year, but found it was too much for her and sold it. She then ran a tourist home and a nursing home and did practical nursing. She was working for a nursing home in Custer, South Dakota, when she was 92 years old. The 85-year-old

Edwin Mitchell

woman who owned the nursing home decided she was too old to keep working and sold the home. This left Mrs. Muckler without a job. "A fine kettle of fish," she said. "Just where can a ninety-two-year-old woman find a job in this day and age?"

A place was found for her at the Odd Fellows Lodge in Dell Rapids, where she takes care of her own needs, follows a busy routine, and employs an 85-year-old secretary to help with her correspondence. Although Mrs. Muckler has three children still living, she would not consider living with any of them. "They have their own lives to live," she says.

It may have been noticed that several of the outspoken statements in opposition to social security were made by blacks. A strongly independent nature is found in many of these black centenarians. Junius Turner of Dillon, South Carolina, says he never had any ambition beyond wanting to be independent, and he feels that he has succeeded. He is living alone and taking care of himself.

"Edwin Mitchell lives on the boundary line between Broward County and Dade County in southeast Florida in a home he built himself during World War II (when he was in his late seventies) and owns.

"Mr. Mitchell was born on a farm in Waycross, Georgia. He never served in the army or navy, but he sailed the ships and worked in the shipyards building cement breakers in both World War I and II.

"Social security is his main income. Mitchell does commercial fishing. He has two outboard boats. He goes fishing four times a week—gets up at 6 A.M. and fishes until 3:30 to 4 P.M. He has two freezers he uses to store the fish. He catches mullet, snapper, grouper, blues, and makes about thirty dollars a month. Besides fishing he keeps his yard in order and cuts wood for the stove."

Andrew Williams was born a slave. He worked on three different plantations and was sold twice as a boy before the Civil War and the Emancipation Proclamation ended slavery. "In those days," Mr. Williams says, "you needed a pass from your master or overseer to go from one place to another. If he'd catch you out, they'd tear you up. When the people were set free, they didn't know where to go."

Mr. Williams says it is a sin when people are not free and therefore slavery is a sin. "I believe in letting everything have its freedom." He pointed to a bird in a cage. "Even a bird would be better off free. Everything ought to have its liberty."

WHEN "TAKES RESPONSIBILITY for life, health" was looked at in the broad context of the psychological repertoire, it registered 30 percent of the centenarians; but when it was considered in a more specific sense as an item illustrating a person's independence, it could be seen to characterize about half the group.

John Stoll, a Wisconsin farmer, took this responsibility seriously enough to quit a job. He quit because he was unable to get milk to drink—he tried the nearby farms in Fort Madison, Iowa, but they all raised grain and had no cows. "He attributes his general good health to drinking milk."

Dr. Leonard Curtis, a retired law professor of De Land, Florida, said, "I have suffered from little things—for instance, I had ulcers once—but I finally decided that if I just worked hard, had constant habits, and lived like a normal individual should, I could live to be

Andrew Williams

a hundred, and that's just what I'm going to do. I have a strong constitution and feel that I am in perfect health myself."

Sarah Ann Page, living alone in Cambridge, Massachusetts, the woman who went to bed by nine but would stay up until ten sometimes when she had company: "You know, about ten years ago I laid in bed for two years with arthritis, and one day I said to myself, this will never do. So I sent for a Christian Science healer, and we read together in secret, and in two weeks I was up and around. How do you explain that?"

Mrs. Matilda Dillin of Sutherland, Nebraska, says that when she was 57 years old she was supposed to have surgery to remove a tumor. "Instead, she treated herself with a patented ointment. She alleges she has used this ointment ever since for various ailments. She believes her long life is due to use of this medicine."

And when Richard Crouthers of Elkand, Missouri, was asked why he thought he had been able to live so long, he replied: "Goat's milk, that's the secret. In 1932 [when he was 71 years old] I was about gone. The doctors didn't seem to do any good. Medicine didn't help. A doctor that people referred to as a quack told me if I wanted to get well, I could cure myself. Otherwise, he said, I'd probably not make it. He told me to get some goats and drink goat's milk. I went home, harnessed up the team to the wagon, and started to look for some goats. Brought three goats home and haven't been without them since. Everywhere we go—and we've moved often—we always take our goats."

Milk, hard work and constant habits, Christian Science healer, patented ointment, goat's milk—the treatment or placebo differs in each instance. But what never varies is that the person took responsibility for his health and did something about it.

"TAKES RESPONSIBILITY for life and health" certainly characterizes William Davis, but this 463rd interview to be processed gave a clue to larger implications of the characteristic. A surprisingly young-looking man, Mr. Davis had a full head of hair, not all of it yet white. He is shown seated in his home at Rogersville, Alabama, reading a paper without glasses. He lives with his daughter in a charming, two-story, colonial house. "Up until last November [four months before the interview] he had remained quite active—doing odd jobs about the house. He mentioned raising a garden each year but doubts if he will this year, due to a fall he experienced last November that injured his leg. He stated, 'I fell and bruised my right leg, but I've got a mighty good liniment that I rub on it that does me a heap of good.'

"In response to a question concerning how he has been able to live so long, Mr. Davis replied, 'I've worked hard all my life and I was always careful about my eating—I was never a glutton. After my wife died, I began eating honey; I believe that has extended my life. For breakfast I use a teaspoon of honey with butter every morning and a small bowl of rolled oats.' "

Certainly he is a man who takes responsibility for his health. But it was not until the brief final paragraph that other dimensions of his independence were revealed: "He is almost stone deaf but does not use a hearing aid. He reads with the assistance of a magnifying glass." A second look at his photograph showed that, sure enough, there

William Davis

was a magnifying glass held close to the newspaper. This revelation of character had the impact of a denouement or enlightenment at the end of a short story.

The importance of this insight was immediately reinforced by the realization that Mr. Davis was not the only centenarian to display a reluctance to use eyeglasses and/or a hearing aid—even though the two most common disabilities were failing vision and failing hearing. The choice of a magnifying glass over eyeglasses was especially puzzling, until one considers that the magnifying glass reduces dependency to an absolute minimum—just to the required visual area and function. We have all experienced how the body adjusts to change, especially those of us who have resorted to eyeglasses. How quickly the eyes adjust to the glasses and to each new increase in the power of magnification, and how difficult if not impossible to reverse the process! A magnifying glass assists in reading, but unlike glasses does not affect any other focal length or any other part of the visual periphery.

Once sensitized to this characteristic of resisting medical aids, an observer can find it in a surprising number of centenarians. Surprising, because one assumes that since so many centenarians are pragmatic as well as independent, in addition to taking care of themselves they would seek to be doubly protected by the medical establishment. Of course, a good number of centenarians do comment that they are glad to have Medicare protection. But they often add that they are happy they have not had to use it. As already mentioned, 42 percent of these very old people do not have any regular, ongoing association with the medical establishment. This statistic, of course, reflects their remarkably good health—a condition that caused many centenarians to express pride or gratefulness. And it is in keeping with statements by Stephen Jewett (Appendix 6)—"The healthy aged are rarely seen in physicians' offices"—and Flanders Dunbar (Appendix 7)—"It is much easier to study sick people and what makes them sick than well people and what keeps them well. The exceptionally healthy people are hard to find in a hospital and they rarely consult a physician."

In many cases, this segregation from formal medical care is stated simply as a fact. Danill Powell said that he had been to a doctor once in his life—when he was bitten by a rattlesnake at the age of 96. But even here there is no word of acknowledgment, much less praise, for the medical help. "They took me to the doctor and he cut on me a little. It didn't hurt so much, though, and I was back to work in three days." And he goes on to tell how he killed the big snake with nine rattles.

An antimedical attitude can be detected in at least eighty-two centenarians. This attitude ranges from a Mr. Davis, who never states it explicitly but who doctors himself and refuses to use medical aids, to the most vehement and outspoken opposition. The following examples suggest some of the gradations found, starting with the mildest forms: centenarians who say they have taken little or no medicine.

Mrs. Elizabeth Randall of Greensburg, Kansas, "had a heart attack several years ago and has some trouble with her hip, so that she is now bedfast. She does get out for a ride in the car about once a week and she likes to go to town and get a 'hotdog.' The doctor advised her not to salt her food so heavy, and she told him he won't live as long as she has so not to try to tell her how to eat."

Arthur Dial of Munford, Alabama, the man who has "worn out six Bibles in my life": "I never was sick much. I doctored myself with herbs and barks when I did get sick. The last time I went to a doctor was about fifteen years ago."

Charlotte Bonner, the happy lady who cheers people at a nursing home near Chicago, "says God is her best doctor and prescribes adherence to the Ten Commandments as the best medicine."

William Hunt of Huntington, West Virginia, at "92 or 93 had a serious operation, but he came through this fine with no complications. The doctor told him that not one man in a thousand would have withstood this surgery at his age. The only medicine he takes is vitamins. He is supposed to take digitalis once a day but he won't take it."

John King of Lancaster, Pennsylvania, "said that he worked on his farm until age 82, and at that time he came to Lancaster to have a kidney removed. After the operation he was told that farming was too strenuous for him so he got a job digging ditches." Sam Furlong of Vinton, Ohio, worked in West Virginia coal mines most of his life. He left the mines "at age 81 and finally retired at age 92, as a janitor, on doctor's advice." But now, in his one hundredth year, he is living on a 42-acre farm with friends. "He raises three acres of corn, two gardens, and has 160 hens, 120 chicks, eight large geese, and fourteen young geese. He is a slim, wiry man about 5'7" and does much of the work himself. He was repairing a shed when the field representative arrived for the interview." In both these cases, the doctors' orders are followed and then unintentionally or unconsciously disregarded.

George Lightburn Kessell saw his physician as adversary. "When social security became a law, Mr. Kessell was employed by Kelly Axe-True Temper Corporation in Charleston, West Virginia. He was 72 years old at this time. He continued to hold this job until he was 87 years old. 'I didn't want to retire then,' Mr. Kessell said, 'but the company made me. A few years before I retired they would send me to Dr. Jarrell for a checkup. He would say, "George, you are too old to work—I'm going to tell them to retire you." He would give me a slip to take back to the foreman with this on it. Those slips never got there and I kept right on working.' "

The physician was seen by several centenarians as the purveyor of negative news. Two centenarians gloated that their doctors had erred in prognosticating their early demise. And David Oglesby of Clay, Kentucky, said that he "has no doctor to tell him that he is not well."

Henrietta Dull of Atlanta, Georgia, "remarked that she doesn't see very well anymore because she has cataracts. 'The doctors want to take them off,' she said, 'but I say no! I don't want them off. I don't want to work anymore and I'm not going to do it. I've retired.'" William Shambow did have a cataract operation, but said he saw better before he had it.

Missouri Statler of Tupelo, Oklahoma, said her health was good. "I last saw a doctor in March [nine months before the interview] and he gave me a small tube of medicine that didn't do any good. He charged me ten dollars for it." She commented about the high costs of all medicines.

"Joseph A. DeMuth has outlived his three doctors, two attorneys, and his dentist. He hasn't used his Medicare card, but his friends have used theirs so he knows the value of it." A resident of Glendale, California, for the past sixty-seven years, Mr. DeMuth composed a poem for his one hundredth birthday. The poem includes this stanza:

> *While talking with a doctor*
> *About accidents and ills,*
> *He said I have lived longer because*
> *I have brushed aside his pills.*

Anthony Kazmierczak of Manistee, Michigan, retired before social security went into effect. "When Medicare was first enacted, he thought about it, but, as he says, 'I never been to a doctor in my life, and I never want to see one.' Not only no doctors, but no hospitals are his credo. 'If I have to die, I want to do it right here in my own home.'"

George Scott, a lawyer of Terre Haute, Indiana, shows how far a centenarian is willing to go to avoid seeing a physician: "When asked about his health, he laughed and laughed at great length and then said he needed to think before expressing himself on his health. 'For the past ten years, I have had a heart condition and I smother if I walk too fast. I am blind in my left eye but can see a little from my right eye. I get dizzy and lose my balance easily, but by being very careful I have yet to fall. I live alone and if I did fall, it would probably be hours before I was noticed.'

"In expressing why he thought he had been able to live so long, he said, 'Because my heart has never quit beating. After I married, I found that my mother-in-law used a medication under the trade name "Dr. J. N. Stufford's Olive Tar." It was composed of olive oil

George Scott

and turpentine. Our family has always used it, and I am presently using it. I have not been able to purchase it for years but still have a small supply for my personal use. In fact, I am using some at the present time for an irritation on my neck. I have spent very little money on M.D.'s.' "

Mr. Scott is one of sixteen centenarians who attribute their longevity to *not* seeing physicians and/or *not* taking medicine. The succinct formula of Nellie Persons of Fort Lauderdale, Florida, for a long life is to "keep away from doctors." Alexis Firm of Fairhope, Alabama, "attributes his long life to the fact that he has never taken drugs of any kind—not even aspirin. 'Drugs are what kill people,' he said." One of the reasons Frank Moore gave for his longevity is that "I have always been allergic to doctors and undertakers."

For the record, ten centenarians did attribute their long lives to their physicians and medical help. Nine of the ten are women. Mrs. Dora Pierce of Springfield, Ohio, "said she never wanted to get that old, but she had been taken good care of by her doctors and nurses." Mrs. Mary Bowman, who spent most of her working life in a drugstore with her pharmacist husband, credits her longevity to "my husband and the doctor taking care of me." When Mrs. Anna Torrel, in a nursing home at Ironwood, Michigan, was asked her secret for living so long, she replied, "I have no secret. I do all I can to please the doctor. I eat, sleep, and drink. I can't ask for anything more, can I?"

Mrs. Minnie Mason is blind and bedridden at the home of her daughter and son-in-law in Sarasota, Florida. "I never thought I would live this long," she says. "I think I owe a great deal to my doctor, especially since I have come here to Sarasota. They have wonderful doctors here, and my health has gotten much better here."

"When asked the secret of her long life, Mrs. [Ina] Braucher replied, 'I always worked hard, kept busy, and lived moderately.' She also gives much credit to her personal friend and physician Dr. Joseph Tushim, who has looked after her health for over twenty-five years." The lone man in the group, Jessie Hoffman of Morgantown, North Carolina, was more impersonal. He ascribed his longevity "to heredity and modern medical practices."

OBVIOUSLY, EXTREME LONGEVITY can be achieved through dependence upon the physician as well as through independence. What these two disparate groups seem to emphasize is the existence of two different modes heading toward the same end. The situation is likely to be either/or because the modes are antipathetic and cannot be easily held at the same time. When centenarians believed themselves to be seriously ill, they pragmatically availed themselves of medical attention; but this dependence did not necessarily last any longer than the need.

That faith and confidence in the doctor are essential to the effectiveness of the therapy was recognized by Hippocrates, who urged physicians to give great importance to their bedside manner. The patient's taking heart at the new source of succor helps him to mobilize and rally his own defenses. The mechanism of dependence is so powerful that it posed difficulties for Freud in his psychoanalytic treatment of mental and emotional illness. After intimate and protracted association between therapist and patient, what Freud called "transference" often occurred: The patient began to confuse the physician with a loved one in his or her personal life.

Evidence that dependence and independence play fundamental roles in health and illness comes from quite another source. Meyer Friedman, a pioneer in the study of Type A behavior, reports that in December 1978 a panel of twenty-five distinguished cardiologists, epidemiologists, and psychologists, meeting under the auspices of the National Heart, Lung, and Blood Institute, concluded that Type A behavior is a serious risk factor for coronary heart disease. That the Type A behavior pattern is conducive to heart disease was proposed as long ago as 1959. The characteristics of the Type A person have been disseminated in the popular media so that they are well known: He is hard-driving, always in a hurry, achievement oriented, meeting deadlines, impatient, quick to anger.

What is far less well known is the underlying basis for the self-destructive behavior. Dr. Friedman: "The Type A behavior pattern is an action-emotion complex exhibited by people who are unable—or unwilling—to evaluate their own competence. Such people prefer to judge themselves by the evaluations of those whom they believe are their superiors. And to enhance themselves in other people's eyes, they attempt to increase the quantity (but rarely the quality) of their achievements. Their self-esteem becomes increasingly dependent on the status they believe they achieve.

"Unfortunately, such people pay a price. Any degree of self-esteem which they gain in this manner is apparently not enough to allay the insecurity and consequent agitation engendered by their 'surrender' to outside criteria, to the authority of others.

"Hoping, nevertheless, to achieve a satisfactory sense of self-esteem, such people incessantly try to increase the sheer quantity of their achievements. And it is this chronic and incessant struggle to achieve more and more in less time, together with a free-floating, but covert, and usually well-rationalized, hostility, that make up the

Type A behavior pattern. The sense of urgency and hostility give rise to irritation, impatience, aggravation and anger: the four components which I believe comprise the pathogenic core of the behavior pattern."

Finally, there is Walter L. Pannell, the centenarian physician I visited in his office at East Orange, New Jersey. He has never relied on drugs, although he is currently taking some vitamin B. "I'm not much on that," he said. I asked him who his physician was and how often he had a physical checkup. "I haven't had the occasion to consult doctors," he replied. He did not have a regular checkup. "I don't feel the need. When you feel all right, you don't hunt for trouble."

CHAPTER 7

Health

The most striking health feature of the group of centenarians is the rarity of the two diseases that kill more than 70 percent of Americans. More than half of all deaths in the United States are caused by cardiovascular disease—heart disease, stroke, arteriosclerosis, high blood pressure. Cancer accounts for about 20 percent of the deaths. Cardiovascular disease and cancer take an even higher toll of Americans 65 years or older—60 percent for cardiovascular disease and about 19 percent for cancer, close to eight out of every ten deaths.

Yet just sixty-one of these centenarians reported having cardiovascular disease and about half a dozen had cancer. Seven percent (of the 836 centenarians who responded to the question "How is your health?" and volunteered information about specific disease) is a remarkably low figure for the prevalence of cardiovascular disease, with cancer virtually nonexistent. Yet there should be nothing surprising about this, for the two diseases are so deadly that they are incompatible with long-term survival.

Only seven of the twenty-six people with heart disease and one of three with high blood pressure were forced to limit their activities. Stroke was far more injurious. Fourteen of the eighteen centenarians who had suffered strokes were bound to wheelchairs, bedridden, or in some other way impaired, as were five of the fourteen people with arteriosclerosis.

The strokes came very late in life. The ages when strokes occurred are recorded for sixteen of the eighteen victims: one in the nineties, one at 95, four at 96, two at 97, five at 99, one at 100, and one at 101 (the latter lived another four or five years). One man suffered a stroke at age 52, became disabled, never worked again, but still

Eleuterio Gomez

was around at the century mark. For those reporting heart disease, one man said he had heart trouble all his life, two centenarians developed heart ailments in their seventies, another in his late seventies or early eighties, and two others in their eighties. Therefore, as far as we can tell, cardiovascular disease appeared in only seven centenarians before they reached their nineties.

Most significant, not a single cardiovascular event is reported in the sixties age group and only one between the ages of 70 and 75. This transitional period from middle to old age was closely watched for the appearance of disease. Sara Harris of the Center for the Study of Aging in Albany, New York, recommended this surveillance in the search for telltale signs of extended longevity. And the perceptive Flanders Dunbar observed that people "who survive the dangerous decade—sixty to seventy—without getting geriatric disease are likely to be long-lived."

The three cases of high blood pressure were women, but most of the victims of cardiovascular disease were men—forty-four of the sixty-one (Appendix 29).

Of the six or seven centenarians associated with cancer, the malignancy of one or two is not certain. It was reported in the preceding chapter that Mrs. Matilda Dillin was supposed to have surgery on a tumor at the age of 57 but instead began treating herself with a patented ointment. Whether or not the tumor was cancerous, she is the only possible instance of the disease reported in a transitional year. One man had a successful cancer operation at age eighty. The other four or five cases occurred in the nineties. Mrs. Nora Swart, the Indiana farm woman who exemplified the orderly life, was reported to have had an obviously successful cancer operation when she was 92 years old. Two men had skin cancer in their late nineties and apparently were able to eradicate this least dangerous form of cancer with treatment. Another man was being treated for small facial tumors, not specifically stated to be cancer; otherwise, his health was excellent. One woman had her right breast removed in her one hundredth year.

While a number of centenarians commented that they had been blessed with good health and forty-four of them attributed their longevity to that fact, only one person perceived that his survival was due to his avoidance of disease in later life. When Sylvester Melvin, a vigorous farmer in Greenfield, Illinois, was asked why he thought he had been able to live so long, he responded: "Main thing is because I didn't have any disease such as cancer that develops in the human system. The only diseases I had were childhood diseases such as measles and mumps."

After cardiovascular disease and cancer, pneumonia and influenza account for 3.2 percent of the deaths in the United States. If the death toll from bronchitis, emphysema, and asthma is added, then the percentage of deaths from lung diseases is 4.5 percent. Diabetes, a major geriatric disease, kills 1.8 percent and liver cirrhosis 1.7 percent. There is not a single case of cirrhosis among the centenarians and just three cases of diabetes. Twenty-one centenarians said they suffered from pulmonary illness at present or in the recent past.

Arthritis is not a killer disease, but it is our leading crippler. About 31.6 million, or one in seven, Americans suffer from arthritis. But that ratio changes dramatically in the aged. More than five in twelve Americans over the age of 65 are arthritic—10.6 million. The ratio for arthritis among these centenarians is less than one in twenty.

There is one other prominent scourge of old age, one that is being paid increasing attention by practitioners of geriatric medicine. This is senile dementia, believed to afflict 5 to 6 percent of Americans over the age of 65, and possibly 25 percent of those over 80 years. This illness inflicts a fearful punishment on surrounding loved ones as well as on the victim, for they must witness the disintegration of the person's mind and personality.

One centenarian of the 1,200 was senile. When she was 93 years old, she went to bed with a cold and stayed in bed until she was too weak to get up unaided. She committed herself to bed. At 99 she was totally senile, and during the last months before her death three months after her 100th birthday, she slept most of the time. This woman was singular in another way. When she was a young woman and pregnant for the second time, with twins as it turned out, her husband deserted her without a word of warning or explanation. There were ten divorces and eight separations among these centenarians, but none of the ruptures, as far as is known, was as traumatic as this one. While most of the divorced or separated centenarians took new mates, this woman stayed unattached for the rest of her life. She raised three children, with the help of her parents until the children were old enough to go to school, and then on her own as a seamstress. Later in life she was called upon to be mother to two young grandchildren after her son's marriage ended in divorce. Hers was a life of labor and stress, but it ended with rest and amnesia.

There are two other references to failing mental powers. One woman was described as "still able to think for herself but becomes easily confused," and the mind of another woman "tends to get a little hazy late in the afternoon when she gets tired." As item 42 on the questionnaire indicates, this group of old people enjoyed superb, almost perfect mental health.

Memory is perhaps our most fragile mental faculty, and becoming an "absent-minded professor" usually is taken as evidence of incipient dotage. Forgetfulness too often is mistaken as a sign of senility. This is not necessarily true and by itself does not mean lessened mental acuity, even if, by its common occurrence, it indicates the most vulnerable part of the mind. But for the centenarians, poor memory was a sign that death was getting close. Twenty-two centenarians whose date of death is known had failing memory at the time of the interview. Only five of the twenty-two are known definitely to have lived longer than a year after the interview. Ninety-nine centenarians had failing memory, but for every one who did, ten others still possessed good memory. A few centenarians won the adjective *amazing* for their powers of recall.

In general, this group of centenarians offers proof, if any is needed, that the chronic or geriatric diseases are pathological states and not requisite expressions of old age. The abnormally reduced presence of disease has the effect of identifying the least durable elements of the human body—those faculties and parts most vulnerable to the wear and tear of living and the attrition with the passage of time. The most common infirmities occurring near the upper limits of the life-span are failing vision and hearing and weak bones, particularly the crucial hip joint.

These are harbingers of death for the centenarians. Not because they are fatal in themselves, but because they foreclose on what has been precious and made life worth living: the prized independence, mobility, the sense and the actuality of being useful, participation in enjoyable and productive activities, and important social interactions. Even so, the centenarians refuse to heed the auguries. Invariably these old people struggle valiantly against their disabilities.

Failing vision is the most common of these afflictions, affecting 338 of the centenarians, 29 percent. The use of eyeglasses was not a consideration for this designation. If a person could see well enough to read and watch television with the aid of glasses, then his vision was not listed as impaired. This was the state of vision for most of the centenarians. Thirty-two of them commented on how especially good their vision remained while 104 subjects still did not use glasses at all. The impairment of sight for the 29 percent ranges from slightly reduced capability to blindness. Forty-nine centenarians were blind, thirty-seven had cataracts, and four suffered from glaucoma. Twenty-one persons with cataracts had operations to remove them; almost all of these operations took place when the individuals were in their nineties, a few as late as the ninety-ninth year.

Three centenarians were blind for a period of years and then had

their sight restored. Two recoveries were the results of cataract operations. To a sighted person blindness would seem to be the most severe of the disabilities mentioned, the most restricting. Yet most of
the centenarians appeared able to cope with this handicap very well.
The story of Leonard Curtis makes the point with the element of
surprise that seemed to be built into a number of the social security
interviews. Dr. Curtis is a retired law professor. The longer-than-
average report on him says that he lives with his 83-year-old sister
and a full-time housekeeper in one of the better sections of De Land,
Florida.

The account then traces his life. He grew up on an Indiana farm
at a place called Ebenezer Ridge, overlooking the Ohio River. He
went to a one-room, red schoolhouse, which he described in detail,
including the readers and other books that were used. "It was in
that same little red schoolhouse that I decided I wanted to become
a teacher." His first job was teaching in that schoolhouse; it was
followed by a long career in education. "He retired from the University of Arizona Law School after thirty-two years there as a professor. On retirement from Arizona, he moved to De Land, where
he intended to remain in full retirement. However, very shortly after
moving to De Land he was approached by Stetson University Law
School regarding a position there, went back to work, and taught for
another fifteen years. He states that he would probably still be there
today except that the Stetson Law School was moved to St. Peters-
burg, Florida, several years back, and he did not feel up to making
the change himself. He has done no work since that time.

"In response to queries concerning his health, his reply was, 'My
health is perfect. My mind is clear, and I think it's because I have
kept up with the times, I am interested in what's going on around me,
and I care what's happening in the world. I have never had any
serious things wrong with me. I have suffered from little things—for
instance, I had ulcers once—but I finally decided that if I just
worked hard, had constant habits, and lived like a normal individual
should, I could live to be a hundred, and that's just what I'm going
to do. I have a strong constitution, and I feel that I am in perfect
health myself.' We might point out that, despite what Dr. Curtis
says, he is almost totally blind. He has no eyesight in his left eye,
having developed a cataract on it several years ago which doctors
were reluctant to remove in view of his age. He says that his right
eye failed many years before that, and as a result, he can only dis-
tinguish light and dark. Despite the fact that he could not even see
the interviewer, who sat next to him on the sofa, he was able to walk

around the house without the aid of a cane or anyone's assistance. When the interviewer said that the way he could maneuver around the house was remarkable, Dr. Curtis replied that he had learned well where every piece of furniture, every door, and every object was, and there was no need for him to have help. He states that, in addition, he takes care of his own room, making up his bed, sweeping it out and dusting it. He doesn't like anyone to tamper with his personal articles in his room, which he uses as a study. He says that he is unable to participate in any activities now; that up until about a year ago he did go to concerts and take part in various meetings around town, but that in the last year he has hardly left the house. He has no hobbies and spends most of his time listening to the radio, chatting with neighbors and visitors or with his sister, who lives there with him. He says there is no ambition he has not realized; that as a very young boy all he wanted to do was to teach law, and he feels that he has realized this ambition adequately after over fifty years in this field."

Because of the prescribed order of questions in the social security interview, the subject of Ella McBride's blindness does not come up until near the end and is not suspected, particularly since the opening statement reads: "Although Miss McBride had some difficulty hearing, she was very alert and articulate." No mention of the more serious disability.

Miss McBride begins by telling about her trip as a 3-year-old in 1865 from Iowa to Oregon via the Isthmus of Panama "on a jerkwater train." She now lives in Seattle. "The most exciting things I've done were climbing mountains. I have made thirty-eight high climbs, including Mount Whitney and Mount Rainier. The most exciting thing to me is standing on top of a high mountain. For years I held the championship of the women mountain-climbers of the Northwest."

She taught school for ten years and was an elementary-school principal for thirteen years. "After finishing my teaching career, I began as a portrait photographer in about 1909 [when she was forty-seven years old]. I did this until I was ninety-one years old. I specialized in pictorial work and have had my pictures in every important salon in the world that has photography exhibits." Miss McBride pointed out two prize-winning items hanging on the wall. One was her "Study of Pavlova" and the other was entitled "Study of a Dogwood Branch."

To the health question, she responded, "My health is wonderful." Among the reasons for her longevity: "I've always enjoyed life so much. I have a keen sense of humor and I have lots of fun."

"What do you do with your time?"

"I retired when I was about ninety-one or ninety-two years old because of my failing eyesight and hearing. I am almost blind now. I cannot see writing. I wear a hearing aid and listen to talking records three to four hours a day. When I was ninety-one or ninety-two, I learned to type by the touch system and I practice one-half hour every day on the typewriter to do my correspondence. I attend the soroptimist meetings at the Olympic Hotel every Wednesday. I also sew and knit. I have a set of dominoes and checkers for the blind. The dominoes have raised spots on them, and the checkers consist of round and square pieces. I have a game of dominoes before going to bed each night. Because of my age, I am now going to bed soon after nine."

"Do you do any work or household chores?"

"I take care of my own room, and I'm able to do my own laundry now that we have nylon things. I hem aprons and dish towels, and I knit washclothes. I live in my apartment with a housekeeper."

"Do you have any outside activities—church, hobbies?"

"I belong to the First Presbyterian Church, and I was active in the church until the point where I couldn't see or hear the minister. I now listen to the services on the radio."

Mrs. Nina Hall, who still manages to live alone in a small apartment in Chicago despite a variety of handicaps, shows the tenacity with which these old people pursue lifelong activities while advancing deeper into the twilight. "Despite failing eyesight, she continues to do repair work on clothing with needle and thread. When first interviewed at her home, she was working on a beaded leather handbag and a man's leather vest, which she was remaking. The vest was of Indian style, with much beadwork. She was also remaking a vest of chamois, which had been her husband's. She said, 'I can't see the thread and needle, but I have a needle threader, and I can also feel with my fingers to get the needle threaded. Once it's threaded, I can sew a straight seam or sew on buttons or things of that sort today.' "

If loss of vision would seem the most dreaded disability, loss of hearing, a secondary sense, would appear to be one of the more preferable handicaps—if a choice could be made. But it turns out that deafness is a severe hardship, for it terminates the primary social activity of many of the afflicted oldsters: going to church. They stop going when they no longer can hear the sermon. Deafness is equally effective as blindness in ending another favorite activity, watching television. This probably is an important reason why reading surpasses television viewing among these centenarians. The penalty of deafness does not end with the curtailment of these activities; the loss of this faculty imposes an unwelcome social isolation that is pervasive. Two hundred and ninety-six centenarians—26 percent of them—suffered some degree of hearing loss.

Twenty-two percent of the centenarians had other restricting disabilities. More than half of these handicaps were some kind of leg trouble, sufficiently common to be a plague to one out of eight centenarians in the entire group. This form of disability is the most onerous, the most difficult for the aged people to cope with. Often, it means not simply the loss of mobility, but the abrupt change from an independent existence to the wheelchair and the bed—or from one's own home to a nursing home.

The most common way such invalidism came about was through the breaking of a hip followed by poor or imperfect healing. This event occurred so often, and usually with such profound effect on the fortune of the victim, as to indicate that the hip is structurally one of the body's weakest links. (Eighty-two centenarians broke a hip, while only six broke a leg, nine broke an arm, and twenty-three others fell and broke other bones; see Appendix 29D.) It is usually the small section of the upper femur that fractures, even though the centenarians say they broke their hip. The patient reports that a fall has resulted in a broken hip, but what really happens, according to Dr. Pannell, the centenarian physician, is that the bone breaks and the person falls. "It's like brick without straw." Whichever comes first, other parts of the hip complex may be fractured by the fall, affecting the extent of the injury and course of recovery.

Osteoporosis is characterized by bones that lose their mass, becoming more porous and fragile. The affliction is implicated in 195,000 hip fractures among elderly Americans each year. Osteoporosis affects one out of four elderly women in the United States, a rate that is twice as high as it is in men. The sex hormones are known to stimulate bone cells to make new bone matter, and although other factors can be involved,* bone production is impaired by the reduced levels of estrogen after menopause. What's more, female bones are less dense to start with, and the female pelvic bones are more delicate, the ridges for muscular attachments less prominent.

---

* The latest research has found a link between vitamin K deficiency and calcium metabolism. Vitamin K deficiency in older people can be caused by bland diets that exclude such foods as green vegetables, cauliflower, potatoes, and liver; and by the use of mineral-oil laxatives and certain drugs. Also the dietary intake of calcium is deficient for most Americans. Bone loss also is associated with lack of exercise. Childbearing and breast feeding may begin the depletion of calcium deposits that are never restored.

There is another kind of selectivity for osteoporosis—by race. A college textbook on anatomy and physiology, *Principles of Anatomy and Physiology* by Gerald J. Tortora and Nichola P. Anagnostakos, states that the disorder affects the "middle-aged and elderly—white women more than men of black or white ancestry and black women not at all." Of the eighty-two centenarians who suffered broken hips, fifty-six of them—more than two out of three—are women. Not a single one of this group, male or female, is black.

On the other hand, there is evidence that a good many of these centenarians are free of osteoporosis. Michael McCullough, a farmer of Gaston, Oregon, "is well known to his neighbors as a man who is still full of life, with a keen mind, and who 'walks straight as a broom,'" My first two impressions when I met Charlie Smith were how neatly he dressed and how erectly he sat, with no support for his back.

Osteoporosis affects the spine, as well as the legs and feet. The spine collapses and curves, causing the chest and ribs to sag, producing the familiar pot-bellied contour of old age. When posture was studied, erectness was observed in 260 centenarians. This is a very high percentage; there were photographs of only 298 of them, and in some of the pictures the posture could not be judged. So the information on erectness comes only from the relatively small number of photos and in cases where it won the attention of the interviewers.

Failure of bone manufacture delays or prevents successful healing after a break has occurred, but in a small number of centenarians recovery was accomplished well. In the case of Ella McBride, the blind Seattle photographer, the word is spectacularly. She broke her hip at age 99. "The doctor said that he had never had a patient who recovered as quickly as I did. I was two months ahead of any patient he had ever had with a broken hip, regardless of age."

If the bodily response of most centenarians is not so memorable, the response of their spirit is. Laura E. Crews is the best example. She is the independent woman who did not want to take social security because she hadn't worked for it. Miss Crews led an extremely active life, working her own farm until she broke her hip at age 85. After she broke her hip and was restricted to a wheelchair, she turned to writing books and articles. She wrote five books, all still in print: *My Kinsfolk; My Kinsfolk Military Record; Memories; Nonsense, Reminiscence by Us Kinsfolk*; and *Original Poems by Us Kinsfolk*. She also wrote the words to the song *The Cherokee Strip*. She recently finished a sixth book, *Tell Me a Story*, "and now spends time writing 'lots of letters.'" With the niece who lives with her, Miss

Thomas Parrish

Crews rented a hall to celebrate her one hundredth birthday. More than three hundred relatives and friends came to the celebration.

"It was always my theory that allowing your mind to become inactive caused senility," says Miss Crews, "so I have tried to keep my mind active."

OF THE 836 centenarians who commented on their health, 13 percent rated it "excellent" and 69 percent rated it "good" (if a centenarian said "fine" or "very good," his health was classified as "good")—a total of 82 percent. An objective evaluation of the health of a larger portion of the cohort, including most of the self-raters, found 87 percent to have good physical functioning. The rating was influenced by the observations and comments of the social security agent; that judgment, in turn, was sometimes influenced by the centenarian's self-evaluation. But if something was evidently and basically wrong with the subject, his health was rated "poor" despite a contrary evaluation by the centenarian or social security agent. As mentioned, the social security people tended to be more impressed with the condition of these aged men and women than were the subjects. Five percent of the centenarians volunteered that they felt great vitality, whereas the field representatives reported this condition in 15 percent.

About a dozen and a half centenarians displayed an agility that had to be seen to be believed. One agent reported that Mrs. Addie L. Barnes, living in a nursing home in Crisfield, Maryland, "feels she is in fairly good health, and can bend over and touch her toes several times (at least eight or ten times)." Mrs. Emma Weaver, living with her daughter in Lakewood, Ohio, attributes her "good health and long life to eating a balanced diet and hard work. She also advocates exercise. She demonstrated one of her exercises for the interviewer. She can bend over without bending her knees and touch the floor with the palms of her hands. She does this exercise ten times when she gets up and ten times before she goes to bed."

Thomas L. Parrish of Milford, Illinois, a nattily dressed man wearing a fedora, is pictured beside an automobile speaking to a younger man. The account begins: "Mr. Parrish lives with his grandson, John Parrish. When we arrived he was sitting in his new 1961 Buick he bought in February after passing his driver's license exam with the Illinois State Police. The records show that Mr. Parrish is the oldest active driver in Illinois and possibly is the oldest driver in the country to pass a formal driving exam. When we arrived Mr. Parrish got out of the car and escorted us to the house. I was immediately amazed at the briskness of his walk, and he went up the three or four steps into the house as fast as the rest of us."

Later in the interview: "When I asked Mr. Parrish how his health was, instead of giving a verbal reply, while sitting on the sofa, he kicked his foot over his head and then reached over and touched the palms of both hands to the floor."

Three-fourths of the 1,048 centenarians for whom there are data were fully mobile. Of the other quarter, about one-half, or 12 percent of the entire group, could get around with a cane or walker. Eight percent were in wheelchairs and 5 percent were bedridden. Not quite one quarter—23 percent—of the centenarians were in nursing homes, a fact that did not necessarily mean they were ill or in poor health. Most of them were not, but they did require support services no longer available to them elsewhere.

Eighty centenarians said they were always healthy or had never been ill in their entire lives. The past health records for most of the cohort are poorly reported. Similarly, there was no systematic attempt to quantify their relationships with the medical establishment. What data are available show that 98 centenarians see a physician frequently or occasionally while 133 of them never go to a doctor. Fifty-six centenarians were in hospitals during the past year, 168 were not; 123 centenarians were in hospitals in later years, 138 were not. Forty-one of them take medical drugs, 130 of them never take drugs or medicine.

One trait appears to be universal; at least no exception to it was seen. Centenarians are well-groomed, clean, neatly and cleanly dressed, the men clean shaven when they have chosen not to wear beards.

Centenarians tend to equate their longevity with good health and often use the terms interchangeably.

THE STUDY OF subjective and objective evaluations of health afforded an opportunity to compare the relative strengths of the internal and external observations by seeing how well they coincided with the length of remaining life. If the self-assessments were accurate, a centenarian who rated his health as "good" or "excellent" should live a detectably longer time than one who rated his health as "poor." A self-evaluation of "fair" or "good for my age" is taken as an indication of change—that the centenarian recognizes a decline in health—so that rating is classified along with "poor" as a negative response. Similarly, the objective assessment of good physical functioning or its absence is a yes-no situation. A "yes" for a long-liver and "no" for a short-liver would both be correct evaluations.

The dates of death some time after the interviews were known for 157 centenarians. In some cases the date was not exactly known, but the death was known to have taken place during a period of a certain number of months or years. Even so, there was a pool of about 130 centenarians whose death dates could be judged with precision in order to test the predictors.

The problem was how to decide what constitutes a long remaining life and a short remaining life for these centenarians. *The Life Insurance Fact Book 1978* states that life expectancy for a 100-year-old person in the United States (judged by the latest statistics from 1969–71) is 2.62 years, or between thirty-one and thirty-two months. A tabulation of the centenarians showed that only about 7 percent of them still were alive thirty-two months after their interviews. Thirty-two months obviously is not the proper point to divide the short-livers from the long-livers in this subgroup, which probably was not representative of the centenarian experience in general or the entire 1,200-member cohort for this inquiry because of the recording of a disproportionately high number of early deaths.

A series of calculations (Appendix 33A) showed that at the end of six months 22 percent of this subgroup were dead, after nine months 35 percent were deceased, at the end of a year 54 percent were dead, after fifteen months 74 percent were dead, and after eighteen months the figure was 84 percent, five out of six of the subgroup. Twelve months, when the numbers of the dead and living were relatively equal, or fifteen months, the first point marking the termination of the great proportion of the centenarians, seemed to be the appropriate places to discriminate between the short-livers and long-livers.

If twelve months is used as the dividing line, 66 percent of the subjective evaluations of health are accurate, 34 percent inaccurate, a two-to-one ratio. The objective rating of health is accurate in 59 percent of the cases and inaccurate in 41 percent, a three-to-two ratio (Appendix 33B).

If fifteen months is used, the self-rating (subjective) accuracy declines to 60 percent, correct three out of five times. The objective rating falls to 50-50, accurate just half the time. Both subjective and objective-rating accuracy get relatively worse the further removed the measuring date, but at thirty-two months self-rating is still correct half the time.

These findings are consistent with those of Eric Pfeiffer, summarized in Appendix 13, that self-perception of health change is an important factor in distinguishing between short-livers and long-livers. This is not meant to deprecate objective observation. For one thing, it was based not on a clinical examination but simply a brief impression of the subject's appearance, behavior, physical circumstances, and apparent amount of vigor. If the division between long-livers and short-livers is moved closer to the time of the interview, to nine months afterward, the subjective and objective ratings are about equal. When six months is used, then the objective rating is more accurate than the subjective.

For these people near the edge of the lifespan, good health is a requirement but not a guarantee for living much longer. For most centenarians, "longevity" is compressed into a narrow future measured in months rather than years.

As the figures indicate, centenarians in general are good monitors of their health and are sensitive to nuances of change. Most of them gauge their health with that same realism that they apply to other matters, and in more than a few cases their prescience is uncanny.

Mrs. Mary Crowell was 101 years and seven months old when she was interviewed in the home of her niece in Brockton, Massachusetts. She told her guest that she ran a department store in Brockton until she was married. "I wasn't married until I was pretty old. I lived with my husband within two months of fifty years. I was ninety-one when I was left a widow. Too bad anyone has to live until that time and lose all their faculties." She is blind and deaf to the point that conversation is a problem, but her health remains good and she takes care of her personal needs. The interview closes: "When I left Mrs. Crowell, I told her I hoped to see her again, and she replied, 'Come back—I'll still be here next year.' " She lived another 14 months.

Albert Damcott made an initial miscalculation in his longevity: "Mr. Damcott actually sold his farm in 1947, when he was 80 years old, with the idea of 'resting awhile before it came my time to pass on.' Farmers then were not covered under social security, so he never thought he would be eligible for benefits of any kind. He had the funds from the sale of his farm and a few dollars in savings to tide him over what he felt would be just a few remaining years at best.

"It wasn't until his daughter inquired a year ago about Medicare benefits that either he or his family was aware that he could be eligible for the special benefits under the Prouty amendment as well as qualify for Medicare.

"This was rather like a windfall, as those 'few remaining years' he planned on at age 80 had stretched to twenty, and his reserve was all but gone.

"Until he suffered a broken hip in December 1964, he was as active as he had been at age 60. The hip only slowed his walking ability, however, and he still gets around with the aid of a walker. His mind continues to be very keen, he can still read a newspaper, and is a great conversationalist.

"Working with the young people of his church, the Abbe Reformed Church [Dutch], has been a life-long interest and, though these past few years have taken him away from it physically, he still continues to read the religious papers and magazines that are published for them. He likes to discuss the teaching methods of today *versus* the methods used in his day. He keeps busy reading and discussing current events with anyone who will take the time to do so. He has no unrealized ambitions—has lived a good full life and is 'ready to meet his Maker anytime.' "

Albert Damcott died six days later.

Sometimes, however, one must listen very carefully. Victor Bergwall was interviewed in the Lutheran Home for the Aged in Worcester, Massachusetts, where he lives with his wife. "On the morning of the interview, Mr. Bergwall was sitting on the rear porch, from where he walked with the aid of a cane into a nearby room, where the interview actually took place." Mr. Bergwall was a pharmacist from the age of 33 until his retirement at the age of 99. At the time of his retirement, he was the second-oldest practicing pharmacist in the country. The report concludes this way: "Mr. Bergwall's energy, alertness, physical condition, and remarkable appearance certainly belie his one hundred years. He was specially honored as 'Druggist of the Century' at the Annual Mid-Winter Dinner of the Worcester Druggists Association last January."

Earlier in the interview, when Mr. Bergwall was asked the state of his health, he responded, "I look much healthier than the rest of the people here." That seemed to answer the interviewer at the moment, but in retrospect it can be seen to be a noncommittal response: It does not hint at his own evaluation. Did Victor Bergwall know something he did not wish to declare? He died exactly seven months later.

"On his 100th birthday, Mr. William H. Miller of Madison, Indiana, was approached by an automobile salesman who was pointing out the various merits of the newer automobiles. This salesman doggedly went through his sales routine without arousing any interest in his prospective customer. Finally, in desperation, the salesman said, 'After all, Mr. Miller, you can't take all that money with you.' Mr. Miller paused slightly, cocked his head, and answered, 'Who's going anywhere?' "

That the point of the anecdote was well taken may be judged from the fact that William Miller retold the story three months before his 105th birthday. Mr. Miller still was active, running the lumber business he had started years ago, still making plans for the future. But in the SSA interview he made no direct statements about his health nor any other assertions about future longevity. Perhaps, as in the case of Victor Bergwall, silence is golden in the information it imparts, for William Miller died ten months later.

MANY CENTENARIANS may have been blessed with naturally good health, but some of them pursued a deliberate policy of taking care of it. Speaking of 105-year-old Mrs. Katherine Franzen in Kinderhook, New York, her daughter-in-law said, "If a hot dog gave you or me indigestion, we'd probably take a Rolaid or aspirin—and keep eating them because they taste good going down, right? If a hot dog gave her indigestion, she would never eat another hot dog." Forty-nine centenarians attribute their longevity to taking care of their health, number 11 on the list of attributions. Many more expressed this careful attitude about matters other than hygiene. They were careful to get proper rest, careful about not doing things to excess, careful about avoiding accidents. Several men refused to operate what they considered dangerous machinery even at the risk of losing their jobs.

With the exception of the twenty-four miners in this group, few of the centenarians worked at hazardous occupations. Peter Wing came from a family of Norwegian sea captains. Both his father and grandfather perished at sea. Mr. Wing declined to follow in the seafaring tradition. But at the age of 19 in 1876 he did enlist in the U.S. Army's "Old First Regiment" and served five years as an infantryman. He is one of only twenty-five of the men to serve in the U.S. armed forces. One reason for the dearth of military experience is that from the close of the Civil War until World War I, the United States was not involved in any major, sustained war. The other reason, obviously, is that these long-lived men did not choose to enlist. Of those who did serve, five reported actual combat experience.

Frank Romero was drafted into the Mexican army in 1876 when he was 14 years old (at the beginning of the regime of President Porfirio Diaz). Mr. Romero spent the next eight years fighting Indians in the northwestern part of Mexico. "Mr. Romero says that his eight years of service in the army were extremely distasteful, and he resolved never again to serve as part of Diaz's military machine. This was a time of great material prosperity for Mexico but was also a time of great oppression and injustice. Mr. Romero became quite bitter when he spoke of it. He says that upon release from the army he returned to his native state of Morelos, but after a very few years was recalled to active service. Because of his great hatred for the army, he ignored the summons and moved to another part of Mexico."

At the age of 48, after twenty-six years of ranching and doing other jobs, Mr. Romero returned to armed combat to fight against the federal army of President Diaz. This was in 1910 when the Diaz regime was crumbling. Mr. Romero's forces fought alongside a group led by Pancho Villa, but after the dictator's overthrow, the rebel forces started fighting one another. Mr. Romero left Mexico for the United States in 1912 when he was 50 years old.

Eleuterio Gomez "remembers fighting with Francisco Madero's troops against dictator Porfirio Diaz during the Mexican Revolution in 1910. He then fought against Pancho Villa, whom he call a 'common bandit.' He remembers a great deal of the Mexican Revolution. He says that Francisco Madero was nominated for president and was elected mostly by peasant votes. During his term in office another revolution took place. This battle was headed by Indian general [Victoriano] Huerta, a Diaz supporter. This battle took place in Mexico City and in the northern and southern regions of Mexico. Mr. Gomez says that it was during this battle that he met Pancho

Villa. Also, while fighting in the southern part of Mexico, he met Emiliano Zapata, who was a revolution leader there.

"His most exciting experience was one of the many times he almost got killed. Mr. Gomez and a friend were sent to burn a bridge. His friend was killed, but he escaped because he happened to be on the other side of the bridge.

"Mr. Gomez has several bullet-wound scars on his legs, chest, and back. Four of his brothers were killed during the revolution. He came to the United States to 'save my life,' he says." He, too, was at the halfway point of what would be a century of existence.

The parallels between Eleuterio Gomez and Frank Romero do not end here. Frank Romero was widowed with no children. He married a second time at age 55, had four children, and spent the rest of his working life in agricultural labor. Mr. Gomez had one child by his first wife and eighteen by his second wife, who is twenty-three years his junior. He, too, spent the rest of his working life as a laborer, mainly in agriculture.

In both of these lives there is a transition at midpoint from an existence of violence and turbulence to one of domesticity and routine. This is a pattern encountered again and again in the centenarian biographies. Although the transformation usually isn't as dramatic as in the stories of these Mexican fighters, once looked for, the pattern is there. For the least venturesome, the risk-taking is completed by the end of the first third of life. The young man leaves his parents' farm when he is 21 years old, hires out to another farm, or goes off on his own. By the end of the next decade or so he has found a wife and earned the money to farm his own land. The young woman works at home or in someone else's household or at some other job until she finds a husband, then assumes her roles as wife and mother. These people are in the grooves they will follow the rest of their lives. When one examines the accounts of exciting lives, one finds that the vividly remembered events almost always occurred before the subject was 40 years old. The intervening years are largely blank. Even the most adventuresome vagabonds have settled down no later than the sixth decade.

Only one centenarian recognized the midlife transition. His statement can be taken literally and as metaphor. Said Dr. George M. Gray, a retired physician and onetime mayor and founding father of Kansas City, Kansas: "You know, a man does not make any friends after he reaches age fifty, he makes acquaintances. He has made all of his friends before he gets to be fifty years old. I do not have any friends now. They are all dead, but I have a lot of acquaintances who come to see me."

The midlife transition is a penultimate decision. Most centenarians must make one further accommodation in lifestyle in order to reach the second century. Near the end of their lives they are confronted with a dilemma that must be faced by anyone who lives long enough. It was sensed by Dr. Pannell when he said, "You can't map out anything. You can make broad recommendations for yourself and for others, but if you are too careful, you get yourself in trouble with worries. If you're careless, things happen, too." The problem for the aged person is to navigate the safest course through ever-narrowing limits.

These old people have sensed that their preservation lies in keeping as busy and active as possible, doing what they have always done as best they can—keeping the franchise. The philosophy was expressed by William Eaton of Des Moines, who said, "If I had sat down and folded my arms I wouldn't be here today. Better wear out than rust out."

This "keep active" philosophy is practiced by Robert Grigsby of Kansas City, Kansas, and by a number of other centenarians. "Mr. Grigsby's daughter stated that his staying active helps her father with longevity, and his tomato patch is his pride and joy. She said that when the snow falls she and Mr. Grigsby may be the first in the block out with a shovel. He is careful, though. He knows when to stop and never overexerts himself, she continued."

There comes a time, however, when no strategy can avail and the open letter of resignation presented to us at birth is called in.

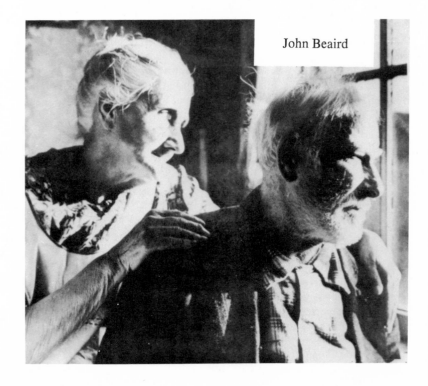

John Beaird

CHAPTER 8
Diet, Sex, and Genes

One food faddist asks, "What do you eat?"
Another says, "How often do you chew it?"
There may be sense in either quiz;
That depends on how you view it.

That's a stanza from the poem that Joseph DeMuth wrote for his one hundredth birthday. Mr. DeMuth believes he lived for such a long time because he "just had good health." He adds, however, that he never drank alcoholic beverages or smoked and hasn't had coffee or tea since he was 37 years old. That makes him one of 118 centenarians who ascribe their longevity in some way to their eating habits, number 3 on the list of attributions for longevity. This consensus really is made up of a variety of reasons related to diet or manner of eating. The subject of diet is not on the list of social security questions (surprisingly) and is discussed in only 263 interviews.

The most common eating habit is consuming three meals a day, observed by 152 centenarians. That's 58 percent of the group for which information is available and fits in with the 63 percent who followed a regular routine of activities or still were working in the "Order" category. In a widely cited study by Nedra Belloc and Lester Breslow, regularity of meals was one of the health practices found to be associated with better health and greater life expectancy (the study is summarized in Appendix 16).

Fifty-nine centenarians said they ate everything and/or followed no special diet, whereas nineteen of the centenarians stated that they watched their diets very carefully. Being careful about what they ate frequently meant eating only what agreed with them. Alexis Ferm

139

"watches his diet, and whenever he doesn't feel good, he says to himself, 'What the hell did I eat'—and cuts it out."

All told, 175 centenarians said they observed some special diet or routine. The most common routine was eating in moderation, another aspect of the orderly life. Forty centenarians said they did not eat to excess. On the other hand, forty-five centenarians said they had a good appetite, ate heartily, or were heavy eaters (see Appendix 30 for diets, foods).

If eating good or simple food (27), eating well (23), eating right (8), eating plain food (5), and good nutrition (2) are lumped together, then that is the most common diet. Of these sixty-five centenarians, forty cited it as a reason for their longevity. Of course, some of those terms are not well defined. When Mrs. Adelheid "Shooky" Schuhnecht of Beaver Dam, Wisconsin, was asked why she had been able to live so long, she said, "Because of my good behavior. We ate good, a bag of potatoes a week." If a balanced diet is added, the total rises to seventy-two. Eating properly, ten more, also belongs with the above group, except that eight people don't explain what they mean by eating properly. To one man it meant no starch and heavy on meat, fruit, and eggs, while to another man it meant eating slowly. Four men attributed their long lives to eating slowly, and one man took small bites as well.

The nature of the plain, wholesome food referred to becomes clearer with a look at the variety of foods cited for their longevous properties or as dietary features: vegetables, fruits, and fresh foods are cited by fifty centenarians, far more than any other type. The emphasis is on fresh, raw, and grown on the premises. Eight centenarians linked their longevity to eating meat, but two of them qualified the meat as killed on the farm. Despite the emphasis on vegetables, there were only four vegetarians (three others said they ate no meat), and only one man attributed his longevity to his vegetarian diet. This lends support to an inference that the meals were balanced even if this were stated explicitly by only a few centenarians.

At least three centenarians commented on the deterioration of food quality. Charley Redd, a Navajo medicine man in Arizona said, "We always had corn and berries that kept us strong and healthy. The store food we have today isn't as good as it was then." Andres Crespo-Bonilla in Puerto Rico "complained about present food, alleging that previous food was of better quality. No fertilizers were used at that time and the food was more nutritive; it took its strength from the ground." Edward Rickman in Springfield, Missouri, said the secret of his longevity is "living as close to nature as humanly possible. Nature possesses all elements necessary for the human body. Man extracts all these elements and puts in harmful preservatives. The result is the human race is slowly being poisoned to death."

These alarms and complaints, the results of experiencing change over a long period of years, coincide with the latest scientific discoveries. Mimi Sheraton, writing in the series "How America Eats" for the *New York Times,* stated: "Much fresh produce is treated with chemical waxes, sealers and antioxidants to improve its appearance, to ripen it artificially or to give it added shelf-life. Although the Food and Drug Administration lists these substances as generally recognized as safe, many scientists and consumer advocates consider them to be potentially harmful." Not only have carcinogenic agents been used as pesticides, but researchers at the University of Iowa were surprised to discover that as an occupational hazard Iowa farmers suffered a greater risk of contracting six types of cancer than did city dwellers. "Cancer is basically considered an urban disease because of smoking habits and industrial exposure," said Dr. Leon Burmeister, associate professor of preventive medicine and environmental health, "yet we are finding that healthy farm-life has its cancer risks."

One other eating pattern emerges from these centenarians, even though the numbers are scanty. Breakfast is the most important meal and probably the heaviest. Seventeen centenarians referred to their breakfasts, often with zest (Appendix 30B). The typical breakfast was bacon, eggs, toast, and coffee with cereal or potatoes added in a few cases. After breakfast, eating tapered off. Only four centenarians referred to lunch and seven to dinner. Only one person said he ate a big dinner. Lunch and dinner for the rest were light. For dinner, one centenarian had only a grapefruit; another had fruit or something light; a third ate lettuce, vinegar, and peppers.

In February 1980 the Department of Agriculture and the Department of Health, Education, and Welfare issued a set of dietary guidelines. This is how the practices of the centenarians, from the information available, compare:

1. Eat a variety of foods. The centenarians do that, with bacon, eggs, bread, cereal, milk (ten said they drink lots of milk, four attributed their longevity to drinking milk), coffee, meat, vegetables, and fruit mentioned most prominently.

2. Maintain ideal weight. Many centenarians did not match a preconception as wizened, wispy people who had been able to live so long because their hearts didn't have to work so hard pushing blood through large bodies. Perry Bradford, a Tennessee man who operated two farms in addition to his "public" work in the mines or on the railroad, was a robust 6 feet tall and weighed 225 pounds. Mrs. Ida Miller, in a nursing home in Springfield, Ohio, is a broad woman.

She told about a market stand they ran for many years in Springfield. "We sold berries, vegetables, chickens, and eggs. I baked bread and pastries to sell. We got up early every Tuesday and Saturday and drove a spring-wagon five miles to Springfield to the market. In those days we got thirty-five cents for a frying chicken. Also, I always wanted to be plump like my mother, so I got so heavy it was hard to climb onto the wagon. People don't want to be fat now." She says she "cleans up" her plate, and that "I could eat more than they give me but I was getting too heavy, so they had to cut down on my food."

Of the 288 centenarians who could be judged for their weight, twenty-six of them—9 percent—were on the heavy side and 48 percent were average. A minority of 43 percent were lean. None was severely underweight or obese. This grouping reflects nicely what scientists now are discovering about weight, health, and longevity. The ongoing Baltimore Longitudinal Study has not been able to show that mild-to-moderate obesity in middle-aged and older people shortens lifespan. The Gerontology Research Center in Baltimore says that evidence from seventeen population studies shows that mortality is lower in elderly people who are mildly or moderately overweight. The National Institute of Mental Health longitudinal study, which examined twenty-three survivors of the forty-seven men it had first tested eleven years earlier, learned that survivors were heavier than nonsurvivors: "Unexpectedly, men with higher weights (but not obesity) survived more frequently than men with lower weights."

The Belloc-Breslow study of health practices found that, for men, being 10 percent or more below desired weight was the factor most associated with mortality, whereas being 10 to 20 percent above desired weight, 5 to 10 percent above desired weight, and 20 to 30 percent above desired weight were the third, fourth, and fifth correlations with the lowest mortality. The correspondence was less pronounced for women, with 10 percent or more below desired weight in fifth place among factors associated with mortality.

Recently, the twenty-four-year study of more than five thousand people aged 30 to 60 in Framingham, Massachusetts, found that the thinnest people had a higher death rate than even the obese, while the lowest mortality rate occurred in those of average weight. This report said that the medical community long had accepted a 1959 insurance-industry study showing that people who weighed well below average had the lowest death rates, outliving people with normal weight. So-called ideal or desired weights were often based on the findings of this study.

3. Avoid too much fat, saturated fat, and cholesterol. The word *cholesterol* is not in the lexicon of these centenarians. Neither do they use the term *saturated fats*. *Fat* is mentioned four times. Dr. Pannell said he ate no fats since a bout with typhoid when he was 20 years old. Edward Ocker, Jr., in a Veterans Administration hospital in Albany, New York, talked of a lifetime favorite: "I like fat. I always did like the fat meat. I guess I'd have no trouble up north eating what they call blubber. Most people don't eat the fat. I do. I eat fat."

Toothless Alberta Pimental was living with a granddaughter at Santurce, Puerto Rico, even though twin daughters lived nearby. The social security agent asked why she chose her granddaughter. "She told me that her children's religion did not permit the use of meat in her home, and there is nothing she likes better than pork, with lots of fat in it." Leslie Carpenter in Rochester, Indiana, gave this reason for his longevity: "I think because I eat a lot of fat pork. I love fat pork."

With the exception of one reference to steak, no other kind of meat is referred to specifically except these most fatty ones: hogmeat, bacon, ham, and pork. One centenarian attributed his longevity to pork and potatoes. And for Jim McEllan, "wild hogs were an important source of food in his early days in Mississippi. He recalled that they would have to feed the hogs on corn a week or more before killing them, in order to rid the flesh of the wild taste and blackened color that resulted from the hogs having gorged themselves on acorns."

Henry Bean didn't use the word *fat*, but his breakfast every morning consisted of "corn bread and tap gravy (lard, flour, and water)."

4. Eat foods with adequate starch and fiber. The variety of foods mentioned by the centenarians indicates they were consistent with this recommendation.

5. Avoid too much sugar. Two centenarians attributed their longevity to eating few sweets (one following doctor's orders), while another thought it was because she ate no rich food. Dr. Pannell gave up sweets as well as fats after his typhoid illness, and another centenarian mentioned avoiding sweets, although neither person connected this abstinence with longevity. On the other side, Mrs. Vincenzina Castelluzzo "attributes her long life to the drinking of black coffee with lots of sugar. She drinks demitasse coffee, black, with several heaping teaspoonfuls of sugar, day and night." Three centenarians named cakes as a favorite food, one mentioned cookies, another candy. Mrs. Katherine Holman enjoys Tootsie Rolls between meals: "The great-grandchildren see to it that the candy supply is never completely diminished."

6. Avoid too much sodium. There are three references to salt. As already mentioned, Mrs. Elizabeth Randall is the woman who reacted to her doctor's advice to cut down on salt by saying he wouldn't live as long as she had so he shouldn't advise her how to eat. Mrs. Mary Jahries in Glendale, California, "believes her long life is a result of good habits and hard work. She drinks a lot of coffee and uses a lot of salt." Joe Shortridge of Circleville, Ohio, "maintains that his long life has been due to 'eating a lot of salt.' He claims his mother always told him that he would stay healthy if he ate a lot of salt, and he 'followed her advice ever since I was small.' "

7. If you drink alcohol, do so in moderation. Most centenarians conform with this advice. Of the 230 centenarians for whom there is information on the subject, 165 don't drink, 8 drink infrequently and 45 drink moderately. A dozen centenarians are heavy drinkers. Looked at another way, about 36 centenarians drink daily, while 30 drink occasionally. As already mentioned in the chapter on "Order," a relatively very high percentage of centenarians attribute their longevity to never drinking during their entire lives: Exactly 129 centenarians gave this reason. On the other hand, 25 centenarians gave the opposite reason: They felt they owed their survival to drinking alcoholic beverages. This conforms with the Jewett-study (Appendix 6) finding: "Drinking: no uniformity. Some drank moderately, some drank too much at times, some abstained."

There is some indication that centenarians who do not drink are more likely to declare that fact than drinkers are likely to acknowledge their custom. For example, this is an excerpt from the interview with Fred Vagele in Gloversville, New York:

"Q. Why do you think you have been able to live so long?

"A. He 'worked hard and ate good.' (He was questioned if he took exceptionally good care of himself. His answer—'Not necessarily, always drank, smoked, chewed tobacco, and ate too much.')"

When a centenarian states he does not drink and never has, there is often the moral connotation of approbation for this type of behavior. Obviously there is a social factor, a stigma attached to drinking, and the question about drinking is rarely if ever raised by the social security representatives.

While several of the centenarians indicated they were hearty drinkers, Thomas Pender is the only centenarian to admit to being a falling-down drunk. This exotic centenarian was interviewed at the Veterans Administration Hospital in Bath, New York. "When the social security representative arrived for the interview, Mr. Pender was in bed taking a nap, but when awakened he quickly roused himself and got into a wheelchair without assistance. He was able to wheel himself to a private office where the interview was held. Mr.

Pender is approximately five feet ten inches tall, stoop-shouldered, and apparently is in good health. His face is remarkably free of wrinkles and he has a very pleasant smile. He has lost his teeth and is hard of hearing. He remarked that the only reason he was in the hospital is that his legs are starting to go bad. He also stated that he felt fine and expected to be around a long time." This was an accurate prediction. Mr. Pender was 101 years old at the time of the interview and lived another two years and nine months, dying shortly before his one hundred and fourth birthday.

"When asked how his health was, he said, 'Outside of not having very much wind I feel very good. I drink plenty of good Irish whiskey. I have a drink every morning—any kind I can get a hold of! I always smoke a pipe, and a cigar once in a while. I guess you could say I lived a full life but always in moderation.'

"When asked about outside activities—church and hobbies—he said: 'Up until two years ago I used to like to spend my time at the downstairs tavern where I lived. Many's the time that I fell off the stool and had to be carried upstairs to bed.' "

Recent evidence shows that moderate drinking offers protection against heart disease and heart attacks. In the 1970s, Arthur L. Klatsky and colleagues at Kaiser-Permanente Medical Center in Oakland, California, found that an unusually high proportion of patients under treatment for their first heart attack were teetotalers. The scientists reviewed the medical records of 120,000 patients to discover that moderate drinkers were 30 percent less likely to have heart attacks than nondrinkers. William J. Darby, a nutrition researcher and president of the Nutrition Foundation, defines moderate drinking as three drinks a day or less. The Honolulu heart study conducted by Katsuhiko Yano and his fellow researchers on 7,705 Japanese men living in Hawaii learned that there were thirty heart attacks per thousand men among current drinkers, forty-four heart attacks per thousand among nondrinkers, and fifty-six heart attacks per thousand among former drinkers. Ronald E. LaPorte and his associates at the University of Pittsburgh reported that an analysis of twenty industrialized countries showed that if the people drank more alcohol, the death rate from heart disease was lower.

One explanation for these correlations is that, as five major studies have shown, alcohol raises the level of HDL in the blood serum. As discussed in Chapter 3, strenuous exercise also produces higher levels of HDL, the substance believed to protect against atherosclerosis and heart attacks. Joseph Barboriak of Wood Veterans Administration Center and the Medical College of Wisconsin found that alcoholics have HDL concentrations that are double the average levels and even higher than those of joggers. If the alcoholic goes on the wagon, the HDL content drops to normal in two weeks. But this benefit of high-frequency consumption of alcohol is outweighed by the greater risk of stroke, accidents, cirrhosis, and other impairments.

Dr. LaPorte, emphasizing the need for moderation, likes to quote a 103-year-old cross-country skier, Harmann Smith-Johannson (not in the cohort for this report): "The secret to a long life is to stay busy, get plenty of exercise, and don't drink too much. Then again, don't drink too little."

Drinking is mentioned most often, negatively, with smoking. Ninety-two centenarians attribute their longevity to not drinking and smoking; these citations often are given as behavioral aspects of living a good, moral life (which many centenarians considered an essential ingredient of a long life).

But whereas twenty-five centenarians saw drinking as such a positive practice that it made their long lives possible, there is a dearth of this kind of testimony for smoking cigarettes. The subject of smoking comes up only eleven times in connection with the question "Why do you think that you have been able to live so long?" Three men say they smoke cigars and a pipe, and three men say they smoke cigars. Of this group of six, three emphasize that they never smoked cigarettes in their lives. A seventh man says that he gave up smoking cigars at the age of 96. One man attributes his longevity to having given up cigarettes and drinking at the age of 82. The ninth man says, "I have chewed and smoked tobacco all my life until about nine years ago. I quit in disgust after seeing a couple of young girls smoking cigarettes and drinking beer." He does not refer to cigarettes specifically. Nor does the tenth man: "When asked to what he attributed his long life, he said that he very seldom drank liquor and began smoking when he was in his late seventies."

That leaves Isaac Burrell as the only defender of cigarettes, and even he does not make a positive statement but uses a double negative. Mr. Burrell is shown seated holding a lit cigarette in a holder. He is a healthy and active man who was to live another three years. This is Mr. Burrell's answer to the question about his longevity. "All our family has lived long lives. My brother in Omaha died in 1952 at the age of one hundred and five. My sister is now in her eighties. There were eight boys and eight girls in our family, and only the two of us are left. One sister died at ninety-six. I think long life is just due to the way you go along. I don't agree with those who say 'Don't drink or smoke.' " So even he isn't saying that smoking prolongs life, only that the practice doesn't shorten it.

These centenarian perceptions of smoking as a life-shortening prac-

Isaac Burrell

tice coincide with the findings of both three-sphere longitudinal studies of aging. In the NIMH study, smoking was one of two key indicators of the nonsurvivors. In the Duke study, "no cigarettes" was fourth among the significant predictors of longevity for men (the NIMH study was entirely composed of men). Cigarette smoking is not such a significant factor for women because it was not so prevalent for the cohorts under study. Of the eighteen centenarians who smoked cigarettes, two were women. One hundred and forty-three centenarians never smoked, an eight to one ratio with the cigarette smokers.

SEX AMONG THE AGED has been unexplored territory until recently. During the past few years, scientists have begun to fill in the outline and some features of the subject. They are finding there is more to it than expected.

Brooklyn College psychologists Bernard Starr and Marcella Bakur Weiner conducted a questionnaire survey of 800 Americans between the ages of 60 and 91. The scientists visited senior citizens' centers throughout the country, explained their study to their elderly listeners, then distributed a 50-question survey to be filled out anonymously. The return of 14 percent of the questionnaires was considered excellent for a survey on sex. What Drs. Starr and Weiner found in this 1980 survey is that an overwhelming majority of the respondents said they were sexually active while 93 percent said they liked sex.

The Baltimore Longitudinal Study of Aging has discovered a wide range in the amount of sexual activity in a group of 188 men from ages 60 to 79 years. The men were divided into three groups of least active, moderately active, and most active, according to the number of sexual events reported during the preceding year. The least active group averaged one event every three months, the moderately active group averaged an event every two and a half weeks, and the most active group averaged one event every six days.

The Baltimore study learned that the amount of sexual activity in later life followed a pattern established during early marriage and the intervening years: The most sexually active had been so throughout their lives, just as the least active were repeating their lifelong habits. The Kinsey studies found this same consistent pattern throughout life in women.

The Baltimore study further learned that the inability to have sex was not necessarily a problem for sexually inactive men because they felt no pressure to perform. "This lack of anxiety made their impotence far less disturbing than this condition is commonly assumed to be." This finding is consistent with the research of Ellen Frank, acting director of the Sexual Behavior Center, and Carol Anderson, director of the Family Therapy Clinic, at the University of Pittsburgh's School of Medicine. Their study of a group of 100 younger married couples suggested that the subjects "often find it difficult to maintain an active sex life. Job pressures, intrusive children, social demands, and just plain fatigue all take their toll in the sexual arena." The researchers continue: "Meaningful sexual relating requires energy, interest, and a minimum of preoccupation. Most of the couples we talked with were not willing to make the sacrifices in the rest of their lives that would be necessary to be constantly sexually active." The lack of sex was not so disturbing because of other pluses in their lives and the emotional security shared by each husband and wife—for Drs. Frank and Anderson were studying *happily* married couples.

The Starr-Weiner survey of elderly people picks up the story, and again there is a consistency. Nearly two-thirds of the group reported that the quality of their lovemaking had improved later in life. Factors involved in this improvement included relief from the pressures of childbearing and the fear of pregnancy, greater privacy at home, fewer inhibitions, and, with retirement, more time and opportunity.

This finding coincides with the Masters and Johnson statement that what is essential for the aging woman to remain capable and effective "is the opportunity for regularity of sexual expression." This is not so easy for older women, because they lose their partners. The women usually have married men who are older and die before they do, or else the male sexual powers decline into impotence. Masters and Johnson have listed six major impediments to performance in the aging man: boredom with a repetitious sexual relationship, preoccupation with career and economic pursuits, mental or physical fatigue, eating or drinking too much, mental or physical troubles either with himself or his wife, and fear of performance.

The Baltimore study also found that much of the sexual inactivity in older men "stems from apathy or indifference to stimuli which previously caused erotic reactions, and not from negative attitudes about sex." Similarly, the study found that physical well-being is associated with the sexually active people.

Several studies, including the Duke Longitudinal Study of Aging, have traced the steady decline of sexual activity with advancing years. The decline cannot be ascribed simply to physiological aging, but to any of the variety of psychological and social reasons given above.

If we are just beginning to find out about sex among the aged, what is known about centenarian sexuality makes our knowledge of the surface of Mars appear encyclopedic. One reason might be that heretofore our society had greater expectations of reaching Mars than of reaching the second century of life. After all, centenarians did not exist for the life insurance industry until 1971. Before that, everyone was considered dead by age 99.

In the 1,200 interviews with centenarians in this inquiry, sex is not discussed directly or explicitly and not even alluded to very often. However, some light can be cast on centenarian sexuality by the data collected and by using what we have learned about sex among the aged as a guide. That some centenarians in this group remained sexually active can be assumed for several reasons. One is that so many centenarians still enjoyed good physical functioning, one of the correlates of sexual activity. Regularity marked many of these lives, and regularity is probably the principal means of preserving sexual capability in advanced age. We know that most of the centenarians were sexually active earlier in their lives. Nine hundred and forty-five of them had children; nearly four hundred had five or more children. Forty-six of them remarried after the age of 60.

There is a way of delineating the size of the sexually active group through the important criterion of opportunity. Two hundred and sixty centenarians were in nursing homes and 560 centenarians lived with children or other relatives. The social circumstances for both groups were such that the opportunities for sex were virtually nil. That's a total of 820. Fifty-four centenarians were bedridden, eighty-eight confined to wheelchairs, sixty-one used walkers to be ambulatory, and fifty-nine others needed canes to get around—all these figures indicating a frailty incompatible with the vigor and physical condition associated with sexual intercourse. That's another 262, for a total of 1,082. That eliminates all but 118, although admittedly the 1,082 figure includes overlaps, with many of the physically handicapped residing in nursing homes or with relatives.

A still more accurate picture can be drawn by looking at those who positively had the social opportunities for sexual activity. One hundred and fifty-four centenarians lived alone. But these people, while independent, were hardly running bachelor pads. With few exceptions there were no signs that the potential opportunity was fulfilled with the regular appearance of partners. That leaves the 118 centenarians who were married. Of that number, 100 were living at home with their spouses. While these 100 centenarians were recipients of companionate services vital to their existence, their physical conditions were such that sexual service was unlikely in many cases.

Considering the married centenarians and those living alone, an educated guess of likely sexual activity was made in cases where social and physical circumstances, allusions, or other factors indicated such a possibility. These estimates of likelihood were made in and conditioned by several contexts. Seen from the perspective that they possessed the physical independence, seventy-four centenarians were considered likely to be sexually active. Judged by independence of personal life, sixty-two centenarians were thought likely to be sexually active. In the context of an independent social life, fifty-six centenarians could have been sexually active. Judged on the basis of their social relationships, fifty-three centenarians were considered likely to be sexually active. The number drops to forty-eight centenarians from the perspective of their biological fitness. The five estimates are encompassed within the narrow range of 4 percent to 6 percent of the 1,200 centenarians.

Carmello Pagliaro

Ernesto Aguiar is a leading candidate. The SSA representative reports: "He told me that he thought social security was the most exciting thing in his life. It is his only income, and with the amount received plus what he still makes as a shoe repairman, he supports his bride of three months, a lady 38 years younger than he.

"He attributes his long life to eating good vegetables when he was young and to the fact that he never had two women at a time. On the other hand, he still smokes a cigar a day, and neighbors tell me he goes for his drinks to the corner bar once in a while, although he denies it."

Mr. Aguiar was interviewed two and a half months past his 100th birthday, so if he married exactly three months earlier, the wedding occurred shortly before he became a centenarian.

John W. Beaird was married, for the second time, right on his one hundredth birthday, in Louisville, Kentucky. The manager of the Louisville social security office read about the event in a newspaper and wrote to Mr. Beaird that he might be eligible for coverage. He was. A short time later, a field representative called on the centenarian to present him with a check for $267.60 and took the opportunity to interview him as well. Mr. Beaird is pictured with his bride, an obviously younger woman. But he doesn't appear to be within decades of 100 years either. He has strong white hair on his head and on his face and under his chin. His face is turned to the side as he looks out a window, squinting into the strong light. His wife is behind him to the other side, one arm and hand across his left shoulder and the other hand cupping his right shoulder in an affectionate semiembrace.

Carmello Pagliaro is what would customarily be called a dirty old man, except that when one is 100 years old the opprobrium in the term is supplanted by wonder and admiration. One of his favorite pastimes is to visit a bowling alley, but, the SSA representative states, "only as an observer; he said, 'I like to see the girls in their short skirts.'" Whether Mr. Pagliaro gives more active expression to his interest is problematical, for he is a widower living in Boston with one of his five children and has no outside activities other than going to a senior citizens club, sitting on a park bench, and visiting the bowling alley. Nevertheless, he is happy. "He loves life and claims an additional extension of it due to the fact that he was a seven-month baby and, therefore, he had had two months more of life than most people." As for living so long, Mr. Pagliaro says: "I ate, drank, and was merry. I took life as it came and never let anything bother me."

Samuel Matkoff expresses the same philosophy. "You want my formula for long life? Live! That's what I have done always. Food? Eat anything. Drink, too. It will not hurt you. Enjoy life, that's my formula." Mr. Matkoff was interviewed by a reporter for the *New York Post* while in Long Beach Hospital on Long Island for a checkup. During the interview, the patient threw back the covers from his bed, hopped to the floor, and began dancing with a nurse. He said he wanted his friends, especially his women friends, at the King David retirement hotel to know he'd be back there in short order. He liked everything about his women friends except the way they danced. "They're too slow for me. I like to dance fast—fox trots and the hustle. So I wait until their daughters come to visit and I dance with them instead." The 101-year-old was shown in a photograph smiling with two young nurses kissing him on both cheeks.

Morris Zone, mentioned in the prologue, liked the company of young women and had a girl friend he called Tootsie. But the closest to an explicit acknowledgment of sexual activity comes from Henry Jones, a West Indian living the bachelor's life in New York City. "Smoking and drinking never held me back," Mr. Jones on his 104th birthday told a reporter for the *New York Daily News*, "and as for the girls, well, there is still a little coal left in the cellar. Never mind the snow on the roof."

There were some poignant laments as well, allusions to glories that have faded from all but memory. "Old age is no fun," said Tolbert Hill, a retired physician. "You lose your hearing and can't appreciate the rustle of a silk skirt anymore." Louis Wiley "has a room in the Parkview Hotel in New York City. He lives there alone since he and his wife are separated. They were married when he was 70 years old and it was his first marriage." That was the opening paragraph of the interview. Then toward the end: "His main problem is that he is blind, so he is confined to his room where he is familiar with the surroundings. He did say he would like to see the good-looking women and it is a 'pretty poor man who doesn't have a nice-looking woman.' "

When the celebrated Charlie Smith was asked if he still had sex, he replied, "Can a dead mule pull a cart?" Of course, he was reputedly long past his one hundredth birthday at that time.

It may have been noticed that in every case the centenarian was a man. Except for one exchange, the subject never was broached or volunteered with the women centenarians. The report on Mrs. Mary Parks, a widow, concludes:

"She lives in a room separated a short distance from her son's house. She spends her time lying in bed or sitting on her rocking chair. She gets about the room without assistance. On Sundays she listens to sermons on her radio.

"Teasingly, the interviewer asked if she had a boyfriend. She hesitated a moment and stated, 'Let's say I have a friend.' Her daughter-in-law then said that a man who is in his eighties comes to see her and they apparently enjoy talking to each other."

Perhaps a future generation of centenarians grown old with the customs of public confession and TV talk shows will not be so reticent.

THE POWER of genetic programming is most evident during the period following conception. By the end of the third week, two cells have grown to an embryo of three millimeters, and the head and tail folds are forming. In another week, the head is at right angles to the body, the tail is prominent, limbs are starting to form, and heartbeat begins. At eight weeks, the tail is almost gone; eyes, ears, nose, and mouth are recognizable; fingers and toes are formed, sex organs are distinguishable. After twelve weeks, the fetus has delicate, pink skin, the brain configuration is almost complete and the head is disproportionately large, blood is forming in the marrow. In another four weeks, the fetus is assuming its human appearance and proportions, the body outgrowing the head; the heart muscle is well developed, and the other organs are taking their places. By twenty-eight weeks, the fetus is developed enough to possibly survive premature birth.

The program of development continues, as we know, with a well-timed regularity from infancy to puberty, the onset of reproductive capability, when the human being is essentially completed biologically. The last dramatic genetic play comes with menopause, nature's way of making sure that mothers will have enough of their lifespan remaining to nurture their last offspring to maturity.

With two exceptions, the connection between genetic inheritance and longevity is not so clear as the genetic role in development. The female of the species—just about any species—lives longer than the male. In our species, women outlive men in almost every society on the planet. In the United States there are three women for every two men by the age of 65. Among centenarians the female advantage has increased to seven to three.

In his discussion of longevity studies, sociologist Charles L. Rose comments on this female superiority: "It is believed by geneticists that the biological influence operates through genetically based female secondary sex characteristics, which produce differences in behavior, metabolism and body structure, rather than through the direct effect of harmful sex-linked [male] genes." Gerontologist George Sacher has found an important correspondence between body size and longevity among mammals. His formula is: the greater the brain size in relation to body weight, the longer the life. While men in the United States average larger brain sizes than women, because of the much smaller female body, women have a larger brain relative to body size, possibly enabling better neural control. In 1980 pathologist David T. Purtillo and pediatrician John L. Sullivan at the University of Massachusetts in Worcester reported evidence that females have twice as many genes that program the making of immunological defense products as males. These genes are located in the X chromosomes, of which females have two and males only one. As a result of this deficiency, the researchers say, males are more vulnerable to a number of severe viral and bacterial infections.

The second clear connection between genetics and longevity is a negative one: Genetic defects curtail lives.

But there is no known set of "longevity" genes. It has been argued that death results not because of genetic programming but because of a lack of any program to ensure continued existence. The genetic blueprint provides sufficient endurance, usually with a margin of safety, for producing and rearing offspring so that the life cycle can be endlessly repeated—but that's the extent of the program. That each species has a fixed maximum lifespan might be explained, as in the case of female longevity, through the theory that duration is a consequence of the specific structures and behaviors resulting from the genetic instructions; to that extent lifespan is genetically ordained. In actuality, this theoretical potential has no meaning in the lives of most human beings. The maximum lifespan of about 115 years is more than half again as long as the average lifespan in the United States.

As for how much influence heredity contributes to the extended longevity of any particular person, there is a saying in gerontology that nature deals the cards but the individual plays the hand (with genetic engineering, human beings are beginning to change the deal). One person born with a good physical deal may behave unwisely while another person makes the most of a poor hand. Implied in the saying is the admonition to conduct one's life to achieve maximum longevity whatever the genetic heritage, but also implied is the impossibility of allotting the precise amount of influence in the interplays of behavior, environment, and genetic endowment.

While this inquiry concentrates on how these people "played their hands" in living the greatest part of the human lifespan, there is evidence of a heredity factor in at least some of the centenarian lives. A genetic factor was objectively judged to be a salient characteristic associated with longevity in ninety lives—7.5 percent of the cohort. Fifty-one centenarians attribute their longevity to being a member of a long-lived family—5.5 percent of those making attributions. However, another forty-four centenarians attribute their longevity to having a good constitution or to good health, and that could be seen to have a genetic component as well—for a total of 10 percent. Sixty-four centenarians said that longevity ran in their families and this could also be true in thirteen other cases where it was not explicitly stated. On the other hand, the family members of at least eleven centenarians were decidedly short-lived. Seven centenarians said they were surprised they had lived so long because their families were not long-lived. Moreover, some of those who did refer to long-lived families gave unimpressive examples, like Egbert S. Van Nostrand. "I give my ancestors the most credit for my longevity; my father lived to be eighty-four, and my mother was about sixty-five when she died." In most cases, only a few examples are given, suggesting that these were well-remembered exceptions while the majority of family members with more average lifespans were ignored.

Of those who volunteered the information, forty-nine centenarians had long-lived mothers while fifty-three centenarians had short-lived mothers; forty-seven had long-lived fathers and sixty-three had short-lived fathers. One man acknowledged parental influences on his lon-

Gonzalo Davila

gevity, but emphasized the social mode over the genetic. He said his parents were good Scotch stock but also good Christians—honest and industrious. He attributed his longevity to his parents' being good Christians. Thirteen centenarians attributed their longevity to having good parents or upbringing. Says sociologist Rose: "One simply does not know whether these parental influences are primarily genetic or social."

Cora McCord gives an example of a parent-child parallel where both modes could be involved. Mrs. McCord said: "Nearly all my folks lived to old age. My mother lived to ninety-two and would have made a hundred if she hadn't broke her hip—but I lived longer than any of my relatives I know of." Mrs. McCord also broke her hip, at the age of 98 as she tried to grab a falling tub of rinse water.

A genetic factor is strongly indicated in the cases of Grant Evans and Sherman Evans. They are centenarian twins, and each man still has all his teeth, a rare trait for the centenarians. Two other men in the cohort were brothers. Several others said they had brothers or sisters who lived to be centenarians. Eighty subjects said they still had living siblings, while thirty-three volunteered that all their brothers and sisters were dead. And there's this interesting set of statistics: One hundred and three centenarians told how many siblings they had and what their position was in the group of children (Appendix 31B). Thirty-seven were the oldest child (in two cases the older of two) and twenty-seven centenarians were the youngest child (in three cases the younger of two). So there was an advantage to being at either end of the sibling group. That advantage can be quantified by considering the odds against middle children: five to three against the children in the middle, and there were a great many more in-between children to start with because the family groups ranged up to fourteen siblings. A total of 213 centenarians told the size of their family groups. Seventy percent had four or more siblings. Just one centenarian was an only child.

A genetic factor may also be gauged from those who come after. Nine hundred and forty-five centenarians had children, and we know what happened to the children in 835 cases. For 305 centenarians, all the children still were living—36.5 percent. All the children of 90 centenarians were dead—11 percent. Two hundred and fourteen centenarians had lost one half or more of their children—25.5 percent. Two hundred and twenty-six centenarians had lost fewer than half of their children—27 percent.

Finally, these notes on late parenting. Mrs. Hannah Jewett of Vancouver, Washington, married at the age of 35 and went on to bear three children, all still living. Mrs. Margaret Wollerscheld of Maynard, Massachusetts, married at 43 and bore one son at the age of 45, but he had poor health and died at fifty. Don Gregorio Duran Baez of Arecibo, Puerto Rico, was married the first time for twenty-five years. "Out of this marriage there were born four children. At this point Don Gregorio made a stirring remark, 'You might as well note, young man, that only four children were born because my wife had twenty-one miscarriages.' " After his first wife died, he remarried in his fiftieth year and had fifteen more children.

Prescott Cogswell of El Monte, California, had three children by his first wife, who died when he was 40 years old. He waited until he was 68 years old before he remarried, then fathered two sons, one 30 years old at the time of the interview and the other 25 years old. But the record goes to Robert Ridley of Cairo, Illinois. The account does not say at what age he married, but he is a widower with four children. The oldest is 33 years old and the youngest is 23 years old. Mr. Ridley became a father for the last time at the age of 77.

CHAPTER 9
Profiles

After processing several hundred interviews, an observer recognizes certain types of recurring personalities and life histories. These configurations were made sharper with assignment of traits in the profile categories and quantification of the traits detectable for each centenarian.

It was discovered that the Order-Freedom (O/F) profile, which was introduced in the first chapter and is based on Sections V and VI of the questionnaire, applied to 1,129 centenarians, 94 percent of the 1,200 cohort, while the Sociopsychobiological (S/P/B) profile, based on the three-sphere model and questionnaire Sections II, III, and IV, was evident in 509 subjects, 42 percent of the group (see Appendix 36).* The O/F profile appeared alone in more than half

---

* After pertinent information from the interview had been transposed to the questionnaire, an assessment was made of each person. The salient characteristics associated with that individual's longevity were itemized; the totals (Appendix 23) have been referred to several times. A decision was made on which profile characterized the person and how well the centenarian matched the items looked for in the questionnaire. Gradations for the number of traits in evidence ranged from incomplete, few, few-to-moderate, moderate, moderate-to-many, many, and very many.

Assignment of the Sociopsychobiological (S/P/B) profile was based on how the subject scored in Sections II, III, and IV of the questionnaire, and assignment of the Order-Freedom (O/F) profile on scores in Sections V and VI.

The fact that each centenarian was alive at the time of the interview was taken as qualification in the "Biological" category. In the "Social" category, Section II, especial importance was given to 23E, "enjoyed work/took satisfaction," and 25A, "takes pleasure from daily activities," because of the findings of the Duke study. In general, what was looked for was high quality of

George Motz

of the people (52 percent), but the S/P/B profile rarely was evident by itself: It was found in 501 centenarians side by side with the O/F profile, but in only 8 persons by itself. Neither a complete O/F or S/P/B profile could be found in 63 people, a little more than 5 percent of the centenarians. The lack of definition in these cases can be largely attributed to paucity of information. The amount of traits for 90 percent of the "Neither" group ranged from "few" downward through varying degrees of "Incomplete" (gradations of the quantification of traits observed are presented in Appendix 36). Even in the groups where the O/F profile is missing, the "Order" category can be recognized in more than 40 percent of the "Neither" group and in 3 of the 8 S/P/B-only centenarians. Clearly, the orderly life is a requisite for longevity.

George Motz is an apparent exception to this rule and is cited here as the one person in the S/P/B-only profile who displayed many longevous traits even as he led the most picaresque and anomalous life of all the cohort of centenarians. He scores highly in the "Free-

---

social life, expressed in references to a happy married life, to having a circle of good friends, being well liked, and so forth. Family relationships and churchgoing were not considered relevant to the "Social" sphere unless there was evidence that they in some way contributed significantly to the centenarian's *quality* of social life. If they were simply routines, they could more fittingly be considered as structures in the person's orderly life.

In the "Psychological" sphere, most importance was given to attitudes, items 33A through L. If a person scored on 33A, "happy with life, takes pleasure from daily activities," or 34A, "harmonious life," because of the Duke and Beard studies, respectively, the subject qualified in the "Psychological" category on that alone. Otherwise, he or she would have to score on several items. What were deemed especially important in item 35, "intelligence/mental status," were "creating new things" and "learning new things," followed by "interest in politics, community, world." Other items were considered in conjunction with the attitudinal and behavioral scores, or the absence of them, in reaching a decision about qualification. The items 34F, "maintains autonomy, independence," and 34G, "makes decisions about own life," although included to fill out the impression of the person's behavior and personality, were not considered in making the judgment for the "Psychological" category because the items signified the "Freedom/Independence" category in the other profile. Similarly, 34H, "has control of life, life well organized," was excluded from qualification because it primarily indicated the "Order" category. And items 34M through O were not considered because adapting can be interpreted as a description or definition of what living beings do in order to continue living. Even in cases where a centenarian exercises such control over his environment that few adjustments in behavior and attitude are required, he cannot prevent the loss of loved ones and the deterioration of his own physical condition. So it could be taken at the outset that adaptability characterized 100 percent of the centenarians. The items were included in order to learn in what ways and to what degrees this trait was discernible in these extremely old people.

dom/Independence" sphere, but his life was not characterized by orderliness—except that he was no stranger to hard work at times and was working late in life. His colorful life and powers as an earthy raconteur make him the kind of grizzled oldtimer beloved by Hollywood scriptwriters, but who in actuality is as rare as, well, one in 1,200.

Mr. Motz's turn of phrase was not always considered suitable for a government publication and was bowdlerized. The field representative writes: "It is rather difficult to quote Mr. Motz, as his langauge is, to say the least, a bit salty, and I cleaned the quotes up considerably, which, of course, means that some of the quotes will not appear as colorful as they were at the interview." The agent explains that the "interview was a difficult one to conduct along the lines set forth in the recent memorandum" because the interviewee swamped the prescribed format with his anecdotes.

George Motz was born in Mondamin, Iowa, in 1856 and he says that before he was 9 years old he drove eight yoke of oxen from Nebraska City, an old steamboat-landing on the Missouri River, to Fort Concho, Texas. He made five trips up the old Chisholm Trail from Texas to Montana as a cowboy: "One thing I remember that was pretty funny. I was punchin' cows for a man named Connors who had a contract to deliver some cattle to the Indians. Well, the trail drive was pretty rough and when we got to the place where they had the scale house to weigh these cattle, Connors said to me: 'George, these cattle won't meet the specifications, they're too thin. What will we do?'

"Well, the way these cattle were weighed, they were driven into the scale house and up on the scales, and weights were put on a beam that run under the platform, and they would weigh six or seven cows at the same time. Well, I figured if we could get a man underneath the platform with a bunch of gunnysacks filled with rocks, that he could place enough rocks on the beam to bring these cattle up to specifications. We filled about seven gunnysacks with rocks, and they nailed me underneath that weighin' platform. As the cows came onto the weighin' platform the bookkeeper would call out: 'Seven cows on the scales.' I'd pick up the seven-cow gunnysack, and it would increase the weight enough so that we wouldn't have trouble.

"Well, one time this bookkeeper called out: 'Seven cows on the scales,' and I picked up the proper stone-filled sack and put her on the beam, and six of the cows run off and left one scrawny calf all alone on the scales. Well sir, that calf weighed thirty-seven hundred pounds. It all got fixed up, though. They figured the scales had stuck and went right on all day. They never got me out of there until late at night and I was so hot and tired that I didn't even feel like dancin' till I'd had a couple of drinks."

His intercourse with Indians was extensive: "I was never in the army or navy, but I worked for the army as a packer for a lot of years. I was a packer with Captain James Walker at the Battle of Wichita. I remember that they sent me with General Johnson to lead the bell mare for the pack outfit. Johnson's outfit ran into a passel of Injuns, and the general got himself wounded, and he was layin' out there on the ground a-bleedin' from a head wound, and ole Ben Chapman, a scout, said, 'Hold 'em off of me, boys, and I'll go git the general,' and he up and went out and brought back Johnson, and just as he got back he took a rifle ball in his ankle. Everybody got all right, though; Johnson's wound was just a crease, and Chapman healed up fine.

"Anyhow, there we were, surrounded by Injuns. Well sir, they decided someone had to go for help, and I up and volunteered. They asked me how I was gonna get through them Indians and I'll tell you I was a slick one in them days—slicker'n a beaver slide. I told 'em I'd put on an Injun warbonnet and ride out through the squaw camp. Well sir, I did just that, and I got across the Wichita River and on the old Chisholm Trail, and I told that ole buckskin to 'take all you can git,' and I went flyin' to Captain Walker's camp and give him the message. Walker wanted me to stay at camp and rest up, but I told him I was a-goin' back to see the fight, so we threw my saddle on another horse, and I got a cup of coffee and some hardtack and mounted up with the troops" (at this point George gives all the army commands to get the troops mounted and moving), "and I went with them to see the fight, and it was a good one.

"The Injuns finally showed a white flag and Captain Walker went out to talk things over with the chiefs. I saw this one chief throw a blanket over his arm, and I cocked my pistol, 'cause they was a tricky bunch. When the Injun got up to shake hands with Walker, he threw the blanket aside, and he had a pistol in his hands and was a-gonna shoot Walker. Well sir, I shot that snake right 'tween the eyes, and they went right on with the surrenderin'.

"I remember another time I got chills and fever, and I packed up and headed for Injun country to stay with the Injuns till I got well. Well sir, the rivers was at spring flood and was roarin' along in good shape, and about four days out I met up with a cavalry outfit, and they was tryin' to git across the river to warn the folk at Fort Sully that the Injuns was on the warpath. This cavalry captain said, 'I'd give a hundred dollars to the man who can get across this river and deliver a message to Fort Sully.' Well, I told that captain that I could swim the river all right, but it was so muddy that I'd have to take all my clothes off so that the mud wouldn't drag me down. Captain told me to go ahead and I swim the river. Well, I got to the other side with a message tied in a sweatband, and it was about two miles to Fort Sully, and I walked as naked as a jaybird. I knocked on the first door I came to at the fort, and some woman opened the door. I never seen such a surprised woman in my life. She called her husband, and I gave him the message, and he got me some clothes, and I went about my business, but I was a hundred dollars richer than when I started.

"Another thing I remember, when General Crook licked Chief Crazy Horse—I was there and I managed to get me a real good pony out of the fracas. Well sir, I took that pony and traded it to the Injuns for four squaws, and I took them four squaws on a trappin' trip and was gone for about two years. I never done any work, made the squaws do all the work. Tell you, that's probably one of the reasons I've lived so long—had squaws to do most of the work all my life."

But even George Motz makes a midlife transition at age 54. "I married a widow in 1910—fine woman—she already had two children by her first husband, and they were wonderful kids. I never had any children of my own." We hear nothing further about the intervening years until the age of 91 or 92 when he goes to work for a gold mine as a handyman.

Mr. Motz is living at a nursing home in Kamiah, Idaho, at the time of the social security interview, but still is able to get around and is not restricted to the place. He sums up: "I knew Wild Bill Hickock very well, and I've seen the James boys and the Youngers and a lot of the oldtimers. Tell you, if I die tomorrow, I sure haven't missed very much.

"I expect to live quite a while yet. I'm in good shape except for my eyes, and I still manage to get around pretty good without help. I don't need very much money, and with my social security and state old-age assistance I get along fine."

At another point, he says, "I rest and sleep a good bit, and every once in a while I go to town and have a few beers and flirt with the girls." In his photograph his right hand is raised, cupping what appears to be a shot glass, in a toast.

Thomas Pender, who often drank to inebriation, is the outstanding example of a centenarian who fit neither the O/F nor S/P/B profiles even though he exhibited many characteristics associated with longevity. He led a roving life at sea, lost his wife and a son in childbirth, and then lost his only other son in World War I. It was not until after that war, when Mr. Pender was 58 years old, that he made a transition from his earlier ways to a more stable life. He left the sea and took a job as a weaver; presumably he kept at this for many years, although that is not stated explicitly. Still, there was no family, no other relatives, no churchgoing or other mentioned structured activities. There was the continuity of drinking, but regularly falling off a barstool is not an activity usually linked with a long life.

For most centenarians there were two main patterns. Rather than show an either-or conflict, the O/F and S/P/B profiles help to reveal how life operates through these long-lived exemplars. The principle is illustrated in nature by the sea anemone. The sea anemone is an animal that looks like a plant, hence the name. The underwater animal consists of a "stub" that becomes permanently attached to a rock or some firm surface, and a cylindrical body made up of clusters of jelly tendrils. The organism is carnivorous, but being stationary must wait for whatever appropriate food passes by. Then the tentacles surround or sting and paralyze the prey, which is fed into a central mouth and gastric sac. When food is scarce, the sea anemone avoids starvation by shrinking in size. When the food supply improves, the sea anemone grows. Its structure is regulated by the levels of energy available.

With the centenarians, it is the size of their lives that varies. The length of their lives is about the same, but there is an enormous range in the social breadth, intellectual depth, richness, variety, interests, and accomplishments. The O/F profile alone is likely to indicate a constricted life. The circumscribed lives presented in Chapter 5 are extreme examples. They do not mean that the subjects are any less happy or have not derived as much enjoyment from their existence as have people with richer experience. The O/F centenarian is just as apt to perceive that he or she has led a full and rewarding life, although perhaps less likely to say so voluntarily. This kind of life commonly is built on the triad of hard work, God or church, and family. That base is sufficient and ample to support a century-long life. In more than a few cases, the support base is contracted still further: work and God, or work and church, or work and family. And there are some cases where existence is honed mainly to just hard work and the independent life that the earnings from that labor support. For the person who is able to adapt to this kind of life, it is an extremely economical existence. In a human parallel to the sea anemone that has shrunk to the core, the individual's resources are taxed a minimum by psychic and social demands.

Of course, the individual's life can expand to a full one within the framework of the O/F profile. In general, though, it is a structured life confined to routine, essential activities and basic relationships. A life that expands beyond the O/F boundaries registers in the S/P/B profile as well. The structure and independence remain, but the life takes on greater dimension. It is like comparing a stove with one burner going to a stove with two or three or all burners glowing. Or, for another analogy, it is like a one-cylinder engine putt-putting along, compared to a four-, six-, eight-, or twelve-cylinder engine purring with power. The single-cylinder engine can go the route as well as the twelve-cylinder one, but the driver gets there in a different style.

While 94 percent of these centenarians were characterized by the O/F profile, 42 percent of them qualified for both the O/F and S/P/B profiles. There is a quantitative indication of the different configurations of these two groups. As mentioned, each centenarian was rated for the number of traits or amount of items scored. Nearly half of the O/F centenarians—about 46 percent—registered "few" items. If the "few-to-moderate" classification is added, the percentage rises to sixty-four—nearly two out of three. Only 3 percent of these centenarians scored on "many" items and 4 percent on "moderate-to-many": 7 percent at the upper end of the scale. Among those centenarians with both profiles, 2 percent scored "very many," 10 percent "many," and 15 percent "moderate-to-many": 27 percent at the upper end, a four to one superiority. Less than one in five gets a "few" rating.

There is also a qualitative index to the lives of centenarians in the O/F and "Both profile" groups. In addition to rating each subject as to the number of traits identified and classifying by profile, the author made a qualitative judgment about each person and the life he or she had led. If the individual was interesting, stimulating, enjoyable, memorable, charming, inspiring; if the person was responsible for noteworthy accomplishments, had done admirable deeds, or made contributions to institutions or community or society; if, in short, the centenarian was a person one would want to visit again and learn more about or had done appreciably more than simply survive—then he or she was given an "elite" rating. Two hundred and forty-nine centenarians, one in five, warranted this "elite" status. Eighty-six percent, seven out of eight, of the "elite" centenarians were in the "Both profile" group, 11 percent in the O/F group.

One-quarter of these "elites" scored on "many" or "very many" items, nearly another quarter registered "moderate-to-many" traits, and with the addition of the "moderate" group, the proportion goes above three-quarters. There is a correspondence between the quality of their lives and quantity of longevous traits.

Henrietta Dull

Henrietta S. Dull is one of nine centenarians judged to be superior even among the elite group. She is selected as an example here because of her blend of orderliness, independence, determination, courage, attitudes, and philosophy, as well as her intellectual accomplishments and contributions to society—an array of traits matched by only three or four others, including Chief William Red Fox.

Mrs. Dull was born on her father's cotton plantation in south Georgia during the Civil War. Her family's prosperity ended with the war. Her earliest memory is picking cotton on the plantation. At the end of her life, she said she had been born on "Hunger and Hardship Creek." Growing up in Reconstruction poverty was hardly the life of a southern belle. "I've done everything but split rails," she said in her one hundredth year, "and I showed a man how to do that once." Her father ensured that she had an education, however. He built a one-room schoolhouse on the plantation and hired a governess to teach his five children.

Mrs. Dull grew up, maried, "and then was left a widow with five young children. She turned to one of the few activities open to a gentlewoman in those days—cooking and the teaching of cooking. She became a pioneer in the field of home economics as a profession for women, and was the organizer of the first department of home economics in the Atlanta city-schools.

"Her cookbook, *Southern Cooking*, published in 1928 (when she was sixty-five years old), has gone into many printings and is still the culinary bible in southern homes. As an expert on cooking, Mrs. Dull was a daily contributor to the *Atlanta Journal* for twenty years. She also lectured and conducted cooking classes.

"Mrs. Dull now spends her time sitting and listening to other people talk. She has no hobbies, and can't get out to church, but many people still drop by to have her autograph her cookbook for them. She lives with her daughter and son-in-law and a full-time companion. She has five children, seven grandchildren, thirteen great-grandchildren (including twins and triplets), and two great-great-grandchildren. Her income consists of her social security benefits, which started in 1956, the royalties from her book, and some stocks and bonds that she has 'saved away.'

"As a recipe for living, Mrs. Dull recommended respect for work and kindness between human beings, and emphasized the importance of gentleness and courtesy. 'Remember,' she said, 'all of us are children of God. That knowledge in itself should keep us striving for the rest of time.' "

THESE FINDINGS in no way detract from the validity of the three-sphere model as a representation of human life. It is obvious that hard work, faith in God or religion, and family* play roles in the biological, psychological, and social areas. And churchgoing has a social component as well as a psychological one. The application of more rigorous criteria had the effect of limiting admissions to the S/P/B profile. In retrospect, what can be seen as a double standard stems from insufficient appreciation initially of the differences in *cultural* background between this cohort and younger Americans. The in-

---

* The extent of family solidarity in the cohort may be gauged by the fact that
. only one centenarian was subjected in youth to the emotional conflict and
turmoil of a broken home.

quiry was designed to discover people psychologically and socially like overselves, not fully taking into account the different effects upon attitudes and behaviors produced by different social environments. A close examination of these life histories was an education on how much American society has changed.

The social area was less important to the survival of these centenarians than it is to the health, well-being, and longevity of contemporary maturing Americans. For every American alive in 1860, there are seven Americans today; there are nine Americans today for every two of the 50 million Americans who populated the land in 1880. With the growth of population, the opportunity for social collisions grows proportionately, or perhaps geometrically. Henrietta Dull may have recommended treating people with courtesy and gentleness from deeply held religious and moral conviction, but it is excellent advice for survival in today's more crowded society. One can pay with his life for a discourtesy on the saturated highways or amidst the jostle of public transportation.

The settings for social friction in contemporary life abound, a situation largely alien to most of the centenarians. About one-quarter of them did live in urban areas, but except for well-established cities like New York, Philadelphia, and Boston on the eastern seaboard, urban centers did not have huge populations nor did they resemble the megalopolitan sprawls of today—much less the unrelieved urbanization from Washington to Boston. Modern Americans are educated in crowds, work in crowded offices and factories, and take their recreation massed in stadiums, theaters, and beaches.

Society has grown in complexity as well as in numbers of people, and the growth of both requires ever greater regulation. After President Garfield was shot July 2, 1881, he lingered near death until he died September 19. There was no crisis in the federal government —mainly because Washington was shut down for the summer. Even a healthy president didn't do anything most of the time, and Congress, now a cornucopia of laws, was in session only a few months each year. It was a tough time for lawyers. This was the experience of Albert Alexander: "I farmed until I was twenty-seven years old— that was in 1886. I decided that I'd go to the university and learn to be a lawyer. I attended the University of Missouri at Columbia from 1886 to 1889. I was admitted to practice before the bar in 1889. . . . After I left the University of Missouri, I accepted a job of schoolteaching at Marshall, Missouri. I was qualified as a lawyer, but I needed a paying job then." Today, laws and lawsuits proliferate, and virtually every citizen chafes under the government's (society's) invasion of his life. Legislation on retirement; disbursement of public funds for jobs, health, welfare, and old-age assistance; regulation or the lack of it for medical costs; supervision of the causes of pollution in food, water, the working place, and the environment in general— all these have a direct bearing on longevity. Today's American is forced to join groups that fight for his rights and lobby for his economic interests, just to stay even.

Perhaps the most radical social-psychological change from the experience of these centenarians has been in the nature of work. Most Americans in the last quarter of the nineteenth century were working on farms to produce the food their fellows ate, and in the fields to produce cotton for their clothing. They were leveling the forests to provide wood for their homes and furniture. Today, it takes only a small percentage of our population to provide these basic raw materials. Only 12 percent of the centenarians worked for large organizations; another 1 percent worked for small outfits. All the rest were on their own or employed in one-to-one and similar arrangements. Of course, the desire for autonomy among so many of these centenarians may have exaggerated the employment proportions, but certainly the opportunities were far greater at that time for a person to work independently. This, and the absence of ambition to climb through the ranks to reach the top of an organization, freed the centenarians from the pecking-order mentality as well as from the bruising struggle to get the better of their fellows.

The most important part of a job today is its socioeconomic status. High pay all by itself can confer high social status, except for criminal activities. But prestige and power are so important that in certain circumstances—taking a position in government, for instance—a person is willing to make a sacrifice in income. All jobs today have finely graded social rankings. The most desirable job is as an executive or a member of a profession. Socioeconomic status is a factor, perhaps the most important one, in the way Americans today regard themselves and others. Many studies have shown a positive correlation between socioeconomic level and longevity—the higher the one, the longer the other. A second Duke longitudinal study of aging (Appendix 14) included virtually the entire older population of Chapel Hill and nearby Carboro, North Carolina. There was a high percentage of retired professors from the University of North Carolina and of farmers and blue-collar workers in the group of subjects. The researchers found a correlation between occupation and longevity: The professors lived longest, white-collar workers next, then blue-collar workers, housewives, and lastly, the farmers.

Awareness of socioeconomic status is absent from the cohort of centenarians, and with the exception of one or two rich people who knew the prerogatives of wealth, the allusions to class distinctions are nil. Even the successful and well-off centenarians never employ or imply the syllogism "I did this or I have that, therefore I must be important." And those centenarians receiving welfare and old-age assistance have a self-esteem and independence of outlook indistinguishable from the rest. The people who worked in humble occupations do not deduce that they are inferior human beings. In contrast to the Duke–Chapel Hill study, the numbers of centenarians in this cohort are in reverse order: most were farmers, then housewives, followed by blue-collar workers, white-collar workers, and, smallest in number, the professional people. These numbers may simply reflect the size of the original groups from which the centenarians survived; the sequence is not offered as a refutation of the Duke study, which deals with a cohort born somewhat later and composed of all elderly people over the age of sixty, not just centenarians.

Other elements of work that are starting to assume increasing importance are the quality of the kind of work being done and of the job environment, and whether the work is enriching for the individual and he or she can enjoy it—whether it is the kind of work the person wants to do. Work satisfaction was the second most significant predictor of longevity for men in the primary Duke Longitudinal Study of Aging. Number three was simply being employed—but if a man was working at a job he didn't like, then it shortened his life rather than preserved it. This finding doubly reinforces the importance of taking pleasure from what one does.

But, again, work satisfaction as a formal concept is unfamiliar to the centenarians. Questions about it are never put to them, and most of them talk matter-of-factly about their work: It is simply the activity one does most of the time in order to earn a living. The nature of the work done by most centenarians was largely determined by sex and circumstances. Occupational training began early, and later changes in vocation usually were prompted only by shifts in employment needs and economic opportunities. By watching closely for the slightest indication of a positive regard for the work they did, work satisfaction could be attributed to 37 percent of the centenarians— three out of eight. Probably, though, if they were questioned about their attitude toward work and made to think about it the percentage would have been much higher. There were no complaints about the work they did and many centenarians credited their long lives to work.

Further indication that people in his generation enjoyed their work comes from Dr. Pannell. He believes the change in the nature of work has been disastrous. He sees mass work-habits as an important cause of today's malaise—of ill health and lack of happiness. "There's not enough work today for man, human and machine. A man gets big pay for putting in a nut instead of being an individual. When I was a kid, it took a year to put up a house. Today one is built in a few weeks, but the doors don't fit." He cites the oldtime tailor who felt sorry for the tailors of today. "Think of the fun I had making things fit." Dr. Pannell recommends a return to the old ways—when a person could take pride and enjoyment from his work—in order to improve the nation's health and happiness. "A fellow wants to have something to be proud of, to be an individual."

Just as most of the centenarians *worked* in relative isolation, so they were not confronted with today's general *social* mobility. Church and school presented the main opportunities for meeting large numbers of people. And for the majority of these centenarians, the school experience was confined to a small group of classmates and to the early part of their lives. Half of the centenarians went to school for less than eight years, and three-quarters of them never went on to high school. Socially, this meant weak peer-bonds. The strong bonds were vertical, intergenerational through the family.

In the centenarians' own self-perceptions, the social sphere was by far the least important in their judgment of why they had been able to live so long. A count was kept of their attributions by sphere (Appendix 32). The one or several attributions of 540 centenarians were limited to a single category. For 346 of them the sphere was biological. Almost exactly half that number—174—gave only psychological attributions. In just 20 cases were the attributions solely social. Two hundred and eighty-four centenarians attributed their longevity to reasons in two spheres: 60 percent of them were psychological and biological, 40 percent either psychological and social or biological and social. Thirty-one centenarians ascribed their longevity to the three sociopsychobiological spheres. Overall, fewer than 20 percent of the centenarians included the social sphere of their lives in making attributions for longevity, whereas close to 70 percent gave biological reasons and 52 percent, psychological causes.

There was virtually no awareness among the centenarians that the physical environment in which they lived had any bearing on their survival. Even though two-thirds of them lived in rural areas or small towns surrounded by open countryside, only twenty-two centenarians attributed their longevity to being outdoors and just three to living in the country and breathing fresh air. Only Sylvester Melvin made the connection between a benign environment and long life as a general rule. This is the same Mr. Melvin who was the only one to perceive that he was long-lived because he had been able to avoid disease in his later years. The longtime Illinois farmer "believes the water and ground where he lives have been contributing factors to his long life. He points with pride to the many 'oldsters' in his immediate community." With industrialized methods and widespread use of chemicals, the farm, sadly, no longer is the healthful environment it once was.

It can also be seen from the percentages of attributions by sphere that the centenarians did not give as much weight to psychological causes as they did to physical ones as having produced their long lives. These subjective evaluations may be partially responsible for the fact that the psychological section of the questionnaire does not show higher scores; in their answers, the centenarians did not stress the psychological aspects of their lives. We know from the Duke and NIMH studies of aging that the psychological area shares significance with the physical one, and the dictum of psychosomatic medicine expressed by Arnold A. Hutschnecker—"Body and mind are one"— makes them coequal.

Undoubtedly, the more important reason for the deficiency of scores in the psychological sphere is that the social security interviews were not intended or designed to probe this sphere. Most of the information in the section is either volunteered by the subjects or inferred from their conversation and behavior. In the most obvious areas, high scores are recorded. The way they conduct themselves and converse with the interviewers makes evident their good mental status and alertness. And their adaptability can be established as they talk about events in their lives. But there were no questions to elicit yes-or-no responses to determine the attitudes listed as items 33A to L (Attitudes), or to determine whether or not the centenarians characterized their lives as harmonious. The scores on these items can be taken as minimal; they should likely be higher.

This judgment is supported by an observation: The greater the volume of information about a subject, the greater the likelihood to get scores on attitudes. Grandma Moses reveals her attitudes forthrightly and at length in her *My Life's History*, and she scores on fourteen of the twenty-four items, in 33A–L of the questionnaire, that were given most importance in the psychological sphere. She was happy with her life and took pleasure from her daily activities; she took satisfaction from her work; she enjoyed life; she lived a placid life; she wanted to live and had a will to live; she had a positive view of life and the world; she had a hopeful outlook; she had no regrets; she accomplished all her goals; she learned never to worry; she trusted in God; she was at ease or content; she lived one day at a time; and she had a positive self-image.

Finally, a breakdown of attributions for longevity shows that three out of five centenarians gave more than one reason for their long lives. A majority of these long-lived people intuited that their longevity depended upon multiple factors, a premise on which both the S/P/B and O/F profiles are based. Notice how the physical, psychological, and social attributions of Mrs. Tekla Scraba of Norwich, Connecticut, intertwine, suggesting that three separate and distinct spheres are, after all, merely human inventions to help us in trying to understand the infinite complexity of life. "I took things as they came and was able to enjoy many happy moments with my family and friends. I further think that proper rest, good standard food, a little beer or wine, and good care also helped me. My pastor visits me every first Friday of the month, and I get a lot of pleasure and comfort from his visits."

CHAPTER 10

Chance

"In so far as the nature of all living things is conditioned by their enemies," wrote William Bolitho in his book about adventure, *Twelve Against the Gods*, "the adventurer is defined by his fight with Order, and his fight with Chance. The first he may win—if he does not, he will go to prison. The second he cannot beat, for it is a manifestation of the universal."

One of Bolitho's adventurers, the renowned gambler in the dangerous sport of *amore* Giovanni Casanova, said: "I have always believed that when a man gets it into his head to do something, and when he exclusively occupies himself in that design, he must succeed whatever the difficulties. That man will become Grand Vizier or Pope. He will upset a dynasty, provided he starts young and has the brain and perseverance necessary. For when a man has arrived at the age that Chance despises he can no longer do anything; for without her aid there is no hope."

Few of these centenarians, it has been noted already, were adventurers; those who were, confined that sort of thing to the first part of their lives. One man was sent to prison for a murder he did not commit and later was released. Another man went to jail for throwing a stone and hitting a man in the eye; the rock was thrown in self-defense after the other man threatened his life with a knife. Those were the only two mentions of prison. One man as a teenager shot another boy and had to leave his hometown. One man said he was a shylock during the Great Depression, and another hinted he used to make moonshine whiskey. Those were the only references to unlawful activities. As we have seen, the centenarians had no

Henry Walker

conflict with order because they acquiesced and lived by it. Neither were these people gamblers. Fewer than a half a dozen of them refer to playing for stakes at games of chance. One person speculated on the stock market.

The routine, conservative, circumscribed, quiet, and nonaggressive behavior of these centenarians in long-familiar surroundings can be interpreted as ways to limit the power of chance. That they managed to live 100 years can be taken, too, as successful defiance of the "manifestation of the universal." But for some centenarians the margin of safety was so narrow that they could never forget.

Mrs. Barbara LeSage was 22 years old when she came to Butte, Montana, in 1885. That was the year a great explosion wiped out the Butte fire department and most of the police force. She was in town on this fateful day and noticed there was a fire. A policeman told her to run fast and get under cover, which she did. The next moment she saw the policeman fall dead; he had been struck by a piece of flying debris.

The experience of Mrs. Rose DeCarli, who was raised on a ranch in Merced, California, was tinged with the malevolence one encounters in an Alfred Hitchcock mystery. When Mrs. DeCarli was asked what was the most exciting event in her life, she said: "My life as a child and as an adult has been rather uneventful. As a child I remember being chased by two men on horseback and carrying guns, as my sister and I walked home from school. It was the scariest moment I could ever remember. I recall leaping a high fence, jumping across a stream, and running into a farmhouse as the men attempted to run me down. Even to this day, whenever I think of that moment many years ago, it just scares me."

Later in life Mrs. DeCarli watched as a notorious bunch of badmen known as the McFarland gang held up the Merced stagecoach. After taking the passengers' money and jewelry, they shot at the people—with what consequence, the report does not say.

This kind of violence in some way touched the lives of three dozen of the centenarians. Amanda Peck came from a pioneer family in California. Her father sailed around Cape Horn to join the gold rush of 1849, nineteen years before she was born. He mined and panned along Deer Creek and struck it rich. Years later, her brother set up the Eureka Stage and Express line. He was slain in a stagecoach holdup on October 30, 1894, when Mrs. Peck was 26 years old.

Zora Harper's father also found gold in California. "Shortly after Mrs. Harper's birth [in 1853 at Waldron, Arkansas], her father left the family to go out west to the California gold rush. Mrs. Harper said that her mother told the children about receiving a letter from their father, saying that he had found gold and was returning with enough gold strapped around his waist to make them wealthy for life. However, on the return trip, the wagon train with which he was traveling was beset by Indians and all the men were massacred. Mrs. Harper's family did not learn the details of this event until many years later. One of the men had survived this Indian massacre. Although he had been scalped by the Indians, he was found alive by a wagonload of settlers traveling west. They cared for him, and after he recovered, he vowed to find the widows of the men who were killed in this bloody massacre. Mrs. Harper recalled: 'I was nearly grown when the man came.' "

Mrs. Mary Muckler's mother died from childbirth in a farmhouse near Kellogg, Iowa, when Mrs. Muckler was 8 years old. Mrs. Muckler's mother "called her into her bedroom and told her to take good care of her brother and sister and to name her new brother Henry. Her mother died and within a short time Henry also died. So Mrs. Muckler, age 8, had charge of the household. She took care of the younger children, helped in the fields, and did cooking and cleaning. . . . One of her most terrifying moments occurred shortly after her mother's death when she was home alone with the two younger children and a band of Indians burst through the door and ransacked the house, searching for money and whiskey. They threw everything out of drawers and cupboards, destroying food and dishes and scaring her 'out of her wits.' Her father then came home from the field for dinner bringing some of his brothers with him. When the Indians saw the men and their guns, they left in a hurry."

When James Cox was in his twenties in the 1880s, he worked in Louisiana swamp timber operations. "He lived in logging camps two months at a time, working seven days a week, and would bring home seventy or eighty dollars' accumulated pay to his widowed mother. He said, 'She always gave me twenty dollars of my pay to go enjoy life before I again returned to swamping.' And, enjoy life he did, with a few drinks and a friendly bit of gambling. However, one time the dice game wasn't so friendly, and he remembers that incident as the most exciting happening in his life. It seems a hard loser started shooting at the participants, including Mr. Cox; two were killed, but Mr. Cox played dead and was unscratched. The killer was never caught or brought to justice."

"The most exciting event that Mrs. [Etta] Matthews recalls is having a runaway with a two-horse team hitched to a spring wagon. She was returning home from a shopping trip to Moran [in Kansas] with her three small children when the team became frightened and started running away. At a sharp turn in the road, Mrs. Matthews and her children were all thrown out of the wagon. Mrs. Matthews was the only one injured. A hedge thorn punctured her left arm, which later festered and had to be lanced. The scar is still visible on her arm."

Mrs. Mary Blakeney of Buffalo, New York, "loved horses and enjoyed driving a spirited horse. Mrs. Blakeney vividly recalls an incident in which her horse and buggy was scraped by a downtown-Buffalo trolley car. This frightened the horse and caused a runaway, with Mrs. Blakeney desperately hanging onto the reins. Fortunately she came through this experience with nothing more serious than several broken ribs."

Even when horses were under control, they could be a menace. Mrs. Emma Cress of Concord, North Carolina, "remembers, also, a big fire at the home of a neighbor on Power Street in Concord. She was hurrying there to see if she could help, when the horse-drawn fire wagon rounded the corner. Someone shouted a warning and she barely managed to jump out of the way of the speeding carriage."

For Neils Neilsen, "the most exciting event in my life was in 1892 [he was 16 years old] when I was a fisherman. I was in a dory with a shipmate. We were setting out nets. A heavy fog came up and we were separated from the ship. We were about seventy miles from land. We drifted for four days, but we were finally picked up by another ship."

Swen Rogeness "was born in Hageson, Norway, and attended school there until he was age 14. Mr. Rogeness was then apprenticed to a cooper, where he stayed about a year. After this, he went to sea as a deckhand aboard a coastal vessel—one of a crew of five. The ship was a sailing ship, and was used in commerce in the North Sea countries. He made trips to England, Denmark, and Germany, hauling various cargoes. On the first voyage the ship made after he left her, it sank with only one survivor."

"Henry Walker was born a slave in Black Hawk, Mississippi, on August 10, 1860. He moved with his family to Madison County the following year and grew up on the DeLoach Farm. . . . About 1880, as a young man, his first regular job was working as a fireman on the Mobile and Ohio Railroad for a number of years. One night he dreamed that he was killed in a train wreck, and was afraid to work the next morning. That same day the train wrecked and several were killed, including the fireman. This ended [Mr. Walker's] railroad career."

For a few of these people who lived a century, the crisis came at the very beginning. Conrad Geitz was born one of twins. "The other baby died shortly after birth, and because the claimant was so small at birth, his father always said 'he would never live to eat bread.' " "Mrs. [Irene] Demoss's mother died one hour before her birth. The doctor, upon arrival, delivered her posthumously by caesarian operation."

The most remarkable—one is tempted to say unbelievable—escape from death happened to Tom Standmire of Waco, Texas. In the words of the social security representative: "His most vivid memories concern the Galveston flood and the time he fell eighteen stories and landed on a steel pipe. He still does not know what prevented his death at that time."

Finally, note the role of chance in the life of Joshua Green and his efforts to deal with circumstances thrust upon him. "Mr. Green was born in Jackson, Mississippi, to wealthy parents on October 16, 1869. . . . Mr. Green's parents lost their wealth in the panic of 1883, and at the age of 14 he went to work in the post office in Jackson, Mississippi, and has been working ever since. Two years later the family moved to Seattle and he immediately took work as a purser on a Puget Sound steamer, the *Henry Bailey*. He observed that roads were poor in the area and that nearly all transportation was by water. After working for just one year he convinced the ship's master, first mate, and first engineer to join with him to purchase a stern-wheel steamboat. This was the beginning of a forty-year career that led to his founding and management of two Puget Sound steamboat companies, the La Conner Trading and Transportation Company with ten steamers, and the Puget Sound Navigation Company operating twelve to fifteen steamers.

"Twice, Mr. Green reports, he was near death. The first time was from an accidental shot from a pistol. The bullet entered through the skin above his left eyebrow, grazed the skull, and left him unconscious for three days. The other occasion was when he was captain of a steamer, guiding his boat loaded with lime in the Straits of Juan de Fuca in a storm. The boat went down by the bow in the heavy swells. The rudder and propeller were out of the water. It was necessary to dump the bow load overboard, to trim and maneuver the boat. Two years later the same boat, under a different master, loaded with lime, in a similar storm in the same area, went down with all hands. Mr. Green is positive the boat would have been saved if the same action he had taken earlier had been followed."

Joshua Green is different from all the other centenarians cited here

for their close calls with death or intimate association with violence—
he links his longevity to the element luck. "On advice to achieve long
life Mr. Green stated that, of course, much of it is luck, next is diet.
'I think cigarettes are bad for a person's lungs, a little liquor doesn't
hurt, but moderation in all things is the best policy. Also, the closer
you come to age one hundred, the more careful you are to reach it."
The element of chance always remains, but the individual can be
alert to it.

Otto Welge is the only other person of the more than one hundred
centenarians who told of narrow escapes or violence close to them
to refer to the element of luck in connection with his longevity. Mr.
Welge came close to death twice. "I remember an eight-button rattlesnake striking within two or three inches of my head when I was
twelve. I remember being desperately sick when I was ten." But these
are not the events he refers to when he answers the question about
his longevity: "Well, son, there are a lot of things that have to be
considered there, but I think no smoking, no drinking either soda
pop or liquor has helped a lot in my living this long. We make some
root beer around here and I drink some of that but not very much,
and I don't drink soda pop more than once a year, and I have never
drank whiskey or smoked. 'Course you know there are other things,
like, no tree ever fell on me, and a horse never rolled on me, and so
forth, but these things people really don't mention of anymore. It's
what kind of a life did you live, and my life has been good."

In all, only eight centenarians in attributing their longevity mention luck or good fortune. William Eaton of Des Moines commented:
"When I look back over my life, it is a wonder I am here. I'm just
happy to be around."

Many more centenarians do acknowledge their good fortune in
other terms. When Henry Walker, who missed the fatal train wreck
because of his prophetic dream, was asked why he had been able to
live so long, he said that he "lived to please the Lord." Tom Standmire, the Texan who fell eighteen stories and lived, said, "I try to
eat like the doctor says, especially few sweets. The good Lord blessed
me because I have tried to live right." About one-quarter of the
people who told of their close calls attributed their survival to God's
will or blessing, to trusting the Lord and serving him.

In our fast-moving civilization, we often are seconds and inches
away from fatal collisions. Terrorists can appear anywhere with
suddenness and irrationality. In November 1979, a man whose mother
had suffered a stroke while singing in the choir of the Haven Memorial

United Methodist Church in Philadelphia fired a gun at a group of people outside the church. One of the three people he killed was a 106-year-old man who had come to attend a birthday party for his 104-year-old sister.

There are too many wild cards in the deck for any strategy for longevity to be covered with the promise "Guaranteed."

CHAPTER 11

Omens

After processing more than four hundred interviews, it became noticeable that "Do you have any ambition you have not yet realized?" was another question that did not always evoke conventional or expected answers. There were repetitions of several different kinds of replies; some of them seemed to be non sequiturs. A number of centenarians appeared to have trouble answering the question. This was odd, because the question did not seem to be difficult.

In seeking an explanation for the unexpected behavior, it was noted that the centenarians took all questions as serious attempts to gain information from them and therefore felt it was their responsibility to respond with thoughtful care. Mrs. Jane Brunton of Aliquippa, Pennsylvania, reacted this way, even when presented with a preposterous question intended for fun. "Asked if she expected to live to age 150, she smiled and then figeted and laughed before saying, 'If I do, I'll need new feet.' She has an arthritic condition in her knees."

More relevant was the realization that the question was inappropriate for many subjects. As already noted, many centenarians deliberately disengaged their lives from ambition. Having ambitions realized or unrealized was not part of their lifestyle, so there was nothing strange (to them) about not having goals at age 100. "Mr. [Cornelius] Ramsey states that he has no unfulfilled ambition, as he long ago learned to forget anything he felt he didn't need or couldn't afford." "I've gotten everything I ever wanted," said Annie Wilkie; "I never wanted much." Harrie Edmonston, the Chrysler Corporation supervisor who practiced the Golden Rule with his workers, retorted to the query: "God no. You don't have any ambition for anything

Catherine Goltzene

Photo courtesy of Sunday News-Sun, Springfield, Ohio

when you get as old as I am." Many centenarians did not think of or conduct their lives in terms of setting and achieving goals.

Even so, most centenarians seemed reluctant to reply to this question in the negative. Some cast about for some trivial thing they still wanted to do, or if the answer was "None," tried to add a qualification or explanation. These kinds of answers led to an understanding that this seemingly lightweight question was loaded with a second, deeper meaning for the old people: A negative response implied that the person's life was over. The question really became, for the interviewees: "Is your life over—yes or no?" If the individual concluded that his or her life indeed was completed, this admission was made only after some consideration. On the other hand, a centenarian might have had no further goals, but by no means believed that his life was finished. In that case, he felt it incumbent on him to try to remove the negative connotation of having no unrealized ambition. It was not a straight yes-or-no situation; it was "No, but. . . . "

A common answer was "None; I have had a full and rewarding life." This, it was gradually learned, was a response that could be interpreted either positively or negatively, depending on what else the centenarian said or on subsequent events. It could mean acceptance without complaint, with the implication that life was completed; but it could also be translated: "Look, I'm happy with my situation just the way it is. Why should I have further ambition?" Said Harry Kordes of Dora, Pennsylvania: "My life has been very rewarding and satisfying, so I have no further ambition. All I want is to sit here, free from worry, and enjoy living." "I can't think of any," said Sherman Parsons of Wolfeboro, New Hampshire. "I'm pretty happy just as I am."

The next discovery was a frequent correlation between the way the centenarian answered the question and, in cases where the date of death was known, the length of life remaining. An unqualified negative response often was followed in a few months by death. Frank Varetto of Baltimore said in November 1962 that he had no unrealized ambitions and no intentions of living to be 200. He died the following February 2. In June an interviewer wrote of Samuel Ladd of Greensboro, Vermont, "He is at rest now, with no unrealized ambitions or interest." Mr. Ladd was dead in December.

Regarding one's life and goals in the past tense and making the answer contingent are other indications that life is near its close. Arthur Hargrave of Danville, Illinois, was a newspaper publisher for sixty years. The social security representative wrote of him: "Mr. Hargrave was rather noncommittal about any ambitions he has not realized. He said he failed to get all the books read that he would liked to have read, and, as is typical of newspapermen everywhere, he had an ambition to write a book. He said he failed to accomplish this." Mr. Hargrave was interviewed in July 1956 and died sometime during 1957. "I planned to travel all over the world," said Myron Stevenson in Ashland, Kansas. "If I get all fixed up so that I can travel, I probably will." He died in eleven weeks.

When a centenarian gave a positive answer, enumerated goals he or she still was vitally interested in pursuing (in a number of cases the unrealized ambition was to go on living), or in some way made it plain that the life was not regarded as finished, the length of remaining life seemed to be appreciably longer. These positive and negative answers did not correlate with remaining lifespans with the consistency of mathematics, but the responses seemed to merit monitoring to find out how reliable they were as predictors.

The possibility of this kind of augury suggested that there might be other kinds. During the course of processing the next hundred interviews, four other telltale signs came to attention. The first involved memory. It has already been reported that ten centenarians had good memories for every one centenarian whose memory was poor. Failing memory was linked with early death often enough to suspect a correlation, and so the state of memory was put under surveillance.

The two most prominent indicators, once looked for, were the closely related items about usefulness (number 52, in the "Order" category) and work (number 59, in the "Independence" category). When a centenarian scored on one of these items, he usually registered on the other. But the two items are not identical and there were some discrepancies. It can be seen that usefulness has four components: 1) work, 2) some degree of physical fitness (in order to perform useful roles), 3) ecological value (in performing the roles whether at home, in the community, or for society at large), and 4) social importance and support. The word *ecological* is used here in terms of the human ecosystem, whether large or in microcosm. The answer of Mrs. Stella Stimson to the question about why she had lived so long should make clear what is meant. "I simply had to," she said, "to take care of others."

The fourth additional precursor to emerge was the centenarian's self-rating of health. This indicator has been discussed in a comparison with the objective rating, in the chapter on health. The objective health-rating was not included as a predictor because the judgment was not based on a physical examination and thus lacked precision. (Two other predictors were tested for—desire to live and the amount of energy a centenarian exhibited—but there were insufficient entries in these classifications, and they were discarded.)

Information about the five predictors was tabulated (Appendix 33). As previously noted, the death dates were known for 157 centenarians. In some cases the death date was not known exactly, but was known to lie within a certain period of time. If, then, a centenarian died between ten and fourteen months after the interview, he would be listed as a "long-liver" when the demarcation point was set at nine months, a "short-liver" when the dividing line was set at fifteen months, and put in the "ambiguous" category when the deciding point was twelve months. That person would not be considered in the twelve-month pool (since it's not certain whether he actually survived more than ten months), but was a participant in calculating the other pools. Even with this certain amount of shifting participants, the size of the pools remained close no matter where the division was set in three-month intervals between six and eighteen months; the pools ranged from 130 at nine months to 136 at eighteen months. At thirty-two months, the number rose to 147 subjects whose death dates were known to have occurred either earlier or later.

Twenty-two percent of the centenarians were dead after six months, 35 percent after nine months, 54 percent after twelve months, 74 percent after fifteen months, 84 percent after eighteen months, and 93 percent after thirty-two months (Appendix 33A). In interpreting the subjective and objective health-ratings, it was decided, as earlier mentioned, that either twelve months or fifteen months would be the most appropriate division points, the former because the group was nearly evenly balanced between living and deceased members, and the latter because this was the first point marking most of the deaths. Discrimination would be lost outside these bounds, because relatively few deaths occurred after fifteen months, while an insufficient number of deaths took place before twelve months.

Several indices (see Appendix 33C–E) show unanimously that the five predictors are most accurate in distinguishing the short-lived from the long-lived when the dividing line is put at twelve months. On average, these indicators are correct 62 percent of the time (Appendix 33E). When the dividing line is put at fifteen months, this accuracy drops to 58 percent, as it does when the line is put at nine months. The decline in accuracy continues as the dividing line is further removed from twelve months—to 56 percent at eighteen months and to 54 percent at thirty-two months.

At twelve months, at least one of the five predictors is correct for 92 percent of the centenarians (Appendix 33E).

These predictors do not register equally except for "work" and "usefulness." There was information on the "work" item for every one of the 157 centenarians whose death dates were known, and for "usefulness" on 154 of them. It could be told whether 132 of them had a good or poor "memory"—84 percent. Next came "self-rating on health"; 120 centenarians made an assessment in this area—76 percent. Even though it was the "goals" item that first raised the issue of predictors (because of the peculiarity of some answers), only 85 of the 157 centenarians gave information on this point—54 percent.

The "work" and "usefulness" predictors are consistently accurate at every stage from six to thirty-two months (see Appendix 33C). So, to a reasonable degree, is "self-rating health," peaking at twelve months and then declining. "Goals" and "memory," however, follow drastically different courses. "Goals" starts out with only a 33 percent accuracy at six months and keeps climbing until at thirty-two months it is an accurate predictor for 82 percent of the centenarians. "Memory" starts at a high of 85 percent accuracy at six months and plummets to a low of 27 percent at thirty-two months. Why does the reliability of these two predictors vary so much?

Of the 85 people who offered information on whether they still had goals, only 16—about one in five—gave unequivocally positive responses. The rest either had no goals (2 said their ambition was to die) or were at least partially negative. At the end of six months, 17 of the 69 negatives had died, but so had 3 of the 16 who did have goals. This is a high rate of accuracy in predicting the very short-lived—17 out of 20, (85 percent). However, 17 is a low percentage of the 69 centenarians who answered the "goals" question negatively. And when the dividing line for labeling the short-lived and long-lived for the entire pool is set at six months, it means that "goals" is an accurate predictor only for the 17 negatives who died and the 12 positives still alive (one answer was ambiguous). Twenty-nine is only 39 percent accuracy for this predictor—because most of the people with no goals still are living. As the dividing line is moved further away, the number of the preponderant "no-goals" people who have died increases . . . and so does the accuracy of the indicator. At twelve months, the "goals" item is an accurate predictor in 62 percent of the cases. What is interesting is the way the two groups divide. By the end of a year, two-thirds of the people who had no goals are dead. The people who did have goals split fifty-fifty. We may infer that for these centenarians, having a positive attitude about their future longevity is no guarantee of living a relatively long time, but lack of goals foreshadows short-term survival.

With the "memory" item, the situation is reversed. For the 132 centenarians on whom there are data, 110 have good memories and 22 have poor memories. This already tells us something about the group, which may be composed of a greater number of short-livers than would be found in the centenarian population generally, or in the cohort of 1,200. The ratio of good to poor memories is exactly half of the 10-to-one ratio for the entire cohort. In response to the "memory" question, most of the centenarians give positive answers, so that at six months, when nearly 80 percent of the subjects still are alive, the indicator shows an accuracy of 85 percent. The percentage plummets as the numbers of dead increase—to 67 percent at nine months and 57 percent at a year. Two-thirds of the centenarians with poor memory have died within a year, and only one of the centenarians with poor memory is known for certain to have lived longer than eighteen months. Failing memory can be taken as a sign of early demise for the centenarians.

About 60 percent of the centenarians rate their health as good or excellent. About two in five rate it poor or fair. These assessments show a high level of accuracy through the shifting composition (live *versus* dead) of the group at the different stages. At twelve months, "self-rating of health" is the most accurate of the five indicators, correct for two-thirds of the centenarians. Thereafter, as noted in the chapter on health, "self-rating" begins a gradual but steady decline.

The superiority of "self-rating" over "usefulness" at twelve months actually is a mere one-tenth of a percentage point. And because there is information on the "usefulness" item for almost every centenarian, while only three-quarters of the centenarians gave a health rating, at twelve months "usefulness" is a correct indicator for eighty-six centenarians and "self-rating" for only sixty-five. Considered in tandem (they are near counterparts), "usefulness" and "work," or "usefulness-work," are the dominant predictors of short-livers and long-livers.

It should be emphasized that one part of the "usefulness" item— 52C, "important to one other person or many people"—had no effect when part B—"performs useful role(s)"—was blank. Three-quarters of all the centenarians studied were important to other people, but when they reached a condition in which they no longer could do anything useful (beyond basic personal services), the end usually was near. Most of them sensed it. When the "unrealized ambition" question was posed to such an incapacitated person, the answer often simply expressed a wish to be able to do useful work again. One woman said she did not understand why she still was here "being of no use to anyone." Earlier examples make clear how much those centenarians still able to do useful things cherished the privilege.

But for those no longer able to perform useful roles, even the pull of their loved ones could not save them. For them, love was not as strong as death.

"Usefulness-work" together could accurately foretell the fates of two-thirds of the centenarians after a year (Appendix 33D). "Usefulness-work" combined with either "self-rating" or "memory" gave correct indications for 80 percent of the 133 centenarians in the pool. And with the four of them together, accuracy rose to 89 percent. When all five indicators were used, at least one—but far more often a majority—of them correctly applied to 92 percent.

"Usefulness" and "work" remained the most consistently accurate of all the indicators through the time span considered. Even after thirty-two months, these predictors still are accurate in 59 percent of the cases. While "goals" was high with an accuracy of 82 percent at thirty-two months, it accounted for fewer than half of the 147 centenarians in the pool, whereas "usefulness" and "work" each correctly applied to three out of five.

Whether or not a centenarian still is doing some kind of useful work is the most obvious sign of how much longer that oldtimer has to live.

CHAPTER 12

Character Facets: The Road Taken

Further reflection upon the "goals" question in conjunction with certain answers led to a realization that the question was more than inappropriate for the centenarians. It was irrelevant.

These were the answers:

" 'Do you have any ambition you have not yet realized?' we finally asked Don Gregorio [Duran Baez, the man who remarried in his fiftieth year and went on to have fifteen more children]. 'No,' he said. 'I think I have lived the kind of life I expected. I have raised a good family, have never done any harm to anybody, have been honest all my life, and people seem to love me. That's enough for the time being.' "

When Mrs. Ellener Jones of Somerset, Kentucky, was asked if she would like to start life over, she said, "I guess not, but I think I've made a pretty good success of this one."

"Mrs. [Sallie] Vandeventer has no hobbies and her only outside activity is in the church. Her only ambition is to go back to Fairmount, Kentucky, before she dies and to be buried there when she does. She said that if she had her life to live over again she 'would live it the same.' "

"Mr. [Amos] Martin states he has a good life and wants for nothing. He says, 'If I had it to do over, I would change nothing.' "

When Mrs. Catherine Goltzene was asked the question, she said she no longer had any unrealized ambitions. "If you are ready to live as you should," Mrs. Goltzene explained, "you will be ready to die."

These responses could be cited as textbook confirmations of Erik Erikson's thesis about the final stage of successful human development. Developmental psychologist Erikson laid out the "Eight Ages of

Dominicus Green

Man" in his book *Childhood and Society*. There are two basic paths through these stages of psychosexual and psychosocial growth: successful or unsuccessful development. Failure at one particular age does not mean that an individual cannot be successful in future stages of development, although the failure will detract from complete emotional maturity. The first six ages are a prelude and preparation for the long period of mature adulthood that Erikson characterizes by the alternatives "Generativity *versus* Stagnation." The person who has developed successfully by this age is able to share love and intimacy with fellow human beings, and he now applies himself to creating and carrying on life and institutions and to other productive tasks.

"Only in him," Erikson writes of the last age, "who in some way has taken care of things and people and has adapted himself to the triumphs and disappointments adherent to being, the originator of others or the generator of products and ideas—only in him may gradually ripen the fruit of these seven stages. I know no better word for it than ego integrity. . . . It is the ego's accrued assurance of its proclivity for order and meaning. . . . It is the acceptance of one's one and only life cycle as something that had to be and that, by necessity, permitted of no substitutions. . . . In such final consolidation, death loses its sting.

"The lack or loss of this accrued ego integration is signified by fear of death: the one and only life cycle is not accepted as the ultimate of life. Despair expresses the feeling that the time is now short, too short for the attempt to start another life and to try out alternate roads to integrity."

That passage applies to virtually all the centenarians. They do not wonder, as did the young poet Robert Frost, about the road not taken. There are no expressions like the famous lines written by John Greenleaf Whittier when he was 47 years old: "For of all sad words of tongue or pen,/ The saddest are these: 'It might have been.' " The centenarians accept their one and only life cycle as something that had to be.

We can also see the congruence with Erikson by what is missing. There is no despair, except for two women who were depressed because they felt their children and grandchildren had forsaken them. Seventy-seven centenarians voluntarily asserted that they had no regrets. Two centenarians were bitter. Four were complaining. And for almost all of them, death had lost its sting. Even though these people knew they were close to the end of their lives, the subject of death rarely came up. Ten people said they thought about impending death a great deal, three centenarians volunteered that they never thought about death, one centenarian acknowledged fear of death, and twenty-two others said they were not afraid of death. The subject of death rarely was discussed—not because the centenarians were avoiding it, but because they had learned to fix their attention on life. Said Harry Lieberman, a primitive artist who took up painting at 80 and still makes a living at it: "I know that I have to die. But why do I have to worry about it? Could I make it not to die? Impossible. Therefore, the best thing, not to think of it."

The Erikson model charts a heaven and hell in this life. The centenarian consciousness takes this into account as well. These people frequently said they appreciated the fact that they had good lives, happy lives, enjoyable lives. They freely expressed their thankfulness, to God or just in general, for their good fortune. Ten centenarians believed they were able to live so long because of their thankfulness. Severo Santiago of San Juan, Puerto Rico, condensed the Erikson model to one pithy sentence. "Life is sweet if you know how to live it," he said, "otherwise it can be very bitter."

AMONG THE CHARACTERISTICS of his long life cited by Don Gregorio (Duran Baez) was that he had been honest. It may be recalled that in the discussion about independence, Rebecca Miller, in receiving social security, was afraid she was going to get something that wasn't hers. And Laura Crews was reluctant to take the old-age pension because she felt she had not earned it. Fifteen centenarians attributed their longevity to their honesty.

Honesty was a trait watched for among the centenarians because Flanders Dunbar had listed it as a typical characteristic. She wrote: "They are honest; thus they can be honest with themselves." Forty-seven centenarians made a point of referring to their honesty. When William Collins of Salisbury, North Carolina, was asked why he had been able to live so long, he replied, "I know only one honest man and that is me."

Elsworth Crawford's "advice to those who would like to reach the century mark is: 'Live honest, don't lie, cheat or steal. Live a clean life and blessings will flow in.'"

Ernest Blackmer wrote form letters for a grocery store in Rockford, Illinois: "He remembers his employer, who also happened to be a church elder, putting beautiful, ripe apples on the top of a bushel basket, with the rotten ones well hidden. He never cared much for Deacon ——— after that." Helen Hasse's first job was as a bookkeeper for a grocery firm in St. Paul, Minnesota. "I stayed only a short time there, however, because they were not honest, and I felt I could not work for people like that."

William Bridendolph's philosophy of life: "I've been good. I've never cheated anyone out of a dollar, and I've helped others when I could. And I have never worried about things over which I had no control." This honesty is all the more striking in light of Mr. Bridendolph's associations early in life. "His first job was in Holden [Missouri] working for fifty cents a day taking care of horses for the James brothers, Jesse and 'the tall one, Frank,' who was his favorite. 'Everyone around Holden was big for the James boys because they did so much for the folks around there. They'd rob a bank but would give the money to some poor farmer who was about to lose his land, to pay off his mortgage.'

"Mr. Bridendolph left home when he was 15 with two dollars his mother gave him. He rode a boxcar to Rich Hill, where he again met Frank James. 'He bought my first dinner away from home [for ten cents] and arranged for me to ride the coach to my destination, Fort Smith, Arkansas.' "

AN UNLOOKED-FOR CHARACTERISTIC was the love of music. Music played an important role in the lives of at least eighty-one centenarians, placing 16th on the list of salient characteristics. This is volunteered information, so the actual number could be appreciably greater. Particularly, the centenarians loved to sing.

Mrs. Anna "Grandma" Groves of Des Moines sang over radio station KRNT every Friday afternoon at 3:15. "The program aired at this hour daily is one entitled 'Party Line'; listeners phone in with questions or comments, and the MC [Bill Riley] has been especially fond of Grandma Groves. She went through her repertoire for me, and sang the following songs in their entirety: 1) *Springtime in the Rockies*, 2) *Abide with Me*, 3) *Sweet Genevieve*, 4) *America*, 5) *That Will Be Glory for Me*."

Edward Swift at Woods Hole, Massachusetts, "has been confined to his bed for the past two years, but hopes to get into a wheelchair this summer. He confided that he sometimes sings in bed."

Henry Fishburn came from a family of homesteading pioneers and has lived on his 353-acre farm in Douglas County, Kansas, for the past ninety-four years. "Mr. Fishburn loves to sing, particularly ballads and hymns. He states he bets he knows 100 hymns. His daughter-in-law says he often sings upon awakening in the morning, sometimes singing for an hour before getting up. His voice is still strong and in key. One of his favorite songs is this ballad, which he learned as a young man, and which typifies the spirit of the pioneer farmers in the West:

Come, boys, I have something to tell you.
Come near, I would whisper it low.
You're thinking of leaving the farm, boys.
Don't be in a hurry to go!

The great busy West has inducements,
And so have the busiest marts.
But wealth is not made in a day, boys.
Don't be in a hurry to go.

Don't be in a hurry to go,
Don't be in a hurry to go.
Better risk the old farm a while longer.
Don't be in a hurry to go.

A good number of the centenarians sang in church choirs. Dominicus Mershon Green, who preferred being addressed by his middle name rather than his first, at the Odd Fellows Home in Princeton, New Jersey:

"I like to sing. I sang in choirs. I sang for one year in the choir of the St. Thomas Episcopal Church at Fifty-third Street and Fifth Avenue in New York. Then I sang at St. Paul's at Vesey Street and Broadway in New York City. This was the chapel of the famous Trinity Church. Washington worshipped there. It was necessary to cut a doorway in the inside wall so he could enter his pew without causing any commotion.

"I go to my church in Princeton every now and then. Until I moved to the home about two years ago, I sang in the choir there. I meet a lot of my old friends there.

"I sing at get-togethers here in the Home. I really enjoy singing."

Several of the centenarians taught or sang professionally. Mrs. Amanda Bonshire "began singing at age 8 in schools, churches, and at other public events. Although she had a fine singing voice she received no lessons until after her marriage and she was the mother of two girls. She was then tutored by such singing greats as Marion Green, then world famous, Harry Wheeler, and Carlyle Tucker, considered the top voice teacher in his day." Mrs. Bonshire did private voice tutoring until she was 95 years old.

Mrs. Lena Brown, who taught music in her home most of her life, said, "I was crazy about music and flowers." Mrs. Josephine Lockwood shared the same interests. She played the piano at Carnegie Hall, loving Chopin's waltzes and *Recollections of Home* by E. B. Mills. She gave up this career when she married at age 21 and began to operate five greenhouses with her husband.

Sadie Smith

Luther Whited of Meadville, Missouri, "began playing the violin before he started to school and fiddled for many country dances in his early days. He still plays the violin and in 1968 (when he was 99 years old) won an impressive trophy as the oldest fiddler in the Old Fiddlers' Contest at Lexington. The engraved trophy is prominently displayed in his living room and represents a highlight in his later years.

"Mr. Whited lives alone near his son and daughter-in-law, Mr. and Mrs. Luther Whited. His hobbies, now that he is retired, are keeping up with baseball through radio broadcasts and playing his violin.

"When he gets a bit lonely he plays a tune on the fiddle, and quite often if his daughter-in-law isn't too busy, she comes across the yard and accompanies him on the mandolin. This makes for a very happy interval in his day."

With all this enthusiasm for music, only two centenarians attributed their longevity to singing. Mrs. Florence McCook composed a message for the guests at her one hundredth birthday party at Pendleton, Oregon, and then recited it from memory. This passage was included: "I learned, long ago, to say 'Never cherish the worries we meet each day, for the better you treat them, the longer they stay. Just pass them by with a laugh or song, and something much better will hurry along. Laugh a bit or sing a song, where they are there's nothing wrong.' "

A. O. Blix, who ran a general store at Turtle Lake, Wisconsin, gave this formula for long life: "Just be satisfied with what you've got if to get more you have to become worried and mean. Enjoy the fresh air, work hard, cultivate a lot of good friends, sing, and make a visit to the hospital every ninety-nine years."

In the sixth century B.C., one of the earliest known historical geniuses discovered that the musical pitch of a vibrating string corresponds exactly to the length of the string. If the node, the point at which the string is held rigid, is shifted from the end of the string to the midpoint, the resulting note is one octave higher. Pythagoras found that basic musical harmonies depend upon simple ratios of dimensions—2:1, 3:2, 4:3, and so forth. Harmony comes from certain precise relationships. All others produce discord.

Pythagoras taught that virtue is a harmony of soul within itself and with God. Harmony of soul is attained through understanding underlying truths and conducting oneself according to the golden mean (a mathematical term) of moderation between extremes. Through fate, the end result of immoderate behavior is retribution:

discord, sin, and tragedy. Health, to this ancient Greek, was a harmony of inner forces. Symptoms of disease appeared when the inner equilibrium was upset by the tyranny of one of these forces. His followers played music to cure nervous disorders.

From the information available, it could be determined for certain that about one-quarter of these centenarians led harmonious lives. And for at least eighty-one of them, part of the harmony, literally, was musical. The relationship of virtually all of these centenarians with music was active—singing, dancing, playing instruments—rather than passive listening.

WE KNOW FROM THREE STUDIES summarized in the Appendix that intelligence is associated with longevity. In the Duke Longitudinal Study of Aging, performance IQ is the most significant of the secondary predictors, but the number-one predictor for eighty blacks in the study. In the NIMH study, the survivors scored higher on intelligence tests than did nonsurvivors. In the Eric Pfeiffer study of longevous elite, IQ score was the top indicator in identifying the long-lived and short-lived women and the number seven indicator for men.

The information gathered here was not designed to test the intelligence of the centenarians in any systematic way. At least a dozen centenarians noted with pride that they were champion spellers as youngsters. The spelling bee appeared to be the primary way to demonstrate intellectual superiority in the days of the one-room schoolhouse. But demonstrations of intellectual excellence largely were superfluous when these people were young. "Work was more important than education then," said Jesse Lane. Ed Wisbey's father told him: "You don't need an education if you are going to be a farmer."

A failure, initially, to appreciate this context of the centenarians' experience led to a misjudgment of the character of their work. Only eighty-five—8 percent—of them were listed as having been engaged in creative work. But this was a contemporary perception of creative occupations, limiting them mainly to cerebral pursuits: the arts, sciences, and professions. Parenting is biologically the most creative work a human being can do. Successful parenting is socially one of the most difficult tasks. The great majority of these centenarians were successful parents. Farming is the creation and protection of life. It may be difficult for a modern observer to see it this way, because our farms are being converted to animal factories and assembly lines for products to maintain our balance of trade so we can buy more oil.

But farming was a creative occupation when these centenarians participated in it. Similarly, the seamstress who made clothes and the carpenter who built homes and furniture were creating things. In this sense, almost all the centenarians were creatively employed—and in very practical ways served the nation's most important needs of the times.

And then they had the wit to survive a century—wit in both senses of the word. Probably the most common phrase used by the social security representatives to describe these old people was that he or she "is very alert and has a keen sense of humor." This latter trait was evident in at least one out of six of the centenarians. More than a few of them in some way alluded to the survival value of humor, like Mrs. Mary Butler. "Find something to laugh at every day," said the Denton, Maryland, farmwife. "A good laugh is better than a dose of medicine anytime."

The most persuasive argument for the centenarians' acumen is their own wit and wisdom, liberally displayed in this report. Here are further entries to the anthology:

A reporter asked Mrs. Dora Spangler how it feels to be 100 years old. "I don't know yet," she replied. "This is my first time."

At Estelle Pollatschek's birthday party in Manhattan, her niece asked a reporter, "She doesn't look like a hundred, does she?"

Miss Pollatschek interjected: "Do I look like a hundred and two?"

Miss Pollatschek recounted a number of historic memories—the blizzard of 1888, rides with her mother in a carriage in Central Park, Lindy's return. When she was asked how she could remember so many details, she said, "Who's here to dispute me?"

In her memoir, *The Fabric of Memory*, Eleanor Robson Belmont wrote after her marriage to millionaire August Belmont: "A private railroad car is not an acquired taste. One takes to it immediately."

Harry Harris, still working as a janitor in Louisville, was asked, "Are you married?" His reply: "Very much so." Mr. Harris "says he isn't ready to die yet—doesn't know what's on the other side—and if there are no women there, he doesn't want to go anyway."

When Robert Wheeler, a Kentucky farmer still busy running his farm, gardening, and attending meetings as a bank director, was asked if he had ever married, he replied, "Not yet."

"I carry the cane," said Aurelia Wilkinson, "to fight off the boys."

Louise Gates, stuck in a wheelchair with a broken hip, "does not do any work or household chores, but does give orders."

John Tintsman's earliest memory was seeing an elephant for the first time, when he was about 4 or 5 years old. "I remember," he says, "I thought that animal had two tails."

"If I knew as much as I do now back in the twenties," said saw-mill worker and farmer Norman Tilley, "I'd have been a lawyer."

Said farmer Louis Washington: "I went through life slow—took my time."

Mrs. Lodema Battershell: "What the world needs is people who are cooperative and congenial. I hope that the world, instead of becoming extinct, will continue to grow."

Morris Seamon's last ambition is to spend his life in discussions. "I want approval of the things I say. I say only reasonable things, and I expect other people to agree with me."

Burrel Falkner, an Alabama farmer, was asked the most exciting event in his life. He replied, "I'll tell you something that might not interest anybody. I raised the largest pumpkin that was ever raised in this part of the country last year. It weighed ninety-six pounds. . . . I never had any public work, but I taught a couple of schools. I seen I'd starve to death if I went to teaching school. Schoolteachers back then didn't get very much. Of course, they didn't know enough to get much."

Mary Kimball on today's youth: "Too many automobiles, too much liquor and cigarettes, and nothing for the youngsters to do. Idleness is the devil's worship."

Walker Harris, a sawmill worker and farmer in Alabama: "I enjoy living—just like a cricket."

Louis Wiley, a blind man: "The work of a man's hand follows him. If you do good, you'll be treated good."

Isaac Jacobson, a New York lawyer who reads the Bible daily: "Immortality is reached when a man leaves a good name behind him. It is attainable by every man."

Joseph Pitrone says he was strong and a leader in his native Sicily, defying the Black Hand before he left for America at the age of 19: "When I was young and full of dreams, it was I who directed the music. Now, that I am old and feeble, everyone else directs the music and I must listen, whether I like it or not."

Severo Santiago, who said life is sweet if you know how to live it: "I am a wonder—I am eighteen years old and I am in love with everything beautiful."

Morris Weisman is a Polish Jew who served in the Russian army and worked at various jobs in Warsaw and Berlin before coming to Chicago in 1912 at the age of 39. He operated a luggage store until he was 95 years old. Now, at age 105 and nearly blind, he leads religious activities at a Jewish home, does intricate handicraft, and cheers up the activities director when she gets downcast. Mr. Weis-man lived by these precepts: "Love your friend like yourself. Be satisfied with what you have. Don't have arguments with anyone. If anyone tries to start an argument, don't answer. In time he will apologize to you. If you let yourself get aggravated, you will have a short life."

This is the complete poem that Joseph DeMuth of Glendale, California, wrote for his 100th birthday and from which two stanzas were excerpted earlier:

> *It has taken a lot of living,*
> *Many times I've blundered;*
> *I have weathered many stormy years,*
> *And now have reached one hundred.*

> *One food faddist asks, "What do you eat?"*
> *Another says, "How often do you chew it?"*
> *There may be sense in either quiz;*
> *That depends on how you view it.*

> *What is your rule for living long?*
> *Your formula? Do tell us!*
> *I have no rule, go ask the birds*
> *That nest in the garden trellis.*

> *While talking with a doctor*
> *About accidents and ills,*
> *He said I have lived longer because*
> *I have brushed aside his pills.*

> *Whatever tasks you undertake*
> *Be not in—SUCH A HURRY.*
> *Take your time and do them well,*
> *And do not ever worry.*

> *The worry bug is rampant*
> *Throughout this "veil of tears";*
> *He's searching for the worry wart*
> *To rob him of his years.*

> *Praise the Lord and keep His way,*
> *Putting evil thoughts to flight.*
> *Delight in His laws both night and day,*
> *And you'll come out ALL RIGHT.*

Anna Mary Robertson ("Grandma") Moses:

"I have found in after years it is best never to complain of disappointments, they are to be."

"My worst memory goes back to the time when I first commenced (at age eight) to realize what the world was like, and I used to worry."

"I felt older when I was sixteen than I ever did since. . . . Even now I am not old, I never think of it."

"I look back on my life like a good day's work, it was done and I feel satisfied with it. I was happy and contented, I knew nothing better and made the best out of what life offered. And life is what we make it, always has been, always will be."

In the first chapter, a field representative described how he had misgivings in calling on a centenarian but was pleasantly surprised when Albert P. Davis, not so decrepit after all, rose to greet him. When the agent asked Mr. Davis about his earliest memory, the centenarian handed him an article he had written, entitled "Second Childhood." The interviewer wrote, "Anyone who reads it will get some idea of the formidable mental powers of Mr. Davis."

This is "Second Childhood," written by Albert P. Davis when he was 100 years old:

"The life of an individual may be summed up briefly—in three stages. Youth, middle life, and old age. Youth is ever looking forward, and planning for the future; middle life is chiefly concerned with the present, caring for a family, earning all he can, and trying to get all he can out of life before old age overtakes him. But what of old age? It has none of these incentives, its aspirations and activities are a thing of the past. Some old people begin to lose their mental faculties while still in good health; they may become peevish or cranky and unreasonable. Some become mild and overly amiable and given to fantastic ideas and pursuits. Such people are frequently referred to as being in their second childhood; I do not agree. I am more inclined to think that these traits arise from an unconscious mental protest against advancing years and the consequent curtailing of activity. The one who lives to a real old age finds himself in a strange and unique situation. With little to strive for, so far as this life is concerned, his problem is how to employ the little time he has left.

"Well, this is a time for introspection, to take inventory of himself, to evaluate the mistakes made and opportunities lost, to recognize and appreciate the many virtues of others that had been overlooked. It is also a time for retrospection, and here begins the real second childhood. To many this is a comforting and rewarding period. He now begins to relive his life backward. He is astonished to see so much beauty in nature, and also in people he has bypassed. He finds it more difficult to recall quite recent incidents than those which oc-

Albert Davis

curred further back; that the further he goes the better his memory becomes until he reaches early childhood, when everything becomes clearly bright.

"Any oldster will testify to the truth of this phenomenon. I remember with amazing clarity an incident that occurred ninety-eight years ago. I was barely two years old. My parents occupied an addition that had been built on to the main house of my grandfather, and what had been an outside door became an inside door between the two families. The dark, weatherbeaten sill of this doorway had not been removed; it was over an inch high and about ten inches wide. It was the first obstacle in my life—I dared not step on it and I could not step over its width, so I got down on my knees and crept over to get in to see my grandmother. I can recall nothing else at that age, and I can account for this memory only from the fact that the experience was repeated daily, and perhaps many times a day over a period of time, and became firmly impressed upon me."

Albert Parlow

CHAPTER 13

In Absentia

Michelangelo portrayed character as much by the marble he removed as by the stone he left remaining. In a similar way, the absence of certain traits helps to differentiate the cohort of centenarians from large segments of our society. They did not, for example, entertain high ambitions. This statement by Albert Parlow is singular among the centenarians: "When I started in the glass-decorating business in 1881 [at the age of 15], it was my ambition to become the best glass decorator in the country. I am proud to say I was considered the best at the time I retired in 1936. I achieved my one ambition."

Albert Parlow is the only centenarian to say he deliberately set a goal to be the best at something. Not that many of the centenarians did not do excellent work, and taking pride in work was commonly expressed. Marshall Grout, a cabinetmaker, built pipe organs for the Estey Organ Company in Brattleboro, Vermont, until he retired on his 95th birthday. The social security representative appended this note to the interview: "An Episcopal priest in the Midwest volunteered the information that many people familiar with organs and their construction have asked him, as a native of Vermont, about Marshall Grout. Apparently his craftsmanship and his fame in the pipe-organ industry are widely known."

The fine crochet and similar work of some of the centenarians drew exclamations of admiration from the field agents. Mrs. Adeline Exum, who lived most of her life in Dyersburg, Tennessee, raised the lowly occupation of ironing clothes to an art. "She takes pride in her ironing. Her daughter and granddaughter remember back just seven years ago, before she lost her eyesight, how people loved the way she ironed for them. She used an old-fashioned, heavy, coal iron and got a brilliant sheen from using beeswax." Grandma Moses, of course, was the best primitive artist in the nation. However, what is absent in these people is competitiveness with others. They worked to the best of their ability and took pleasure from it. Today's preoccupation with being Number One is alien to the centenarians.

Similarly, they are not stage-center people. Celebrities are rare. Few centenarians were in the limelight, few were in positions that called attention to themselves, and few followed the pursuits most familiar to today's mass television audience. There were no career actors and actresses; only one ex-vaudevillian. If crime was almost absent, there was only one career policeman and a couple of men who were sheriffs for parts of their lives. The limited number of adventurers settled down after a certain age. There were few politicians, three men in the management of large corporations, and two career newsmen. They are not selfless people, but neither are the centenarians egotists.

As mentioned, there was one case of senility, little evidence of despair, few complaints or signs of bitterness, and not much expressed fear of or even thought of death. Also virtually nonexistent: any neurotic traits or signs of anxiety. To these can be added an omission that is startling because the characteristic is so commonly associated with old age: There are no expressions of self-pity. In the first vignette recounted in the prologue, Mrs. Constance Oerter states: "Growing old is a terribly hard thing because a person loses all his friends. They die and you're left alone." The next, and final, sentence in the social security report reads: "She said this without self-pity, just a statement of hard fact."

Donal McLaughlin, a retired architect, was living in a geriatric center in Manhattan on his one hundredth birthday when he said: "Self-pity is the biggest disease we have here." This was the 1160th interview to be processed, and he was the first and only centenarian to express a realization that his attitude was starkly different from that of other aged people. The distinctive attitude first came to attention early in the investigation, but it appeared only intermittently at great intervals. The centenarians expressed no awareness that there was anything unusual about their attitude, and this lack of emphasis tended to obscure the significance. It was the accumulation of repetitions that prepared receptivity for Mr. McLaughlin's penetrating observation.

Mrs. Ada Bell Kobilka, the 105th interviewee, lived with her 63-year-old granddaughter in a small apartment in Toppenish, Washington. Mrs. Kobilka had lost her husband early in life, and her only daughter died when Mrs. Kobilka was 86 years old. Her granddaughter was her only descendant. "Although Mrs. Kobilka is chair-ridden and has little use of her hands as the result of four major strokes, she is mentally alert. Regarding her health she said, 'I have always been well.'

"Regarding her present activities, Mrs. Kobilka said: 'I just listen to everybody I can hear. I can't read on account of my eyes—the letters all kind of run together. I enjoy my friends who come in all hours of the day and lots of them. My granddaughter reads to me.' "

At least Mrs. Kobilka was on the "outside." Mrs. Minnie TerVeen was in a hospital room with somewhat crippling arthritis and other restricting ailments. "I am in good health, but I can't see well enough to read, and I can't hear, so I don't get to go to church services. All I do now is sit in my room. I miss the good times we had when I lived in the other building with all the women. We used to make things together and have such fun." Mrs. TerVeen still knits nufflers for friends and for sale in the hospital gift shop. "She manages to do this by feel alone, and says that she plans to make many more of them." She was interviewee 217.

Number 435, Herman Bade, was confined to his room in a nursing home because of blindness. He was one of the few centenarians who were separated from spouses; six of his nine children were dead, and only one of the remaining three lived nearby. Mr. Bade spends his time with a parakeet, playing "talking magazines," and listening to the radio.

Mrs. Cora Cashwell, number 454, was in worse straits, in a Fayetteville, North Carolina, rest home. Widowed, she never had any children and "is bedridden and practically blind. Most of her time is spent in bed, but she is occasionally put in a wheelchair. . . . She has no ambitions but she does enjoy sitting in her wheelchair listening to the Sunday-school classes in the home."

Under such circumstances, a little self-pity or a bid for sympathy would be understandable. It became a challenge to find a centenarian who yielded to the indulgence.

Mrs. Diantha Wheeler, interviewee 671, a longtime stitcher in factories, was divorced with no children or relatives. She spent all her time in a boardinghouse bed, stricken with rheumatoid arthritis. "Her regular schedule is to listen to the radio from 7:00 A.M. to 11:00 A.M., then rest, and then she listens to the radio again from 4:30 P.M. to 10:00 P.M. . . . I found Mrs. Wheeler most interesting. She had clear ideas on all subjects and spoke directly to the point. . . . To me, the really touching story is the relationship between Mrs. Katherine MacDonald, the landlady, and Mrs. Wheeler. Mrs. MacDonald is in no way related to Mrs. Wheeler, yet it seemed to me that the affection between these two is as tender and as deep as between mother and daughter. Mrs. MacDonald, who became a widow of a railroad worker in 1960 [the year of the interview], said that Mrs. Wheeler had roomed and boarded with her for so many years that she would not allow her to leave the house for fear she would soon die of homesickness."

"Mrs. Hedges [number 848] has been bedridden for the past nine years. One would think that alone would dampen the spirits of even the most hardy individual—but not Rhoda Hedges. She is a very small, frail person, but not sickly in appearance. Just the opposite. She has a ready smile for everyone and will talk at the drop of a hat."

Finally, Mrs. Josephine Long in a nursing home in New Brighton, Minnesota, number 875. She is a widow and both her children are dead. She has poor eyesight and her left arm shakes constantly. "She has no hobbies now and doesn't attend church services. She would like to visit Chicago, but her main desire is to pass on so she will no longer be a burden to anyone. . . . She doesn't see well enough to read and just sits and thinks about past events. This gives her 'lots of fun.' " This woman was reduced to her last resource—her memories. Still, no "woe is me," no feeling sorry, only the constructive use of that final resource.

That this attitude and behavior have social survival value is evident from the case of Mrs. Wheeler in the boardinghouse. At a time when the commitment of old people to institutions by uncaring children has become common fare for magazine articles and television drama, this woman was cared for by a nonobligated nonrelative.

"The greatest blessing I have had in my old age," said Mrs. Arista Hewitt, "is a dear daughter and son-in-law who are so good to care for me." Mrs. Hewitt said that her daughter sometimes allows her to help with the dishes, and that makes her feel she can be useful around the house. The daughter added, "Mother sometimes says she can't see any use in living this long, but I tell her that God has left her here for me, to be my pleasure in life, and she is."

When a centenarian is committed to a nursing home, both parent and child usually understand and accept the fact that because of physical infirmity there is no viable alternative. Even when they do enter institutions, as earlier examples have shown, the centenarians' uncomplaining, pleasant attitudes make them favorites of staff and residents, creating an environment congenial to continued existence.

THE ABSENCE OF ONE characteristic was puzzling for a long time. The centenarians rarely expressed grief or bereavement. A few mentioned that they missed their spouses or children who had died, but they were exceptions to the rule. The departed relative might be praised or the fact of the death stated (matter-of-factly), but almost never was there a reference to the emotional impact upon the centenarian himself. This became particularly noticeable in the case of one man whose lifetime mate had died just the month before. The report of her recent death was the only reference to her. Otherwise, the centenarian never mentioned his wife, the interview was indistinguishable in tone from any other, and the social security representative seemed unaware of any bereavement in his subject and impervious to the fact that the absence of any sign of sorrow might be highly unusual.

The date of death of a mate was at least somewhat more removed in other cases; nevertheless, this apparent neglect of the person who must have been important to the centenarian's life, welfare, and survival made these old people seem callous and flinty, even ingrates —characteristics that are at odds with what had been learned about the centenarians in all other areas.

The first possible explanation—since nothing was offered in the interviews—was that what appeared to be neglect simply was a matter of omission: The subject never came up. The government interviewers regarded personal loss and grief, like sex, as private matters. Such information was unsought, and the centenarians may have been laconic in discussing close, personal relationships; 456 centenarians were married for very long periods of time, but there were only 56 references to happy marriages.

Upon reflection, the following explanation, however, is offered as the main reason for the suppression of grief and bereavement. The explanation is based only on inference and the premise that these old people had become acute monitors of their state of health and well-being while their survival was a *de facto* demonstration of their devotion to life. Bereavement is the normal—indeed, unavoidable— human reaction to the loss of someone dear. But bereavement and grief also are life threatening. Psychologist Arthur C. Carr and psychiatrist Bernard Schoenberg state in *Loss and Grief: Psychological Management in Medical Practice*: "The concept that bereavement is associated with increased mortality is supported by numerous studies." The first study they cite compared the immediate relatives of 371 people who had died to a control group of immediate relatives of 371 living people (matched by age, sex, and marital status). "Bereaved relatives were found to have a much higher mortality rate during the first year of bereavement. Increased risk of mortality was greatest for widowed people. For example, during the first year of bereavement 12.2 percent of the widowed people died, compared with 1.2 percent in the control group."

The risk of death for widows and widowers is ten times greater than it is for their peers who have not lost a mate. When this multiplication is applied to the already high death rate for very old people, then the odds against surviving the death of a spouse become virtually insuperable. The odds can be quantified. For Americans in their mid-nineties about one-quarter die and three-quarters normally survive another year. But if that 25 percent is multiplied by ten, the number of deaths rise far beyond 100 percent to 250 percent.

In the course of living a century, virtually all of these people have endured the death of not merely *one* beloved person but of many such people, including parents, spouses, brothers, sisters, and children —most of the deaths bunched into the last part of the centenarians' lives. Many centenarians, such as Louisa Gardner, also mention friends: "I had a lot of friends but they are all gone. I'm like a soldier left on the battlefield." These emotional shocks are the surest and severest penalty in living 100 years.

The inference is that the centenarians sense that at their advanced age indulgence in prolonged grief is fatal. This is innate wisdom; the scientific literature connecting bereavement and a heightened risk of death is recent, and in any event it is unlikely that the centenarians would have been aware of such literature. Bereaved old people have a life-or-death decision to make. They can choose loyal attachment to the beloved spouse, and death; or they can close their minds to the event and its meaning, and survive. The case of Barney Richards of Rumford, Maine, suggests that this is what happens. "Mr. Richards has been married twice. His first wife died of consumption, leaving him with five children. He married again, and there were seven children by the second wife. After sixty-five years of marriage to the second wife, she died. . . . After his second wife died the family suspected that the effect of his bereavement might be too much for him and that he might not live long, but he promptly pulled himself together."

ACTS OF COURAGE in the conventional sense of derring-do are atypical of these centenarians. Only one centenarian was decorated for an outstanding act of bravery during wartime, and that was not for combat against the enemy but for potentially saving the lives of fellow Americans. Edward J. Ocker, Jr., the man who loved fat and was living in a V.A. hospital in Albany, New York, was awarded the Distinguished Service Medal for saving a cache of ammunition at

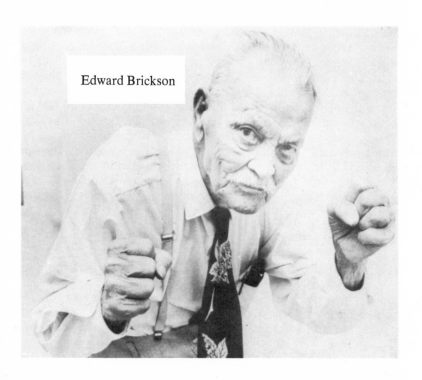

Edward Brickson

Ponce, Puerto Rico, during the Spanish-American War. "The Spaniards over in Puerto Rico set our ammunition house on fire," says Mr. Ocker. "There were a lot of powders, a lot of explosives, some of them in wooden boxes. I ran right in there and put it out. The officer of the day came around, and when he saw the fire he ordered everyone to run. Everyone ran away from that fire but me."

As a young man John Williamson was on a riverboat excursion when a little girl fell overboard. He jumped in and saved her. Joseph Pitrone defied and fought against the Black Hand in his native Sicily. William Wilkie as a young man defended a Salvation Army girl from a bully who was abusing her. He broke his right wrist in the fight. With a few exceptions, these incidents exhaust the list of conventionally brave acts.

Actual physical fighting took place in only two of the four cases cited above. Edward Brickson's fight could be considered either an act of courage or of foolhardiness: "This was when he was about 17 or 18 years old [in 1884 or 1885]. He had been up in North

Dakota working on bonanza farms for about a year prior to this. On his way home he had stopped at Fargo, North Dakota, to visit a brother. While there John L. Sullivan came to town offering half of an evening's gate to anyone who could stay in the ring with him for five rounds. Mr. Brickson wasn't too excited about getting into the ring with John L. Sullivan but friends of his advised him all he had to do was stay away from Mr. Sullivan for five rounds. This Mr. Brickson managed to do for three rounds. 'In the fourth round he hit me real hard,' Mr. Brickson said, 'but luckily enough it was high enough on the ribs that it didn't knock the wind out of me, and I was able to keep away from him. I did manage to get one punch in, and that was like hitting a bull.' Mr. Brickson managed to last the five rounds and collected his money. He then remained in Fargo for two years working in the Northern Pacific warehouse and picking up occasional fights." When Sullivan was the first heavyweight champion, from 1882 to 1892, they fought with bare knuckles.

In 1883, Clark B. House was 20 years old, living on a farm in upstate New York with his father and two brothers. "The farm contained a 'hop yard,' where hops were grown and processed for the malt-beverage industry. One night a group of six or seven men invaded the farm and attempted to steal some of the processed hops. The intruders were armed with guns and clubs, and a wild melee ensued, during which Mr. House, his brothers, and his father attempted to repel the invaders. Many shots were fired, and his father was shot in the arm and shoulder. A series of fistfights took place, and Mr. House stated he 'got in some mighty good pokes.' "

Frank Lester of Deford, Michigan, "stated he was a 'champion all through school' at fighting and especially wrestling—'I was ugly' and he likes to brag about it. He was also champion 'finger puller' (this is a tug of war with index fingers, which he tried out on the interviewer —he's still pretty strong). He was beaten in finger pulling only once, and this was as an adult. The fellow 'pulled so hard that rheumatism acted up (in the finger) and I had to quit.' "

One case of physical fighting in the hundredth year is reported. The combatant was Edward G. Snyder, at the Masonic Home in Alma, Michigan. "On a few occasions this spring Mr. Snyder wandered away from the home and was the subject of a more or less intensive search by home personnel. On another occasion he became involved with another guest and in the ensuing scrap broke two of his opponent's ribs with his cane."

But to balance these encounters are about an equal number of admissions of fear and prudence. When Chris Jungck "was handling freight for the army, the battle of Wounded Knee occurred. This particular incident has stayed in his memory because of his fear of the Indians while he was transporting freight to the military post." The event William Scarborough remembers is walking along a street in Tacoma, Washington, one night when he was 40 years old. "It was dark and a big fellow jumped out and said, 'Boss, give me a dime.' I think my heart must have stopped beating. I was really scared, but I told him I didn't have a dime for him and walked on by. I expected him to jump me, but he didn't."

Samuel B. Shepard, the president of an independent telephone company in Bar Mills, Maine, and a leader in the state's Republican party: "In 1885 [he was 28 years old] when I first came to Bar Mills I joined the local volunteer fire company. In those days much of the local social life revolved around the fire company. Shortly after, there was a murder in Bar Mills. In those days we didn't have the elaborate police protection we have today. I received a letter from the county sheriff appointing me a deputy sheriff to head a committee to investigate the murder. I refused the appointment on the grounds that it would be inconsistent with my practice of getting drunk at the monthly fire company meetings. Besides, I was always a coward, and I wouldn't have dared arrest anyone anyhow."

An extremely common answer by the centenarian men to the question of whether they ever served in the armed forces was that they either were too young or too old. There is, however, a general impression that most of these men were well satisfied with the fact that they never saw military service. It is more than an impression, in a few cases. "The Spanish-American War stands out as the most historical event in the life of Mr. [James] Hollis. He recalls being too young to enlist without his parents' consent, and his mother would not sign for him. World War I came along and he was too old; therefore, he never entered military service." Actually, Mr. Hollis was 29 years old when the Spanish-American War started.

"For one war I was too young," said William Collins, "for one I was too old, and the rest I guess they figured I was just no-account." Mr. Collins also was 29 years old at the start of the Spanish-American War.

"When asked if he had ever served in the army or navy, Mr. [Leon] Hodges said that he had 'escaped everything.' The only war which he was eligible for was the Spanish-American War, but the fact that he wasn't in it was all right with him since he wasn't a fighting man."

All told, twenty-five centenarian men enlisted in the United States Army or Navy. Three of them saw action at the famous battle of San Juan Hill in the Spanish-American War. One of the three was Thomas Pender, who lived at the V.A. hospital in Bath, New York, and who sometimes got falling-down drunk. A second was John A. White, who was asked if he had seen any actual combat or had met Teddy Roosevelt. "Ted came up one side of the hill with his cavalry, and we were coming up the other side. I was covered with blood. I didn't have a scratch myself, but blood from the enemy." Frank James fought with Roosevelt's Rough Riders. Mr. James says he "crawled up the hill through eight inches of blood."

For both Thomas Pender and John White, the charge up San Juan Hill was the most exciting event of their lives, but Rough Rider Frank James's "most exciting experience was his discharge from the army and return to his father's farm."

CHAPTER 14

Rosetta Stones

The 700th interview to be processed was with Mrs. Sophia Cobbum, who was living in a nursing home in Goshen, Indiana. She was another centenarian who loved to sing. "When she was wished a happy birthday, she replied with a mischievous smile and sang the 'Happy Birthday' song to 'Mrs. Cobbum' in a clear, steady voice that would put many a younger vocalist to shame."

Mrs. Cobbum was born on a farm in Ohio, one of sixteen children. She did not go to school very long because her parents needed her at home to help take care of her younger brothers and sisters. Other people tried to adopt some of the children, but the parents turned down all offers. However, in the custom of those days, Mrs. Cobbum went to work and lived with another family early in life, giving her earnings to her parents. She married, had two children, and returned to outside work at the age of 68, with a rubber company in Goshen. She was widowed when she was 73 and continued to work until age 77, when she was able to retire on social security payments. In other words, hers is a fairly typical centenarian biography. That is, until this sentence in the final paragraph: "She couldn't give a reason for her long life unless it was that she thrived on hard work."

Thrived! Work satisfaction is a pallid phrase beside that verb.

I turned back a dozen interviews to one with James Baxter of De Funiak Springs, Florida. Mr. Baxter lived a tough life. His parents were poor, and when he was 16 years old he "struck out on my own." His first job was in a sawmill 30 or 40 miles away. He was a sawmill worker or railroad section-hand until he was 43 years old, when he came to Florida because he heard "they were paying good money to

John Newhard

turpentine workers and there was plenty of jobs." That work continued until "the hard times hit" in the 1930s, when he was about 70 years old. After that, it was scratching out a living with yard work until he managed to qualify for social security.

This was a circumscribed life and these were menial jobs. Nevertheless, there was this passage about his life as a turpentine worker: "It was hard work in all kinds of weather, but I liked it. Me and some of them big old rattlesnakes out in the piney woods growed old together."

The cultural bias that blinded me to the creative aspects of labor also prevented me, until this point, from believing or understanding that anyone could get deep, genuine, soul-fulfilling enjoyment from routine, repetitive, intellectually unchallenging work.

Then these examples came to mind. Mary Redmond, a black woman living in Hattiesburg, Mississippi: "She has never been employed in commercial or industrial work, but from the age of about 20 to about 80 she did considerable household work for white families, most of which consisted of washing and ironing. She used to work on a farm, and among the most pleasant jobs that she remembers was picking cotton."

And Gonzalo Davila in Caguas, Puerto Rico: "In those days, you had to work hard all day long. I first started working as a water boy, hauling drinking water for the men who planted sugar cane and weeded the fields. I used to get twelve cents a day and had to work from sunrise to sunset. I still remember the old ox driving the sugar cane presses. How times have changed! Later on, after working as an agricultural laborer for several years, I worked my land as a sharecropper. I planted sweet potatoes, corn, and tanniers. I had a wooden plow and would borrow a team of oxen from a neighbor— you have no idea how happy I felt while plowing my land, thinking on the produce I would collect."

These are paeans to work, love songs to work. An unusual attitude toward hard work and labor. Hard labor is the vocation of slaves and punishment for criminals. The cultural bias against it goes back a long way. In Genesis, God's penalty against Adam and Eve and their descendants is expulsion from the Garden of Eden to labor in the fields: "In the sweat of thy face shalt thou eat bread. . . . (Has anyone ever suggested that the passage is simply a brilliant description of the human transition from gathering fruits and nuts to agriculture as a way of earning a living?) In 1899 Edwin Markham restated the curse in his poem "The Man with the Hoe, Written after seeing Millet's world-famous painting of a brutalized toiler in the deep abyss of labor." It begins:

Bowed by the weight of centuries he leans
Upon his hoe and gazes on the ground,
The emptiness of ages in his face,
And on his back the burden of the world.

But for two centenarians, the hoe is the symbol of life, the staff of continued living. Harmon King of Enid, Oklahoma, "says he has never retired. Because his legs are unsteady, he sits in a chair and hoes weeds in the flower garden." Ed Wisbey in Vancouver, Washington, says, "As long as I can have the hoe to hold me up, I can keep working."

The difference between these men with hoes and Markham's man with a hoe is the gulf between the independent American farmer and serfdom. Could it be that the difference between the American farm workers who lived a century and the other American farmers is precisely the difference in their attitudes toward their work? The question of hard work had been perplexing. Unquestionably, strong physical exertion practiced regularly confers benefits for longevity. But all farmers must have worked about equally hard. Why these few centenarians out of the millions of farmers? There's no way of knowing, of course, the attitudes of the shorter-lived hard-workers. And very many members of this cohort do not express themselves one way or another on how they felt about their work. With the closest scrutiny, it could be said that three out of eight of the centenarians in some way indicated work satisfaction. But it can also be said that none of the centenarians spoke negatively about the work they did. By today's standards, these people were workaholics; but this latest pejorative term—indicating that their work was excessive, compulsive, neurotic, and barren of pleasure—is another foreign word for the centenarians.

About a hundred interviews after Mrs. Cobbum's was a report on Alvan Couch, who lived most of his life in Kansas—the man who presented a reasoned argument against sending Americans to the moon. "Mr. Couch taught in a one-room, country schoolhouse for twenty-four years. He said he worked from 4 A.M. until late in the evening seven days a week, working the farm and teaching school. 'When I was teaching, I had as many as twelve different groups. We had blackboards all around the classroom, and I would send the students to the blackboard, arranged by groups. The little ones would be practicing their numbers, and I would progress through the groups until I was giving problems in business and arithmetic to the older ones. It was a very busy classroom.' . . . In discussing the secret of his longevity of life, Mr. Couch smiled and said, 'I have never worked hard in my life. True, I worked seven days a week, eighteen and nineteen hours a day, but always in an activity that I enjoyed, which you cannot consider work.' "*

Mrs. Eleanor Robson Belmont refined the formula to two crucial elements. The way to live to be 100 years old, she said, is: "No diet, no special care, nothing like that. It's doing what you want and doing it happily."* Most of the centenarians, unlike the enormously talented and wealthy Mrs. Belmont, did not have much liberty to choose what they wanted to do for a living, but they did have the ability, and they learned to be content with their lot. Again, not a single centenarian described his or her life in negative terms, even if from the available information only about half of them positively could be said to be happy.

For Mrs. Susannah Edrington, happiness all by itself is the key.* "When asked what her formula was for persons who want to live to be 100, she replied, 'The important thing is to be happy, and I have some sayings which I remember, use, and live by.' " These were her sayings:

> *Sing instead of growl,*
> *Smile instead of frown,*
> *Look up instead of down.*
>
> *A sigh adds a nail to your coffin, no doubt.*
> *A chuckle, however merry, draws one out.*

After Mr. Couch's use of the word *enjoyed,* I began to become aware that I had overlooked how often the centenarians used this particular verb. The reason for this oversight, I believe, is that the term I had used in the questionnaire is *joie de vivre.* This term connotes a spiritual high, and this kind of frothy excitement is not the emotion experienced by the centenarians. Indeed, could anyone sustain life at that pitch for a century? The enjoyment expressed is as undramatic as the unspectacular activities that the centenarians described. (See Jewett's remarks in Appendix 6: "They had a capacity to enjoy life. All had a degree of optimism and an unusual sense of humor. They responded to simple pleasures available.")

---

* These attitudes match perfectly the principal findings of the Duke study that work satisfaction and employment are the most important psychosocial factors in longevity for men, while happiness is most important for women.

By this time, about two-thirds of the interviews had been processed. By going back through notes and excerpts on some 800 questionnaires and monitoring the remaining 400 interviews, it was found that at least 200 centenarians used the verb *enjoy* to describe what they did in their lives. "Enjoys" was a salient characteristic for 168 of them, number 6 on the list. And 32 centenarians said they had been able to live so long because they enjoyed life.

CHAPTER 15

Will

Walking along the corridors of the Adventist Nursing Home, a large and well-run center for old people in Livingston, New York, I observed an array of residents. Some were dressed in normal street clothes and were moving about; some in pajamas and robes were in wheelchairs, lost in private reverie; some were engaged in animated conversations; others were reading. Three centenarians were in the home. I wondered if I could pick them out of a group as a witness selects a suspect in a police lineup. I knew I would look for the most cheerful, open-faced person, one who appeared to be kindly (or least grouchy).

Since the staff members of the home would be well acquainted with their wards, I put the question to social worker Mrs. Susan Robinson. She said the difference between the centenarians and other residents "is that the centenarians have not given up." A head nurse, Mrs. Wanda Ferrari, said, "The difference is that the centenarians are strong willed," whereas most others were docile and acquiescent. She gave as an example Miss Lillian Boehmer, one of the centenarians I had come to see. The nurse had difficulty persuading Miss Boehmer to keep her room neat. Mrs. Ferrari said that after one attempt, Miss Boehmer stamped her foot and said, "You will drive me crazy."

The nurse replied, "You have lived a hundred years and still are not crazy."

Miss Boehmer's rejoinder was "But there is still time."

This is Miss Boehmer's version: "My nurse doesn't like the looks of my room. 'Well,' I said, 'there shouldn't be any rules for anybody a hundred years old.' She said, 'What am I going to do with you?' I said, 'Well, don't do anything with me.' "

Charlie Smith

Based on my intimacy with three teenaged children, Miss Boehmer's area didn't look very untidy to me. But based on my knowledge of the importance of order in the lives of centenarians, I was interested in her comments on her own perception of her disorderliness. "I wish I could be neat and tidy. You know, order is one of heaven's first laws. And I think sometimes—how will I get to heaven? I'm not orderly."

One of Miss Boehmer's earliest memories relates directly to nurse Ferrari's observation of strong will. At about the age of 3, Miss Boehmer was sent to bed and punished, but she didn't know why. She lay in bed crying and gasping until her parents finally came in to see her. "I know they would not have found a live child if they had not come in to console me."

This was reminiscent of other tests of wills. Grandma Moses told of one occasion when her family had company. She was not permitted to sit at the table even though a younger brother was. "I started to bawl." Her father commanded her to stop crying, provoking greater howls. At this, he threatened to whip her, even though he and his wife did not believe in corporal punishment. However, her grandfather was present, and he did believe that children should be seen and not heard. Her father took her by the arm to the shop. He picked up some shavings to whip her, "and that made me mad, I stamped my foot, and I shouted, 'If you strike me with that, I will never like you again.' " She could see her father smile under his beard "as much as to say 'You little imp.' " He took her back to the table, and someone put a plate in front of her.

Ella McBride, the Seattle photographer and mountain climber, said: "I remember when I was about three years old and we were coming out to Oregon from Iowa. We didn't come straight out. We went to New York and took a steamer from New York to the Isthmus of Panama. We crossed the Isthmus of Panama on a jerk-water train. We then went to San Francisco and took a steamer to Portland. We then took a riverboat on the Willamette River to Albany, Oregon. I remember that when we were crossing the Isthmus of Panama I cried most of the way over because I was so thirsty. They gave me water, but I wouldn't drink the lukewarm water—I only liked the cold water."

Will to live was a quality included in the questionnaire and watched for. It was not until after the insight of the Adventist Home nurse, however, that I began to realize that will is not simply another trait in the centenarian repertoire, but the centerpiece. And that was a reminder of the central concept of Arthur Schopenhauer. Schopenhauer was the intellectual pioneer who opened the way for the modern understanding of human mentality. Before him, thinkers solemnly considered man to be the rational animal. But Schopenhauer showed that reasons are merely rationalizations for whatever we want to do. Our behavior is not driven by a sense of logic: The power to reason is used to justify and explain what we do. The mainspring of the individual—any individual in any species—is the will to live. This will is the essence of life and is universal. The birth of a human being is the objectification of will. Thereafter, the individual desires to live, desires to perpetuate life, desires endless existence.

If this is the case, the will to live should be especially strong in centenarians. Its *de facto* presence in these people could be taken from their record of successful survival. That its importance was not so readily noticeable may have been due to several factors. For one thing, it is usual to think of a person's being strong willed in the Nietzschean sense. Friedrich Nietzsche, Schopenhauer's successor in philosophy, decided that the essence of life is not the will to live but the will to power. Strong will in this sense is exhibited by dominating others. Hitler acted upon the Nietzschean will and became an apostle of death, whereas centenarians are exemplars of life. Centenarians are notable for the absence of the desire for power over their fellows. Their strong wills are confined to themselves and their own lives. Miss Lillian Boehmer did not try aggressively to impose her will upon the nurse, but employed it instead to defend her status quo. The situation was somewhat similar in the case of the young Ella McBride, and Grandma Moses was fighting a perceived injustice to herself.

Subsequent to my visit to the Adventist Nursing Home, I came upon two dramatic demonstrations of the will to live. Mrs. Dora Spangler, living alone in Wichita, Kansas, fell in the middle of the night, gashing her head severely. Although she was bleeding profusely, she managed to crawl from her bedroom to the kitchen and pull the telephone down to the floor by its cord. Then she calmly told the operator to call her daughter, an ambulance, and the fire department, because her doors were locked and her rescuers would have to break in.

Arthur Dial of Munford, Alabama: "The most exciting thing that happened to me was when I was about eighty years old. I was walking across the L & N Railroad trestle near Jennifer—a very high trestle— and didn't think a train was anywhere around until I heard the whistle behind me. When I looked back, that train was right on me and looked as big as a tree. I had to do something in a hurry. I scrambled over to the outside edge of the crossties and lay down. The engine and several cars had crossed the trestle before the train got stopped. I was scared all right, and I got up and climbed on top of a boxcar, 'cause I was shaky some. The train people—the engineer and fireman—started looking around everywhere for me, under the trestle and the train, and then one of them said, 'There he is—up there!' That was a close call."

Most examples of will, once looked for, were undramatic—in keeping with quiet lifestyles. John Newhard, who at 100 years still was working as a cemetery manager, said everybody thought he was going to die from typhoid pneumonia in 1900. "But I was only thirty-four then, and figured there was a lot of new things coming, and I wanted to be around to see them." Elza Wynn "thinks he's been able to live so long because he just made up his mind to live. He said he was thinking about dying about 1945 (when he was 77 years old), but decided he'd wait a while yet." When Mrs. Sadie Smith was asked why she had been able to live so long, she said: "I think I had quite a lot of ambition. I had broken bones six times, and I was just determined to get back up and around."

The responses of Mr. Wynn and Mrs. Smith are rare. Very few centenarians associated their long survival with a strong will. This may be because they assumed the will to live is the same for everybody. They know only their own interior reality. A number of centenarians stated they could not understand why they had lived so long, because they were the same as everybody else or no different from anybody else. This failure of the centenarians to recognize their own strong will further diminished the visibility of this quality.

I was aware of the characteristic in the centenarians I had interviewed earlier. But it was only in retrospect, after talking with Mrs. Ferrari, that I was able to appreciate its paramount role. Strong will all by itself can explain the strange interview I had with Mrs. Katherine Franzen.

The interview took place in the home of her daughter-in-law, Mrs. Rudolph Franzen, in Kinderhook, New York. The centenarian was not on the scene at the appointed time, and the daughter-in-law said she still was at her toilet, grooming and preparing herself. When she finally did appear, her entrance was in its way a dramatic one. She moved into the room quietly, slowly, like a pale wraith, stopping after each step to advance the walker ahead another few inches. I felt an impulse to leap up to help her; but the younger Mrs. Franzen showed no concern, so I stood up in place. The 105-year-old woman was small, thin, and frail; but upon closer observation her skin was not so much pale as luminously laved. Her hand was soft to the touch. She seemed befuddled even after the daughter-in-law introduced me and tried to explain who I was. This was cause for concern. The daughter-in-law must have briefed her beforehand about my visit. She should not have been so puzzled if her mind were clear.

The daughter-in-law interrupted her explanation to tell the old woman to turn on her hearing aid. Again, the same attitude of incomprehension, as Mrs. Franzen looked from one to the other of us. The daughter-in-law's frustrated instructions became pleading, and then the woman understood. She turned on her hearing aid. The daughter-in-law motioned toward a large armchair and, mixing in German words, urged her to be seated, saying I wanted to talk to her about herself. Still she hesitated, and there was a moment of doubt that she would consent to the interview at all. That would have been disappointing to me, because accessible centenarians are not commonplace. But after a few repetitions, she seemed to agree, progressed slowly to the chair, and sat down without assistance. When she turned to face me, I introduced myself, told her I was trying to learn about centenarians, and asked a question. She gave no indication that she knew what I was talking about, and remained silent. I tried several approaches and different questions, assisted by coaching from the daughter-in-law, with the same result. Mrs. Franzen was confirming my earlier apprehension that the interview would be a zero.

I was about to turn my attention to the daughter-in-law, when Mrs. Franzen began to speak. She described volubly and with great emotion the death of her 77-year-old son from a heart attack the year before. She discoursed on this subject at length in an uninterrupted monologue. When she finished, she fell silent; she uttered nothing more except to say "Goodbye" and smile when I was leaving. In between, I learned about her life from her daughter-in-law.

That frail old woman was in control of the situation from the start. Her delayed entrance emphasized who the important person was. She used her weaknesses—her frailty, her deafness, her seeming inability to understand—to enforce her control. We waited for her decisions. She discussed only what she wanted to and was adamantly unresponsive to everything else.

There was nothing in the interview with another centenarian that particularly called attention to strong will, but at a later time a relative of the centenarian's wife told me: "He does what he wants when he wants to do it. He always considers his wants first."

My interview with Charlie Smith could be interpreted as an encounter with will. I first heard of him in May 1973 when an official at social security headquarters wrote me that "the oldest person receiving monthly benefits is Mr. Charlie Smith, 965 Laurel Street, Bartow, Florida. Mr. Smith is 130 years of age, based on a date of birth of July 4, 1842." As already mentioned, the *Guinness Book of*

World Records and scientists do not accept such great antiquity. Gerontologists believe the human lifespan terminates somewhere in the twelfth decade.

According to published articles sent to me by the Social Security Administration, Charlie Smith was born Mitchel Watkins in a coastal town in Liberia. When he was 12 years old, his mother gave him permission to visit a ship docked at the boat landing. A man invited onlookers to come aboard the ship to see the "fritter tree." Down in the hold was a tree covered with fritters dripping with syrup. The man said that these trees were all over his country, and that when people got hungry, they just went up to a syrup tree and picked a fritter.

When Charlie came up from the hold, the ship was at sea. "I never saw my mama again." He was bought at the New Orleans slave market by Charles Smith, a rancher from Galveston, Texas. The transaction is supposed to have taken place on July 4th, and Smith assigned that day as Charlie's birthday. Charles Smith had three sons and treated Charlie as a fourth, even giving the black youth his name. In 1863, after the Emancipation Proclamation, Smith told Charlie he was a free man and could leave. "But as it was, I felt free all along. Some slaves had a bad time, some had a good time." Charlie chose to stay, since the ranch was his home. A few years later, Smith, on his deathbed, asked Charlie to swear he would keep his name. Charlie Smith promised.

Charlie spent several winters on the Smith ranch, then worked elsewhere in Texas and the West as a cowboy. Charlie says he acquired the name "Trigger Kid," because he was quick to draw his .45 and not reticent about pulling the trigger. He was no stranger to gunfights. He says he rode with Jesse James to pick up the man who tried to shoot the president [*sic*]. There is another version of how he got the name "Trigger Kid"—that somewhere along the line he acted in silent movies.

There are reports that he worked as a guard and laborer on the Panama Canal (a French company tried and failed to build a canal during the 1880s) and on a construction project in Nicaragua. He became a logger in Mississippi, did odds jobs in Alabama, and then about the turn of the century he came to Florida, first to work in wood mills and then as a citrus picker. He was married three times and had one son from the first marriage. "During President Hoover's time I was in Groveland running a bar and living with my third wife 'til I shot at her and run her off. That's the only time I remember missing anything with a gun. I was sure fed up with that woman. She was stealing my whiskey and running 'round with other men."

Charlie Smith first came to public attention in 1955. He was one of twenty-five extremely aged people gathered for study at the Spears Chiropractic Clinic in Denver. The researchers accepted an affidavit from an Auburndale, Florida, citrus grower that a birth record showed Charlie to be 90 years old in 1932. That made him 113 years old in 1955. That same year, a payroll clerk discovered that Charlie had no social security card. When the social security people received his application, they thought a mistake had been made in the birth year. They found in the Polk County Courthouse the document signed by his employer: "According to Charlie Smith [*sic*] Birth Record he was 90 years old when he worked for me 1932." The social security people stopped him from climbing ladders, and he eventually ended his work career operating a candy store.

When I arrived in Bartow, Florida, in January 1977 (Charlie Smith reputedly was in his 135th year), I learned from a local newspaper editor that Charlie was in the Bartow Convalescent Center. Alarmed that my visit might be too late, I asked how he was. "He is lucid," said L. L. Frisbee of the *Polk County Democrat*, "and eager as ever to talk to visitors."

I reached the convalescent center at noontime, so that the receptionist taking me to see Charlie first scanned the dining area, already filled with residents. He was not among them, so we went to his room. Charlie sat on the side of his bed, buttoning his shirt and jacket. I had two immediate impressions. One was that he was more formally dressed than other residents. He wore a trim, black-and-white checked, lightweight jacket over a patterned shirt, open at the collar, and dark trousers. He was neatly dressed, the jacket hanging smartly on his trim frame. The other impression was of how erectly he sat.

Seen in profile, tufts of white hair grew thickly at his temples and, more sparsely, around the back part of his head. The front top of his head was bald. He was clean shaven. His skin was wrinkled but not overly so. He appeared to be of indeterminate old age. There were no eyeglasses, hearing aid, or cane. My guide introduced me to Charlie and explained that I wanted to interview him. I asked for and received permission to tape record the interview and went to my car for the equipment.

When I returned, Charlie was sitting alone. I set the tape recorder on a small table that stood in front of him and pulled over a chair to sit across from him. His first distinguishable words to me were that I could not put my recorder on his table. He said he needed the table for his things. Since the tabletop was bare, I took this gambit as a warning signal to proceed with caution.

I put the recorder on the floor and then saw that the wires were so tangled that I could not get the microphone high enough to rest it on the table top. I had to hold the microphone in my left hand, several feet from him. This made it difficult for me to balance a pad on my lap and write on it. I wanted to take as complete notes as I could, because my experience has been not to rely solely on a recorder. If for some reason it is faulty, and you have not taken adequate notes, it becomes impossible to reconstruct a long interview.

Juggling my journalist's tools as best I could, I began.

"How do you feel, Mr. Smith?"

"How do I feel?"

"Yes."

"I feel all right. How are *you*?"

Was there a note of belligerence in his question? Not betraying any reaction to what might be construed as an unfriendly retort and trying to turn this opening course of the dialogue to advantage, I said that I was fine. "And I'm pleased to meet you. I've heard about you. You're probably the oldest person in the United States."

"I don't know about that. My name's all over the world, I know."

"Why do you think you've lived so long?"

"You say you've heard about my name. But what about my name?"

"That you're the oldest person in the United States."

"I don't know about that."

Undeterred: "And that you were born way back in 1842, social security says. Why do you think you've had such a long life? Why do you think you've lived so long?"

"How come I've lived so long?"

"Yes."

"I dunno. I ain't the Lord."

Stalling: "Huh?"

"I ain't the Lord. Why are you askin' such a question as that? How come I'm living that long. How come you living as long as you living?"

"Yeah." I refused to be drawn into that. I hadn't traveled a thousand miles for him to interview me. But I was having trouble fighting down the start of a feeling of despair. When an interview starts this way, with a person who doesn't want to communicate, it only gets worse.

But Charlie was not accepting my noncommittal response. "Why are you living as long as you living?" he persisted. "I dunno how come I'm livin' as long as I is. I hope I won't never die, as far as that's concerned." (There—that's more like it. A positive attitude toward life!) "Nobody don't know how long they be livin'. Me, you, and nobody else."

I seized upon the positive aspect of the statement. "You're still looking forward to the future?"

"Huh?"

"You're still looking forward to the future?"

"A teacher?"

"No, the future . . . to what's coming up. Looking forward to tomorrow."

"What kind of future? What coming up tomorrow?"

Determinedly: "Well, what *is* coming up tomorrow? I mean, I was asking you if you're looking forward to that."

"Well, you've got eyes to look just as good as I is. You shouldn't ask me. You can look just as good as I can look."

No doubt about it, he was hostile. The adversary mode is the worst to get into with a subject if you're seeking information rather than trying to produce theatrics for a television or radio audience. The interviewee becomes uncooperative and the interview unproductive. Somehow, I seemed to have turned a lovable raconteur into a word miser. Furthermore, a testy grouch did not fit my preconceived notions of a centenarian.

But I was here, so I might as well make the best of it. "How long have you been here?"

"I been here a week or two."

I knew he had been at the center much longer than that. Was his mind going? "What do you do each day here?"

"What I'm doing now. I been doing it all my days. What I'm doing now. The same thing. I'm a State man. The United State. I go where they send me."

I had no idea what he meant by that, so I said quickly, "How's your sight? Do you see well?"

The eyes were the part of Charlie Smith that intimated extreme age. The whites were rheumy around the edges, the pupils a milky blue, as though they were slowly clouding over. They were like two star sapphires. They weren't lifeless, like the gem, but the fires of life that burned in them seemed banked low and greatly recessed.

"I see like I been seeing all my days. I ain't no different in my eyesight that I knowed of. If there is, I ain't found it out."

A nurse looked through the open doorway and gesturing toward him stage-whispered to me that it was time for his lunch. Charlie's back was turned toward the doorway, and he did not see the nurse. I told Charlie it was time for him to eat.

"Huh?"

"The nurse said it's time for you to go and eat now."

"How do you know?"

"The nurse just came here"—I was almost pleading for him to believe me—"and said for you to go and eat now."

"She ain't told me nuthin' about it."

The point I wanted to get at, and I asked him, was whether I could stay while he went to eat so that we could talk further afterwards— although, I thought to myself, God knows why.

"I ain't been going there to eat," he replied to my request. "They been bringing what I eats . . ."

"Oh, they bring it in here. Oh, I see." And at that moment an attendant entered with a trayful of food and set it on the table in front of Charlie.

"Hi ya, Charlie," the attendant said. "How are you?"

That was the first time I realized that Charlie Smith knew something I didn't know. The second thing I realized was that he wanted to keep his table clear for a reason quite important to him: That was where he was going to eat his lunch. And, thirdly, he wasn't about to believe some stranger who told him he was supposed to go to eat in the dining area.

I arose and went over by the doorway to allow Charlie to eat in some privacy. Bright sunlight streamed into the room through a large window. Outside was a pleasant court and just by the window a palm tree.

Although Charlie was toothless, he appeared to have no trouble chewing. He ate deliberately, with single-minded concentration. A nurse stopped at the open doorway to comment to me, "Charlie eats everything we put in front of him and never eats anything he shouldn't eat." She went on to say she hoped that he hadn't been cranky, because sometimes he had been getting that way lately. I mentioned that he would not talk about past details in his life. "That's only happened in the past few months that his memory has begun to fail." This was disappointing news. "He still gets around, though, unaided. He takes his teddy bear and his pocketbook"—and for the first time I noticed those items on the bed behind him—"and goes for a walk. He's still a little disoriented because he was just moved to this room recently from the opposite hall." There was the logical explanation for his saying he had been here—here in his present room—only one or two weeks!

The nurse leaned into the room. "Hello, Charlie," she said affectionately. "How're you doing?"

Charlie answered the greeting with a minimum response, a sort of regal acknowledgment of his due. The same ritual was repeated when the director of the center and the program director came to the room. There was genuine fondness and respect in the way they addressed him. No question but that Charlie Smith was a Very Important Person at the Bartow Convalescent Center.

That was another mistake I had made: I had called him Mr. Smith when to everyone he was Charlie.

After he had finished lunch, he put on a tall-crowned, ten-gallon, white cowboy hat. I soon found that his good humor had returned. Well, it was understandable for a fellow to be out of sorts when he was hungry. Charlie had changed in still another way. He felt like talking. I let him go, deciding not to "structure" the interview, but let him take me where *he* wanted to go.

To my dismay, that was right back to the business of his being a "State" man. "The United State send me places. The United State take care of me. The United State pays all my bills and everything. The United State. Nobody don't give me nuthin'. The United State sant me right here. The United State sent me places. The United State man always tol' me: Anything I've got to have, don't never let it give out. Enjoy your income when you're livin'. For you can't enjoy it when you're dead. The United State. Anything you got to have, git it. Before it give out."

And then he introduced four items that were to dominate the rest of whatever it was we were having together. He shifted two pairs of shoes that had been on the bed beside him to the table between us. He apparently kept all his possessions grouped close to him on the bed. Beside the teddy bear and pocketbook were an attaché case, which he called his "suitcase," a large book, and the two pairs of shoes.

"These are my shoes. They don't cost me nuthin'. Here are two pair and I got on a pair. They don't cost me nuthin'. The State takes care of me. The United State. They don't cost me nuthin'. This is a pair. And this is a pair. And I got on a pair. Don't cost me nuthin'. The world don't give 'em to me. The State takes care of me. They send me different places. Sant me here . . ."

The monologue was developing a rambling quality, as he touched the same bases and kept making the same points. I was reluctant to interrupt him, but I was appalled at this childish discourse and his repetition of "This is a pair and this is a pair and I got on a pair."

I asked Charlie about the book beside him.

"It's a history. Oh, that's a history."

"Are you in there?"

"I guess so." He opened the book and held it upside down. He can neither read nor write. The book, filled with pictures, was *The West*, edited by David R. Philips. Philips wrote in the book, "For Charlie Smith with Best Wishes." Said Charlie: "The reason I show it to people or just tell 'em about it . . . the way they go off, they say, 'Oh, that's a damn lie. He ain't got nuthin' to show for it.' That's what they'll say. I don't have to buy these shoes. I don't have to buy nuthin' I got on. I got on a pair. And here's a pair. Here's two pair . . ."

I asked him if he knew why people came to see him.

"Oh, the people read about me. You hear my name before you ever seed me."

"That's right."

My concurring with him pleased him and for the first time he chuckled. "Well, you heared my name before you ever seed me. Not only you, everybody. Seed my name before they ever seed *me*." And then he was back to the shoes and how some people said it was a damn lie because they didn't believe that he possessed three pairs. "You tell 'em you seen 'em. There's a pair and . . ."

I persisted in asking him why he thought people came to see him.

"I don't know about that . . ." But he was pleased to return to the subject. He laughed with pleasure. And when he did, his eyes twinkled. The wrinkles from the corners of his eyes curved downward. His smiling mouth curved upward at the corners, so that his face seemed to be wreathed in an oval of creases. "People just read about me. They hear tell of me, and don't *believe* it. They say, 'I'll go see.' Well, they comes to see me. All my State shirts are in the cleaner. Sent 'em to the laundry to have 'em cleaned and pressed." He pinched his shirt between his fingers. "That my top shirt, what you call a State shirt. Ain't got 'em on now, they're in the laundry. All that's State clothes. Don't cost me nuthin'. Some folks say, 'Oh, he's a damn liar. I don't believe he got no damn show for it.' " He laughed again with pleasure. "That's the reason I show the people my clothes."

I asked what he had in his briefcase, and he produced an 8- by 10-inch color photograph of himself receiving a Citizen of the Age of Enlightenment award. He was wearing an elegant cowboy shirt for the ceremony, and he made sure I appreciated it.

Next he showed me a frayed, dog-eared *Ripley's Believe It or Not* cartoon dated 1955. There was a drawing of Charlie with the legend: "Oldest working man in the world. Auburndale, Florida. Still employed at the age of 113, has worked regularly for 100 years—submitted by Dr. Leo L. Spears, Denver, Colorado."

As I handed the cartoon back to him, he said, "That's the reason I show it. They say, 'He telling a lie. He ain't got nuthin' to show for it.' " Then he laughed with satisfaction. "That's the reason I show my shoes . . ."

"Charlie, everybody seems to like you." He laughed again, and now I knew I was right on target. I finally was getting through to him. "You know it?"

"What?"

The devil, he was forcing me to repeat it. "Everybody seems to like you."

"What?"

"You must be a nice fella."

"Well, I know how to *treat* people. And I know how I *want* to be treated. And I treat people like I want them to treat me."

Then he was back to those shoes again and asking me to tell the people about them so that nobody could say he was a damn liar. And now, for the first time, I deliberately looked at the shoes. Each pair was different, each pair in excellent condition. They were worth being proud of. And then I got it. I finally understood what he had been trying to tell me. "These are more shoes than you've ever had before, aren't they?"

His face lit up brightly at my understanding. After all his dogged efforts and all my baffling, frustrating obtuseness, he had finally gotten through to me! "Yeah! I got more than I had before. Yeah. And they ain't cost me nuthin'. Shirts the same way. Top shirts same way. You see they can put them in the laundry and have them cleaned up. You see, like that!"

What he had been trying to tell me all along was that after his long life of work and vicissitudes, here he was better off than ever. He enjoyed a pleasant environment where kindly people looked after him. All his needs, including a splendid wardrobe, were provided free —because he was such a noteworthy person that the United States itself took care of him. Indeed, the United States—through the Social Security Administration—did provide for his needs. In a hallway showcase devoted to Charlie Smith's memorabilia was a letter from the president of the United States congratulating Charlie on his 134th birthday, and messages from Florida's two United States senators praising him for the honorary high-school diploma he was awarded two months before his birthday.

Charlie had only one worry when it came to his role in society, I finally came to understand: He needed to be assured that people knew he was telling the truth. The shoes were tangible evidence of his word. But the deeper meaning and concern stemmed from the difficulty in proving his age to the doubters. A human being does not grow rings like a tree. Where was the birth certificate? That disbelief, of which he was aware, challenged his integrity, his identity, what he was and what he had done. He wanted me to spread the word that he was an honest man and was what he said he was.

I came to him imperiously. I was the college-graduate reporter, armed with electronic paraphernalia and information about what I intended to seek and extract from him. I called on him at my convenience, with no advance word, expecting him at once to oblige my wishes. When he failed to serve my purposes, I quickly concluded it was because of mental deficiencies. He was an institutionalized, illiterate, frail old man no longer able to sustain an independent social life. But he so dominated our meeting that at the end I was able to understand him on his terms. At the end, he had converted me into an agent for his purposes.

Whether or not Charlie Smith's true age ever will be verified, he was an authentic exemplar of life's most wonderful characteristic. He was indomitable.

John King

CHAPTER 16
Conclusion

As this investigation progressed it uncovered a surprisingly large number of conscious or unconscious strategies and characteristics, bewildering in their variety and unrelatedness: the various forms of order, hard work, trust in God and faith in church, the Golden Rule, pragmatism, quiet and circumscribed lives, no high ambitions, strong personal independence, taking care, midlife transition, balanced diet, devotion to family, content with lot, love of music and harmonious lives, sense of humor, wisdom as a sign of innate intelligence, no self-pity or regrets, absence of grief, noncombativeness and few heroics, enjoyment of work and life, and a strong will to live.

No single centenarian exhibited all these traits; nor did the traits appear in the group with equal strength. Some centenarians manifested many traits, some survived with few, and there were various combinations. Obviously, there were many routes to becoming a centenarian.

It was not until the final discoveries about enjoyment of work and strong will that a common denominator emerged. The catalyst for the discovery of the synthesis was Norman Cousins. The onetime editor of *Saturday Review* told in a television interview of his unorthodox battle against a rare disease that was causing the deterioration of connective tissue in his spine and elsewhere in his body. At the time, in 1964, the disease was believed to be irreversible and fatal. Taking responsibility for his own life—a trait observed in the health crises of several centenarians—and with confidence that he would be successful, Cousins went on a regimen of massive doses of vitamin C and laughter. He looked at Charles Chaplin movies and found that ten minutes of solid belly laughter gave him two hours of pain-free sleep. Physical tests showed that each dose of laughter slightly improved his body's ability to fight inflammation and that the improvements were cumulative. "I was greatly elated," he wrote after his experience, "by the discovery that there is a physiologic basis for the ancient theory that laughter is good medicine." While the laughter therapy got the popular attention, Cousins explained in the interview that "laughter was just a metaphor, a symbol for a number of other things that were being done, most of them having to do with the positive emotions: will to live, hope, faith, love, all the things that are involved in one's attitudes."

Cousins was talking about recovery from a single case of illness and not about longevity, but the parallel between his strategy and that of the centenarians was unmistakable. It was apparent to Cousins that stress was a factor in bringing on the disease; it appeared after a stressful trip to the Soviet Union. His defenses were down and he was vulnerable. He remembered reading in Hans Selye's *The Stress of Life* that negative emotions—fear, suppressed hate, rage, hate, exasperation, frustration—produce negative chemical changes in the body. "Well, it seemed to me that the body just didn't work one way, that if the emotions had an effect, they would have an effect on the upside as well as on the downside. And if negative emotions produce negative chemical changes in the body, it stood to reason that positive emotions would have to produce positive chemical changes."

I went back to read more by Selye (Appendix 17). I had included *The Stress of Life* among the research supporting the main studies used as the basis for the questionnaire. Selye's work has been given great attention in terms of health and illness, but not much consideration with regard to aging and longevity. He is not an authority of the field of gerontology. But this time I looked at the relevancy of stress theory to longevity. After all, a number of centenarians equated their longevity with their good health. Longevity is simply the product of continued good health.

Selye first published on the stress syndrome in 1936. He was working on a project attempting to find a third female sex hormone. Various extracts of cow ovaries were injected into female rats. Selye performed autopsies on the rats looking for some kind of change in their sex organs. Instead he found:

1. An enlargement of the adrenal glands, with signs of increased hormone-producing activity
2. Atrophy of the lymphatic system, including the thymus (which at

that time was not yet known to be an important organ in the immunologic defense system)
3. Peptic ulcers of the stomach and upper intestines, especially the duodenum

When other substances, including poisons, were injected into the rats, subsequent autopsies showed the same syndrome. Rats exposed to severely cold weather suffered in the same way. Selye began to wonder if there could be a common *nonspecific* cause of most diseases. Intolerable strain expressed itself in different ways in different individuals, with the breakdown appearing in the weakest bodily part. Selye had a simple analogy: When intolerable pressure is applied, a chain breaks at the weakest link.

This was a highly original approach to determining the cause of disease. At that time, medicine—buoyed by the breakthroughs that followed in the train of Pasteur and Robert Koch—was searching for specific causes of disease. Scientific minds were not receptive to stress theory, and many years were to pass before it would gain a medical acceptance that is far from complete today. But evidence in support of stress theory has been piling up in recent years as scientists have been learning more about how the mind and the nervous and endocrine systems work.

To Selye, biological stress "is the nonspecific response of the body to any demand." If we walk from a warm room to a cold room, an adjustment must be made. Such adjustments, or adaptations, are happening all the time. More stressful situations would be cutting a hand, getting the flu, finding a burglar in the house, and losing a job or beloved person. These require considerably more of what Selye calls *adaptation energy*, different, he says, from the usual metabolic energy.

Selye has called the stress reaction the *general adaptation syndrome* (GAS) and says it occurs in three phases:

1. Alarm. There is a dip in resistance, and if the challenge is strong enough, the result may be death.
2. Stage of resistance. If the challenge is of less than lethal strength and if it continues, bodily signs of the alarm reaction disappear and resistance rises above normal.
3. Stage of exhaustion. Prolonged exposure to the continuing challenge, to which the body has become adjusted, eventually exhausts adaptation energy. Signs of the alarm reaction return, but now they are irreversible and the individual dies. This stage can be avoided if the challenge is removed in time.

The three stages correspond to the stages of a person's life:

1. Childhood—low resistance and excessive responses to any kind of stimulus
2. Adult—adaptation to most common challenges; increased resistance
3. Old age—characterized by irreversible loss of adaptability and eventual exhaustion, ending in death

The body must adapt to any changed situation in order to continue functioning properly. This is accomplished through complex communications, primarily among the brain and the nervous and endocrine systems. Minor adjustments take place all the time below the level of consciousness. Some adjustments—removing a hand from a hot iron, for instance—occur faster than conscious deliberation. But let us take a potentially stressful situation germane to the discussion.

There is a clap of thunder. This is a stimulus. The cerebral cortex makes an evaluation of the event's meaning for the individual. One person, working in a large steel-and-concrete office building, hears the thunder but doesn't give it a second thought; he is indifferent to it. A farmer greets the noise with hope, joy, and thankfulness; the thunder signals to him a break in a drought and the possibility of saving his crops. To a third person, who has had a close call with lightning, the sound is a warning of the approach of extreme danger.

The importance as well as the variations of individual perceptions of stimuli make stress difficult to assess and quantify with scientific exactitude. In the hypothetical situation above, the third person's fear triggers the stress mechanism. The hypothalamus in the brain stimulates the sympathetic nervous system and sends chemical signals to the pituitary, and the master gland alerts the endocrine system by emitting hormones into the bloodstream. The main hormone in this case is ACTH, which notifies the outer parts of the adrenal glands to produce and send out steroid hormones, called corticoids by Selye (the best known is cortisone). The purpose of the corticoids is to tranquilize the tissues in order to block overreactions that might be harmful. The hypothalamus signals, via nerve pathways, the inner cores of the adrenal glands to inject epinephrine and norepinephrine into the bloodstream. These hormones help elevate the amount of energy available to the system, reinforcing the actions of the already turned-on sympathetic nervous system. The sympathetic system quickens the heartbeat and constricts visceral and peripheral blood vessels. This elevates blood pressure and diverts more blood to the muscles. At the same time, digestion is inhibited. The breathing rate increases and the bronchia to the lungs dilate, providing more oxygen, which is rushed to the muscles by the speeded-up blood flow. Increased perspiration cools the body heat generated by the accelerated metabolism. We readily recognize the hyped-up, tense feelings produced by these changes.

The body is now prepared for flight or fight, whichever course the brain may dictate. Of course, that decision may be influenced mainly by the emotional coloration assigned to the stressful challenge. Anger, rage, hatred, or desire for revenge would motivate one kind of action; fear, another kind. This bodily preparation is proper and necessary for emergencies. But when the stress is prolonged or constantly triggered, the chemistry is abnormal and harmful. Meyer Friedman, the pioneer investigator of Type A behavior, was quoted earlier as saying, "The sense of urgency and hostility give rise to irritation, impatience, aggravation and anger: the four components which I believe comprise the pathogenic core of the behavior pattern." Dr. Friedman goes on to ask: "What is the mechanism·by which this behavior pattern might effect eventual arterial damage, infarction or sudden death? We do not yet know. But the elevated serum corticotropin and norepinephrine level so often observed in these patients is strongly suspect. . . . I suspect that the metabolism of these hormones may be disturbed by dysfunction occurring in the limbic system and certain hypothalamic centers of the nervous system."

Different meditation techniques as well as the "relaxation response" (a term originated by Herbert Benson) deactivate the sympathetic nervous system, and an opposite set of bodily reactions takes place. Heartbeat is slowed, blood pressure is lowered, oxygen intake and metabolism are reduced, and a torporlike calmness spreads over the body. Some people practice these techniques for one or two brief periods during the day as an antidote to the stressful pressures of contemporary life. (Obviously, a person could function no more effectively if he spent his entire time in a torpor than if he were propelled by hyperactive energy.)

Dr. Selye has taken into account stress levels as a way of life for the long term. While there is no way to avoid stress, for it is the mechanism that keeps us adjusted to our life situations, we can regulate the level of stress expended. A person can be an underachiever and try to avoid all challenges. However, Selye states that those who are content to live a purely vegetable existence are exceptional. And so are the people, he says, who are willing to give all their time and energy in an attempt to achieve some extremely difficult goal. Most people fall somewhere in between: There are at least a limited number of things they want and are willing to strive for. Different people have different stress levels. One person may be happy at some passive activity while another may seek stress in the form of challenge or competition, even when playing. To the person aiming at a goal, leisure activities could be more stressful than his work. Once stress is understood, each person can be his own best physician, because he knows his needs better than anyone else. He must learn the stress levels at which he functions best and stay within those limits. This requires self-observation. Some people cannot recognize the boundaries until the danger signals appear—insomnia, irritability, indigestion, headaches, depression.

Just as there can be too much or too little stress, there are two kinds of stress: bad stress and good stress. Bad stress, or *dis*tress, is what we invariably mean when we use the word *stress*—coping with unpleasant and trying situations. This kind of stress is harmful. Good stress is beneficial, and while it is not a familiar term, we all recognize it in ourselves. It is the good feeling we get from doing activities we like, the satisfaction from a job well done, the pride and enjoyment of attaining a goal, the pleasure of being among friends and people who love us. Selye says the individual should strive for as much good stress as possible and try to avoid as much distress as possible.

The best way to avoid harmful stress is to select an environment— wife or husband, boss, friends—that meets one's preferences and to do work that the individual likes and respects. For many old people, the most difficult part of retirement is the feeling of being useless. "Man must work. I think we have to begin by realizing that work is a biological necessity." Most people believe they work for economic security or social status or a successful business career, only to find that when these are gained and there is nothing further to fight for, they become bored. The Western world is being pressed by insatiable demands for less work and more pay. Stress is associated with every kind of work, but distress is not. The question is what kind of work suits us best. An effective way to remove worry is to displace it with other thoughts. A person who undertakes some strenuous task that needs all his attention accomplishes this displacement. Unpleasant thoughts can be erased by conscious concentration on pleasant ones.

In seeking good stress and the avoidance of distress, we should know that biologically there are three—and only three—types of feelings or attitudes toward events:

1. Positive feelings can be described as love, in the broadest sense. Gratitude, respect, trust, admiration for the excellence of important

achievements—all of these amount to goodwill and friendship. Our security in society is best assured by arousing positive feelings toward us in as many people as possible. As far as science can determine, the ultimate aim in life is the maintenance and enjoyment of life itself.

2. Negative feelings include hatred, distrust, disdain, hostility, jealousy, and the urge for revenge: the very attitudes that endanger one's security by encouraging aggressiveness in other people who fear they will be harmed.

3. Feelings of indifference can lead at best to an attitude of tolerance, making peaceful coexistence possible, but nothing more.

Selye explains that these positive, negative, and indifferent attitudes are built into the very substance of living matter. They regulate adaptation on all levels of interaction—among cells, human beings, nations.

Selye does not believe it is possible to propose a code of behavior equally suitable for everyone. We are just too different. But in seeking the goodwill and friendship that help to promote individual survival, one of the wisest and most generally applicable behavioral laws is the Golden Rule and its variants. Selye does not believe that its extension to "love thy neighbor as thyself" can be carried out, because biologically we are not made that way. He advocates what he calls *altruistic egoism*. A person should do good things for other people with his own self-interest in mind—so that they will want to further his welfare by doing good things for him. Selye says that the principle behind altruistic egoism is "Be necessary."

THE CORRESPONDENCE between the traits, attitudes, and behaviors of the centenarians and the theory of stress is clear and persuasive. Such a finding was unexpected and unsought. No centenarian makes a reference to stress theory, nor is the word *stress* ever used. But a recapitulation shows that the achievement of the centenarians can be explained in terms of stress (and that this coincides with the findings of Flanders Dunbar, Appendix 7).

The centenarians held positive attitudes and emotions while extirpating negative ones—even to the point of appearing callous in relinquishing grief for a lifetime mate who died. "I don't think I ever lost my temper and got real wild like some folks, even when I was young," wrote Grandma Moses. "When I get angry, I just keep quiet and think 'Ishkabibble'—what the meaning of 'Ishkabibble' is I don't know—but it's quite a byword, something like 'the devil take you.'

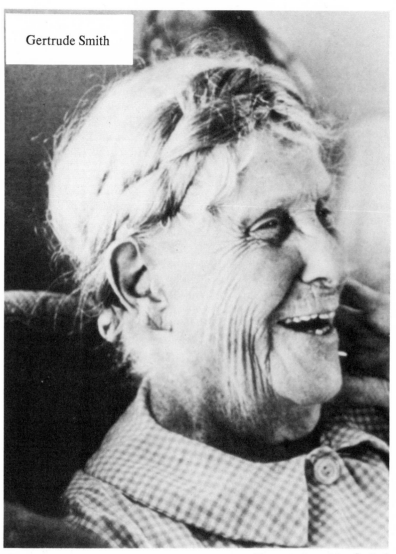

Gertrude Smith

Photo courtesy of Sun-Sentinel

If you lose your temper, you do something and say something which you wouldn't if you waited a few minutes. (But a flash of temper is sometimes better than to brood over things and feel revengeful, that kind of poisons your mind.)"

Mrs. Esther Gould intuited a direct connection between distressful emotions and truncated lifespan. Mrs. Gould "attributes her long life to temperance and remaining calm. She specifically stated that she is a strong believer that jealousy, anger, and other emotional upsets can shorten your life." Mrs. Sarah Runyan made the same connection once it was suggested to her. The social security interviewer states: "I asked Mrs. Runyan about her health, and she said she never has aches or pains and never grumbles. She couldn't think of any reason why she has lived so long; but when I suggested that it might be the fact that she never grumbles she said, 'Young man, that's it—I'm easy going, I don't let troubles bother me.'" And Mrs. Nan Mays's explanation for her long life is: "Never let it bother my mind —no way."

We have seen that a great many centenarians avoided strong emotions altogether. Excitement was not part of their low-key lifestyle. When Sarah Page was asked about the most exciting event of her life, she replied, "Of course, you probably mean something that stirs you up, but I don't let things stir me up." This corresponds to what Selye says is the function of the corticoid hormones on the cellular level: to avoid overreaction.

Stress theory makes visible one more—and probably the most important—benefit of work. Work, particularly hard work, and keeping busy, focus the mind, not only blocking out negative preoccupations but enforcing a discipline that combats mental entropy or disorderliness. As shown in items 41A and B of the questionnaire, *all* centenarians were associated for at least part of their lives with hard physical work or conscientious work, and the great majority of them for most of their lives. The method of meditation or of "relaxation response" is simply to concentrate on a single phrase, word, or number, blotting out all other thoughts. But anyone who has tried to do this knows how difficult it is, at least initially, to keep the mind from wandering over errant byways—particularly if one is involved with a pressing problem.

Some centenarians explicitly recognized this particular value of work. Henry Raines "is sure it helped [in living a long life] that he always found a job or a chore to do, and kept himself 'too busy to let any worries bog me down.'" Joseph Augustaukis said, "I think I have lived so long mainly because I have kept busy, and perhaps I just don't have time to think about getting sick." John Newhard, still working as manager of Greenwood Cemetery in Allentown, Pennsylvania, "pays attention to his work—'It keeps the mind and body active,' he said."

Independent work habits, working alone, being one's own boss bypass stressful frustration with superiors and inferiors in a business organization. An independent, self-reliant attitude safeguards one from Type A behavior, which is associated with destructive stress. Active physical work is less stressful (or not distressful at all) than sedentary work that requires body positions to be held for long periods of time. A positive attitude toward work produces good stress, whereas a negative attitude toward work produces bad stress.

The orderly life reduces stressful friction, the disorderly life increases it. Moderation can be defined as a course set between excessively high or low levels of stress. The chapter on profiles noted the variety of energy levels on which these centenarians lived: Some lived constricted lives, some led expansive ones. They all were behaving according to Selye's dictum: They were matching stress levels to what suited them as individuals. We have seen that they were sensitive monitors of their bodies and states of health.

The antimedical attitudes observed in more than a few centenarians can also be interpreted in terms of stress. Going to a hospital as a patient can be stressful in and of itself. Norman Cousins said he didn't think a hospital is a good place for a person who is sick and needs a lot of rest. "I knew I would have to find a place somewhat more conducive to a positive outlook on life," he said. He removed himself to a hotel room to carry out his successful therapy. Going to a physician for a checkup can carry its own burden of stress, conjuring fears and anxieties. David Oglesby explicitly made this point. "He said he feels good and does not need to have a doctor so he 'has no doctor to tell him he is not well.' " The centenarian physician Dr. Pannell expressed this philosophy when he said: "I haven't had the occasion to consult doctors. I don't feel the need— when you feel all right, you don't hunt for trouble." Dr. Selye said that when a person understands the nature of stress, he can be his own best physician.

Herman Lemmermann, who owned and ran a grocery store for thirty-seven years, shows how acutely attuned to stress some centenarians can be. Whereas most people see the automobile as a means of transportation, a status symbol, a vehicle for enjoying travel, Mr. Lemmermann regarded it as a stressor. "When asked the reason for his longevity, he replied, 'I've never driven a car. There's too much to worry about when you're driving—I let the other people worry.'

He added a wink at the end." Ten percent of the centenarians expressly said they followed a policy of not worrying, one of the most corrosive negative emotions.

At the same time we have seen that the centenarians embraced positive attitudes and emotions, enjoying their activities, being happy or content. "A good thought never hurt anyone," said Miss Page, the woman who never allowed herself to be stirred up. "Don't worry, be thankful, and give everyone a good thought. There's too much criticism today. I don't go into anyone's house to criticize. If it wasn't for the good thinkers of the world, today, we'd be in a fine fix. You know, you can't live without the good thought."

Jim Kilgore's daughter-in-law "stated she believes Mr. Kilgore has lived 100 years because he is so good. In the discussion she said, 'I've lived with him in this house for seventeen years and have never seen him angry or heard him say an unkind word.'" Mrs. Sarah Romeling "attributes her longevity to the love and kindness of friends and family. Her motto is 'If you will be a friend and be kind to others, they will be kind and a friend in return'—and this brings about contentment and long life." An explicit declaration of Selye's altruistic egoism. We have seen that many centenarians practiced the Golden Rule and many more recognized the vital importance of what Selye said is the core of altruistic egoism: to be useful or necessary to others.

Being thankful and delighting in song, humor, and laughter are among other positive attitudes and behaviors evident in a sizeable number of centenarians. Another prevalent characteristic is their ability to feel good about themselves; they feel comfortable with the record of their lives. This was expressed in a variety of ways. Fifty-seven centenarians attributed their longevity to their good behavior or doing right, another fifty-five to living a good, clean life. Other centenarians believed they had been able to live so long because they were good Christians, because of the Lord's blessing, because they served God, or because the Lord had rewarded them for their goodness. All together, these responses account for nearly one-quarter of the centenarians' attributions. In addition, there were those centenarians who said they accepted their lives as they had lived them and would change nothing.

This recognition of deserving to feel good about oneself as a requisite for long life is a point made dramatically by Flora Whisenand, even though she expressed it in a negative fashion. Mrs. Whisenand is the bedridden woman who, after deliberation and contrary opinions delivered by other women in her room, said she was a centenarian because "nothing has transpired in my life that I am ashamed of." Grant Gray acknowledged this same passport to continued existence. "He has no remaining ambitions except 'to do nothing wrong.'"

Albert Damcott came to this understanding in the most poignant episode recounted in the thirteen volumes of the SSA series. Mr. Damcott died just six days after his interview, so the story survives because of that sliver of survival in his long life. "When Albert Damcott was just past 5 years of age, his mother, who was on her deathbed, called her children about her and calmly explained what was about to happen. She also told them to follow the laws of God in their own life and they would have no regrets to consider when their time came.

"That was more than ninety-five years ago, and, to his present age, Mr. Damcott has tried to follow her directions—succeeding quite well, as can be noted from the summary of his life."

The strong inference is that guilt, remorse, and regrets are incompatible with long life. If these emotions cannot be assuaged, expiated, and excised, their punitive oppression is relentless to the point that life becomes insupportable. A person must live in accordance with his own code of conduct. This suggests that further investigation of the link between personal morality and longevity might be useful.

Studies being carried out at the Gerontology Research Center in Baltimore suggest an explanation—in terms of stress—for the value of the transition that centenarians make to quiet, routine lives after the first third or half of their lives. A National Institute on Aging publication states: "Medical scientists have known for a long time that hormones, circulating in the blood stream, send signs to body cells which call for certain functions, such as metabolism of fats or to help the body in adapting to stress. They have known too that these signals are received from the hormones by small receptors located either outside or inside the cells. The Baltimore researchers find that the receptors definitely change with age, decreasing in number in both humans and animals." The centenarians have tailored their lives as if they were aware of the body's declining ability to handle stress—and almost all of them escaped the diseases that characterize the transition from middle to old age.

This does not mean, however, that the centenarians have lost their adaptability. Late in life, more than 90 percent of them still exhibit the ability to accept change and to deal with loss. The mechanism and physiologic price for maintaining adaptability, the hallmark of living creatures, is stress.

The conclusion of this inquiry is that the secret of the centenarians' longevity is their ability to deal successfully with stress during a major part of their lifetimes. What science knows about stress today is the result of a massive amount of research. Each centenarian worked out his salvation alone, with only his intuition and native intelligence. "The few centenarians in our population today," said Flanders Dunbar, "have apparently achieved their longevity by something like a stroke of genius."

Charles Spaulding

Life Is Sweet When You Know How to Live It

The quality of sweetness is universal in the faces of babes. At this early age, the quality is associated with innocence. Infants do not yet know that they are not the centers of existence, that they some-day will have to earn their survival, that they will have to die; they have not yet lost a beloved person, or been betrayed, rejected, defied, tested, hit with all the other slings and arrows of experience.

The quality of sweetness fades with advancing years and is rarely seen in faces beyond childhood. The adult human face has other qualities that are recognized and admired. Foremost is beauty that blossoms to its fullest in young women and virile handsomeness in young men. But eventually these qualities, too, fade with the passage of time.

So in surveying photographs of these centenarians, it was astonishing to see the return of sweetness, and with that quality a unique kind of beauty. This sweetness shines not from the unlined, cream-soft, supple faces of babes, but from faces that are creased and mottled.

Wasn't Severo Santiago revealing the recondite knowledge surely won in the process of becoming a centenarian when he said, "Life is sweet when you know how to live it, otherwise it can be very bitter."

Tatzumbie
DuPea

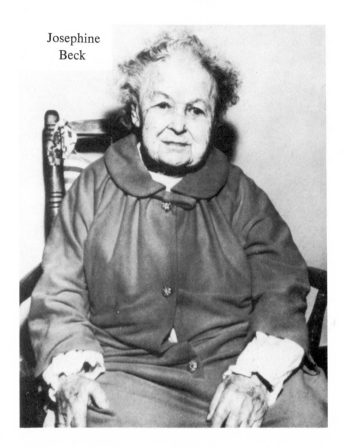
Josephine
Beck

Elizabeth
Barton

Rheem Wetzel

Alice Stamm

The Questions

APPENDIX 1

THE QUESTIONS SUGGESTED TO SOCIAL SECURITY FIELD REPRESENTATIVES FOR USE IN THEIR INTERVIEWS WITH CENTENARIANS

1. What is the earliest thing you remember?
2. What historical event stands out most in your mind?
3. Do you remember some of the presidents you have voted for in your lifetime?
4. Where were you born?
5. Did you ever serve in the army or navy?
6. What was the most exciting event in your own life?
7. What were your schooldays like?
8. What was your first job?
9. What kind of work did you do most of your life?
10. What kind of work did you do to earn your social security credits?
11. What were your reactions when you first heard about the social security program?
12. Did you think that you might someday get payments yourself under this program?
13. What do your social security checks mean in your life today? Are they the main part of your income?
14. Are you (were you ever) married?
15. Did you have any children? How many? Where are they now?
16. How many grandchildren and great-grandchildren do you have? Any great-great-grandchildren?
17. How is your health?
18. Why do you think that you have been able to live so long?
19. What do you do with your time?
20. Do you do any work or household chores?
21. Do you have any outside activities—church, hobbies?
22. Do you have any ambition you have not yet realized?

APPENDIX 2
AUTHOR'S QUESTIONNAIRE

I. GENERAL

1. Number:
2. Name:
3. Address:
4. Born:
5. Date of interview:
6. Age:
7. Died:
8. Final age:
9. Birth month:
10. Zodiac sign:
11. Sex: Male_____ female_____
12. Photograph:
    Smiling_____
    Smiling face_____
    Pensive, interested_____
    Unanimated_____
    Sour_____
13. Marital status:
    A. Married_____
       Widowed_____
       Single_____
       Divorced_____
       Separated_____
    B. How many times remarried_____
       Remarried at age(s):
    C. No data_____
14. Progeny:
    A. Number of children_____
    B. Number of grandchildren_____
    C. Number of great-grandchildren_____
    D. Number of great-great-grandchildren_____
    E. Number of great-great-great-grandchildren_____
15. Number of siblings:
16. Position among siblings:

17. Race:
      White_____
      Black_____
      Other_____
18. Height:
19. Weight:

II. SOCIAL SPHERE

20. Socioeconomic status:
    A. Wealthy_____
       Comfortable_____
       Independent, makes ends meet_____
       Poor_____
    B. No data_____
    C. Social Security only source of income_____
    D. No data_____
21. Education:
      None_____
      One year or less_____
      Less than 8 years_____
      Elementary_____
      High school_____
      Some college_____
      College degree_____
      Postgraduate_____
      Doctor's degree_____
      No data_____
22. Social status:
      Highly regarded/well known_____
        a. Respected because of age_____
        b. Respected because of past achievements_____
        c. Both_____
        d. Other_____
      Average_____
      Low status (low regard, shunned, disliked)_____
23. Work:
    A. Vocation:
    B. Still working_____
    C. Retired_____
        a. When:
        b. How long worked:
    D. Creative work_____
    E. Enjoyed work/took satisfaction_____
    F. No data_____

24. Relationships:
    A. Living with spouse_____
       Living with child_____
       Living with grandchild_____
       Living with others_____
       Living alone_____
       Nursing home_____
       Other_____
    B. Family important_____
    C. Happy marriage_____
    D. Fabric of friends_____
    E. Likes people_____
    F. Appears well-liked_____
    G. Sexual_____
    H. Isolated_____
    I. No data_____
25. Activities:
    A. Takes pleasure from daily activities_____
    B. Gainfully employed_____
    C. Church_____
    D. Other_____
    E. No data_____

Environmental

26. Life locale:
    Rural_____
    Small town_____
    Town_____
    Suburban_____
    Urban_____
27. Outdoors lover:
28. Workplace:
    Outdoors_____
      a. Farm_____
      b. Other_____
    Indoors_____
      a. Office_____
      b. Factory
      c. Store
      d. Shop_____
      e. Home_____
      f. Other_____
    Both_____

29. Work arrangement:
    Alone_____
    Own boss_____
    For others_____
    Small outfit_____
    Company_____

Hereditary

30. Influence of:
    A. Mother_____
    B. Father_____
    C. Siblings_____
31. Parents were hard workers:
32. Parents kept regular lives:

III. PSYCHOLOGICAL SPHERE

33. Attitudes:
    A. Happy with life, takes pleasure from daily activities_____
    B. Takes satisfaction from work_____
    C. Loves life_____
        Loves, likes people_____
        Joie de vivre_____
        Life has been exciting_____
    D. Wants to live, will to live_____
        Has something to live for_____
        Positive view of life, people, world_____
        Hopeful outlook_____
    E. No regrets_____
        Accomplished (all) (most) goals_____
        Feels fortunate_____
    F. Doesn't worry_____
        Everything in God's hands, trust in God_____
        At ease_____
        Sense of humor_____
    G. Lives one day at a time_____
    H. Looks to future_____
        Still has goals_____
    I. Expected long life_____
    J. Ambition to be 100_____
    K. High self-esteem, positive self-image_____
    L. Believes in Golden Rule_____
    M. Takes responsibility for life, health_____

265

N. Ethical_____
O. Religious_____
P. Reverent without narrow sectarianism_____
Q. Toward death
    Thinks about it constantly_____
    Never thinks about it_____
    Fears it_____
    Not afraid_____
R. Longevity a matter of luck_____
S. Bitter_____
T. Complaining_____
U. Anxious_____
V. Depressed_____
W. No data_____

34. Behavior/personality:
    A. Harmonious life_____
    B. Does what he likes, likes what he does_____
    C. Does no chores_____
    D. Escaped conflict with authority_____
    E. Doesn't hurry_____
    F. Maintains autonomy, independence_____
    G. Makes decisions about own life_____
    H. Has control of life, life well organized_____
    I. Daily activities well organized_____
    J. Honest_____
    K. Excels in something_____
    L. Does useful work_____
    M. Ability to accept change_____
    N. Ability to deal with loss_____
    O. Ability to vary schedule_____
    P. Ability to modify role_____
    Q. No data_____

35. Intelligence/mental status:
    A. Curiosity, interest in life_____
    B. Learning new things_____
    C. Creating new things
    D. Interest in politics, community, world_____
    E. IQ achievements_____
    F. High awareness_____
    G. Useful activities_____
    H. Orientation to himself, time, place_____
    I. Memory: good_____ poor_____
    J. Neurotic symptoms_____
    K. Senile_____
    L. No data_____

IV. BIOLOGICAL SPHERE

36. Physical:
    A. Still performs physical activities_____
    B. Exercises_____
    C. Looks younger_____
    D. Good personal care_____
    E. Erect posture_____
    F. Weight
        Obese_____
        Somewhat obese_____
        Average_____
        Lean_____
        Gaunt_____
    G. Young skin, few wrinkles_____
    H. Good muscle tone_____
    I. Hair:
    J. Vision very good_____
    K. Still has teeth_____
    L. Signs of strength_____
    M. Hearing excellent_____
    N. Works at job_____
    O. Sexual activity_____
    P. Disabilities
        a. Hearing_____
        b. Vision_____
        c. Arthritis_____
        d. Other_____
    Q. Uses cane_____
    R. Needs walker_____
    S. Wheelchair_____
    T. Bedridden_____
    U. Does not wear glasses_____
    V. No data_____

Health

37. Subjective evaluation:
    A. Excellent_____
        Good_____
        Fair, good for my age_____
        Poor_____
    B. Vitality/energy
        Strong_____

Moderate_____
Weak_____
C. No data_____
38. Objective evaluation:
   A. Good physical functioning_____
   B. Mobile_____
      With cane, walker_____
      Wheelchair_____
      Bedridden_____
   C. Vitality/energy:
   D. No data_____
39. History/profile:
   A. Disease
      a. At present:
      b. In middle age:
      c. In youth:
   B. Disability
      a. At present:
      b. In middle age:
      c. In youth:
   C. Eating habits
      Same as in past_____
      Changed from past_____
   D. Weight
      Same as in past_____
      Changed from past_____
   E. Reliance on health care
      a. Sees physician frequently_____
         occasionally_____ never_____
      b. In later years saw doctor frequently_____
         occasionally_____ never_____
      c. In middle years saw doctor frequently_____
         occasionally_____ never_____
      d. In hospital in past year_____ never_____
         In later years_____ never_____
         In middle years_____ never_____
      e. Never takes drugs/medicine_____
         Takes occasionally_____
         Regularly_____
      f. In later years never took drugs/medicine_____
         Took drugs/medicine_____
      g. In middle years never took drugs/medicine_____
         Took drugs/medicine_____
      h. In youth never took drugs/medicine_____

Took drugs/medicine_____
    i. No data_____
F. Sleep
    a. Hours of sleep_____
    b. Hours of sleep in later years_____
    c. Hours of sleep in middle years_____
G. Alcohol

	Present	Later Years	Middle Years	Youth
Never				
Infrequent				
Moderate				
Liberal				

	Present	Later Years	Middle Years	Youth

H. Smoking
    Never
    Occasionally
    Less than 1 pack
      daily
    1 pack daily
    2 or more packs
      daily
    Cigars
    Pipe

40. Diet:
    A. Three meals a day_____
    B. No special diet, eat everything_____
      Followed special diet
        a. No meat_____
        b. Vegetarian_____
        c. Moderation_____
        d. Ate carefully_____
        e. Other_____
    C. Watched calories, low calories_____
    D. No/low salt_____
    E. No/low sugar_____
    F. Coffee:
      Never_____
      Infrequently_____
      One cup a day_____
      Two cups a day_____
      Three or more_____
    G. No data_____

41. Habits:
    A. Hard physical work: still_____ until recently_____
       Most of life_____ in middle life_____ in youth_____
    B. Conscientious work: still_____ until recently_____
       Most of life_____ in middle life_____ in youth_____
    C. Keeps active_____
       Sedentary_____
    D. Exercises_____
    E. Arises early_____
       Arises late_____
    F. Goes to bed early_____
       Goes to bed late_____
    G. Alcohol
          Never_____
          Occasionally_____
          Daily_____
    H. Smoking
          Never_____ moderately_____ heavily_____
          Cigars_____
          Pipe_____
    I. No data_____
42. Mental/emotional:
    A. Healthy_____
    B. Neurotic traits
          a. Sleeplessness_____
          b. Nervous_____
          c. Anxious_____
          d. Depressed_____
          e. Other_____
    C. Sleeps well
    D. Memory: good_____ failing_____
    E. Senile_____
    F. No data_____

Genetic

43. Longevity runs in family:
    A. Mother's age:
    B. Father's age:
44. Sibling longevity:
                    Number

    Centenarian
    Over 90:
    80–90:

70–80:
Under 70:
45. Children's longevity:
    A. Number of children alive_____
       Over 80_____
       70–80_____
       60–70_____
       50–60_____
    B. Number of children dead_____
       Died over 80_____
       70–80_____
       60–70_____
       50–60_____
       Under 50_____
    C. No data_____
46. Stock:

V. ORDER/DISCIPLINE

47. Organization:
    A. Organized daily activities/routine_____
    B. Organized lifetime activities/goals_____
    C. Harmonious, integrated life_____
    D. Managing life in own house_____
    E. Three meals a day_____
    F. Followed disciplined regimen_____
    G. Realized all or most goals_____
    H. Still has goals_____
    I. Looks to future_____
    J. No data_____
48. Regularity:
    A. Still working_____ or regular routine of activities_____
    B. Regular social visits, meetings, recreation, etc._____
    C. Arises, retires same hour every day_____
    D. Three meals a day_____
    E. No data_____
49. Moderation:
    A. In eating_____
    B. Moderate weight_____
    C. Use of alcohol_____
    D. No smoking_____ or cigars_____ or pipe_____
    E. Use of coffee
    F. Drugs/medicine_____
    G. No data_____

50. Stability:
    A. Continuous place in family_____
       a. Still married_____
       b. Lives with child, grandchild_____
       c. Sees children_____
       d. Sees siblings, relatives_____
    B. Continuous place in community_____
    C. Continuity in work_____
    D. Continuity in interests_____
    E. Living in same house_____
                    town_____
                    area_____
    F. Traveled extensively_____
    G. Married very long time_____
    H. No data_____
51. Social:
    A. Strong family fabric_____
    B. Structure of friends_____
    C. Structure of neighbors_____
    D. Scheduled meetings, regular get-togethers, etc._____
    E. No data_____
52. Usefulness:
    A. Still gainfully employed_____
    B. Performs useful role(s)_____
       In home_____ for community_____
       for society_____
    C. Important to one other person_____ many people_____
    D. No data_____
53. Work:
    A. Worked hard_____
    B. Worked long time_____
    C. Has easy life now_____
    D. Had easy life_____

VI. FREEDOM/INDEPENDENCE

54. Physical:
    A. Still does physical work, exercises_____
    B. Takes walks_____
    C. Good physical functioning_____
    D. Still mobile_____
    E. Mobile with cane, aids_____
    F. Drives car_____
    G. Travels_____

H. Sexual activity_____
I. Freedom from disability_____
J. Freedom from disease_____
K. Freedom from health establishment_____
L. No data_____
55. Intellectual:
    A. Still creates_____
    B. Still learning_____
    C. Curious, interested in immediate world about
       him/her_____
    D. Solves puzzles_____
    E. Reads_____
    F. Attends meetings_____
    G. Watches TV_____
    H. Listens to radio_____
    I. No data_____
56. Psychological:
    A. Makes decisions_____
    B. Autonomous life—freedom from dependence (on medical,
       physician, nursing home, social services)_____
    C. Freedom from stress, anxiety_____
    D. Flexible, adaptive_____
    E. No data_____
    F. Attitude toward social security:
57. Personal life:
    A. Takes responsibility for life, health_____
    B. Manages own home_____
    C. Living in own place alone_____
    D. Living at home with spouse_____
    E. Living in home of relative_____
    F. Nursing home_____
    G. Sexual activity_____
    H. Freedom of choice_____
    I. No data
58. Economic:
    Wealthy_____
    Comfortable_____
    Independent, makes ends meet_____
    Poor_____
59. Work:
    A. Freedom of choice_____
    B. Still works at chosen vocation_____
    C. Works part-time
    D. Able to perform useful role(s)_____
    E. No data_____

60. Social:
    A. Freedom of choice_____
    B. Still meets new people_____
    C. Variety of friends_____
    D. Takes part in group activities, meetings_____
    E. Family_____
    F. Sexual activity_____
    G. No data_____

VII. INDIVIDUAL

61. Attributes longevity to:
62. Philosophy of life:
63. Present goals:
64. Crises in life:
65. Most difficult time:
66. Most vivid memory:
67. Other pertinent characteristics:
68. Idiosyncracies/differences from others:
69. Comments (quotations, anecdotes, Americana):

Summaries of Scientific Research upon Which the Questionnaire Is Based

APPENDIX 3
DUKE LONGITUDINAL STUDY OF AGING

Conducted from 1955–79 at Durham, North Carolina, the study included 268 volunteers, mostly middle class. The subjects were somewhat above average in socioeconomic status with a remaining life expectancy one year more than actuarial expectancy. Ages at time of first testing ranged from 60 to 94 years old with the median at 74 years. Sex, race, and occupational ratios matched the area. The state of health was not made a precondition for selection except that all subjects were ambulatory and noninstitutionalized.

The subjects were examined for 788 physical-psychological-social qualities. During two days, they were given a physical examination with laboratory tests, a psychological and psychiatric examination, and social history interviews. The factors tested for were 75 percent medical and social, 25 percent psychological and psychiatric/neurological.

The subjects were reexamined ten times, at four-year intervals in the beginning and one-year intervals toward the end.

Significant predictors of longevity:
Men:
1. Physical functioning
2. Work satisfaction
3. Employment (but a negative factor without no. 2)
4. No cigarettes
5. Secondary group contacts (churches, clubs, etc.)
Women:
1. Physical functioning
2. Happiness rating

Other significant but secondary predictors:
1. Intelligence—performance IQ (no. 1 for the eighty blacks in the study)
2. Self-health rating
3. Usefulness
4. Health activities
5. Non–group activities

6. Education
7. Prestige feelings
8. Leisure activities

The study found no correlation between the subjects' longevity and parental longevity.

NATIONAL INSTITUTE OF MENTAL HEALTH (NIMH) LONGITUDINAL STUDY

The study began in 1956 at NIMH in Bethesda, Maryland. The study was controlled for good health and all volunteer men were screened, but all completely healthy subjects could not be found. The researchers settled for twenty-seven healthy men free of any pathological symptoms and twenty men who were essentially healthy but who had mild asymptomatic abnormalities. The men ranged in age from 65 to 91 years with a median age of 71 years.

The subjects were measured for more than six hundred characteristics in four areas: medical and physiological, psychological, social-psychological, and psychiatric. The researchers said their aims and methods were close to the Duke study, that the two studies complement one another, "and where their findings are similar, their validity may merit much confidence."

The subjects were reexamined eleven years later. By this time, twenty-four men had died, twenty-three survived. The average age of the survivors was 81 years. In a comparison of the two groups' records, the survivors were found to be superior to the nonsurvivors in every category where there was a significant statistical difference. But two key items could, taken by themselves, correctly indicate the groups' members in 80 percent of the cases.

Significant indicators between survivors and nonsurvivors:
1. Organization of behavior (a social-psychological measure of the amount, planning, and complexity of daily activities)—survivors scored higher
2. Non–cigarette smoking—higher for survivors

Other indicators:
3. Mental status (psychiatry)—higher for survivors
4. Intelligence tests (psychology)—higher for survivors
5. Social involvement—higher for survivors
6. Adaptation (psychiatry—a measure of resourcefulness in meeting needs and of self-esteem)—higher for survivors
7. Environmental loss (social psychology)—less in survivors

In the follow-up study, survivors reported that their energy had decreased from the time of the previous examination.

APPENDIX 5
SOCIAL COMPETENCE OF CENTENARIANS

This is a study of one hundred centenarians by Dr. Belle Boone Beard, a sociologist recognized by gerontologists as the authority in the United States on centenarians. The research was published by the University of Georgia at Athens, in 1967.

Findings:
1. The centenarian "shows exceptional ability to make social adjustments."

   This major finding was based on the Activities and Attitudes Inventory worked out by Cavan et al. in 1949, and Burgess, 1954, and given to 2,924 people in the fifth and ninth decades of life. Beard found that the centenarian scores were higher than what would have been expected in a logically extrapolated downward curve with age. Cavan's adjustment shows successful changes in behavior in reaction to changes in the social situation. The person restructures his attitudes and behavior in such a way as to integrate his aspirations and the demands of society.
2. Centenarians have knit their lives into a harmonious pattern. They seem to have learned how to eliminate loose ends to create what could be called an integrated life pattern that is characterized by lack of conflict.
3. The centenarian is characterized by an absence of frustration.
4. The centenarian seems able to resolve problems and make adjustments without worry—a learned reaction to life experiences. When asked the secret of longevity, the most frequent answer is "I don't worry."
5. The centenarian is average in most things, habits, traits, and abilities "but usually excels in one or two traits which bring him recognition and prestige." The centenarian is a normal person who remains himself.
6. The centenarian is characterized by the absence of neurotic traits and by the persistence of normal behavior patterns and wholesome activities.

ALL CENTENARIANS tested showed some capabilities for self-maintenance, social competence, psychological competence, and for flexibility, adaptability, and creativity.

Work:

Gainfully employed: 20. This included 10 women who made pin money from knitting. Six were employed full-time: 2 farmers, 2 insurance directors, 1 lawyer, 1 cosmetics manufacturer.

Health:

Excellent	17
Good	39
Fair	35
Poor	6
Very poor	3

No days in bed last year: 46. A few days in bed last year: 27.

Nervous or neurotic symptoms (sleeplessness, bad dreams, feeling blue, tiring too easily, etc.):

None	33
One	29
As many as four	11

Marital status:

Married	9
Widowed	81
Single	7
Separated	2
Divorced	1

APPENDIX 6

LONGEVITY AND THE LONGEVITY SYNDROME

A personal study of seventy-nine individuals, most within the ages of 87 to 103 years, by Stephen P. Jewett, M.D., a former professor of psychiatry at New York Medical College and Chief Consultant and member of the board of trustees of High Point Hospital. His findings were published in *The Gerontologist*, a journal of the Gerontological Society, in spring 1973. Jewett was interested in observing characteristics common to longevous people.

Findings (not necessarily in order of importance):
  • The healthy aged are rarely seen in physicians' offices, never in nursing homes, seldom in homes for the aged.
  • Facts appear to indicate that individuals who escape catastrophic diseases of mid-life and the diseases of senescence are likely to have an excellent chance of living out a good part of their potential life-spans.
  • Physical characteristics:

> Average height, male: 5′ 7½″
> Average height, female: 5′ 2″
> Overweight or underweight: None
> Little variance in weight during lifetime
> Good general muscle tone
> Skin looks younger
> Good grip
> Still drives car and engages in physical activities

  • Superior native intelligence, keen interest in current events, intellectual interests, good memory.
  • Freedom from anxiety. Few illnesses. Never prone to worry.
  • Independence of choice in their vocations: They tended to be their own bosses, had more freedom than the organization man, retirement at 65 was not forced on them. They worked at farming and in the nursery business, and at the professions of law, medicine, and architecture; they headed small businesses of their own, and in a few cases, large businesses. The majority did not retire early.
  • They were in their fifties and sixties when the Depression hit, so that many of them had to start again and build for their futures.

- They had a capacity to enjoy life. All had a degree of optimism and an unusual sense of humor. They responded to simple pleasures available. Life seems to have been a great adventure. They could see beauty where others saw only ugliness.
- Great adaptability. While many cherished childhood memories, none wished to return to them. All preferred living in the present with its many changes.
- They were not preoccupied with death.
- They continued living with satisfaction from day to day.
- All may be described as being religious in the broad sense, but none exhibited religiosity or extreme orthodoxy.
- They were moderate eaters but willing to experiment. No special diets. Diets included a wide variety of foods high in protein, low in fats.
- All were early risers. Average period of sleep was between six and seven hours, although they rested for eight hours.
- Drinking: no uniformity. Some drank moderately, some drank too much at times, some abstained.
- Smoking. Some abstained, a few had smoked very moderately but had long since given it up, a few were inveterate pipe smokers.
- Medication. Less medicine used in their lifetime than many people use in a week.
- Most drank coffee.

Jewett acknowledges an indebtedness to Flanders Dunbar for the similarity in a number of their observations and for the term *longevity syndrome.*

IMMUNITY TO THE AFFLICTIONS OF OLD AGE

This address was delivered by Flanders Dunbar, M.D., Med.Sc.D., Ph.D., to the American Geriatrics Society, May 3–4, 1956, and later published in the society's journal in December 1957. Dr. Dunbar served as Director of Psychosomatic Research at the Columbia University College of Physicians and Surgeons and at Presbyterian Hospital, from 1932 to 1949, and was editor emeritus of *Psychosomatic Medicine*. She emphasizes a number of points in preparation for her main thesis:

• People who survive the dangerous decade—60 to 70—without getting geriatric disease are likely to be long lived.

• It is much easier to study sick people and what makes them sick than well people and what keeps them well. The exceptionally healthy people are hard to find in a hospital and they rarely consult a physician.

• There are two periods during the growth process when psychosomatic changes are accompanied by unusual stress: adolescence and middle age. The adolescent is concerned with finding, the middle-ager with losing, himself or herself vocationally and sexually.

• The term *homeostasis*, introduced by Walter Cannon in 1929, describes the capacity of the living organism to maintain a stable equilibrium.

• Stress, as defined by Hans Selye, is a nonspecific deviation from the normal resting state; it is caused by function or damage and it stimulates repair.

• About all that is known of coronary disease and hypertension is that they have something to do with body chemistry, autonomic balance, and patterns of response to stress.

• Those in the dangerous age and approaching retirement must face the mass conviction that for them life is over and from now on they are of no particular use. Feeling helpless and unwanted of themselves increase susceptibility to illness and injury.

Personality and stress:

A study of centenarians and "nimble nonagenarians" reveals "what appears to be one healthy pattern of reacting to stress and so maintaining homeostasis in senescence." "The indications are that they have avoided some types of stress whenever possible, but that they have actually sought out others."

Characteristics of the centenarian-nonagenarian pattern:

1. Centenarians and nonagenarians have shown ingenuity in avoiding frustration.

    A. They have escaped conflict with authority—some by seeking vocations where they are their own bosses. Also, they don't want to boss others. They prefer small businesses to large corporations. If they are professionals and artists, they have their own offices or research projects or they associate with groups that have much in common.

    B. They value independence and try to apply principles of democracy as a basis for cooperative and productive living. When this is impossible, they are likely to start anew, unembarrassed by any sense of failure.

2. They have worked long hours and hard, but usually managed not to punch a time clock.
3. They are rarely interested in getting to the top.
4. They like people and appear to be well liked. They are sociable, have a sense of humor, and are disinclined to argue.
5. They are good fighters about major issues but are not combative about little annoyances and disagreements.
6. They do not worry about things beyond their control.
7. Although they do not always sleep long, they sleep soundly.
8. They are extraordinarily active.
9. They are rarely overweight.
10. They avoid acute illness almost completely.
11. They are honest; thus they can be honest with themselves.
12. They have been able to handle catastrophe in stride.
13. While most of them have experienced emotional shock, a history of physical injury is rare.
14. They are rarely in a hurry.
15. They remarry very late in life. The divorce rate is low. (Ninety-eight percent had been married, 30 percent more than once.)
16. They contrive to transform marriage from a stress situation to a healthy state of living.
17. The last stress situation—death—does not seem to trouble them. They assume living to be natural and often are annoyed by questions about their longevity.

Other noteworthy traits:

1. They are religious but avoid the extreme of orthodoxy.
2. They are disciplined, but
3. They are more interested in being creative than being perfect.

4. They are interested in the development of new ideas.
5. They are never at a loss about what to do with their leisure time.
6. They increase their ability to develop new projects, are more interested in the new than afraid of it.
7. They keep their lines of communication open. "They combat entropy by remaining curious."

Prognostic signs of potential centenarians:
1. Unlike most older people, the precentenarian responds creatively to change. Perhaps this more than anything else makes her or him seem like a different kind of person.
2. Freedom from anxiety. Anxiety inhibits a person's ability to improvise and create.
3. The continued ability to create and invent.
4. Adaptive ability. High level of adaptive energy.
5. Integrative capacity.
6. He or she wants to stay alive.

APPENDIX 8

THE BALTIMORE LONGITUDINAL STUDY OF AGING

This study began in 1958 and is now following a population of 650 men and 150 women, all volunteers, ranging in age from 20 to 103 years. The Baltimore study basically tries to look at the effects of aging on different organs and their related structures—to delineate the physiological, psychological, and pathological changes that occur in normal aging. Subjects under 70 undergo two and a half days of tests every second year, those 70 or over are tested every year. The study has yielded a great amount of literature on the declines that accompany aging.

Major recent findings:
1. Variation among individuals increases with age, and in the 80- and 90-year-old groups, says Dr. Nathan Shock, is "just tremendous."
2. While performance always declines with age when measured as a group average, such a standard decline does not necessarily apply to all individuals in all areas. The Baltimore study has documented the absence of decline in kidney function and problem-solving ability. About a dozen people actually have shown improvement in kidney function. The maintenance of problem-solving ability occurs in people who do that as a way of life—an example of the dictum that you must exercise the franchise in order to keep it. Some subjects also show little decline in lung function while others show no decline in learning and memory.
3. The most complex organs, such as muscles, are the first to diminish.
4. The main reason for reduced work capacity is loss of muscle tissue.
5. The study has not been able to show that mild and moderate obesity in middle-aged and older groups shortens life span. Dr. Reubin Andres has presented evidence from seventeen population studies showing that mortality is lower among the elderly who are mildly or moderately overweight.
6. A Baltimore study of 188 males aged 60 to 79 showed that the most active sexually had been so throughout their lives. Sexual

events during the previous year for the least active group averaged 3.8; for the moderately active group, 20; for the most active group, 62.3. Most subjects rated their current marital situation as highly successful and considered regular sexual activity important for good health.

7. Men in their sixties were as efficient as men in their twenties in measurements of light to moderate exercise, but the older men had to use a higher percentage of their total capacities.

8. Alcohol is metabolized as efficiently in the aged as in young adults, but at the same blood levels older men have greater declines in intellectual functions (such as decision making, memory, and reaction time).

9. Heavy smoking is related to reduced lung function. Average test results for a heavy smoker are similar to those for a nonsmoker who is ten years older. When smoking is stopped, function returns to near normal in eighteen to twenty-four months.

10. High levels of cholesterol in the blood peak at about age 55.

11. Sugar tolerance diminishes with age, but that does not mean the oldtimer is diabetic.

APPENDICES, SECTION III
Supporting Research

APPENDIX 9

ALEXANDER LEAF

Alexander Leaf, M.D., Jackson Professor of Clinical Medicine at Harvard Medical School and Chief of Medical Services at Massachusetts General Hospital in Boston, investigated three populations with reputations for extreme longevity: the isolated village of Vilcabamba in the Andes Mountains in Ecuador; the province of Hunza in the Karakoram Mountains bordering on Afghanistan and China, and controlled by Pakistan; and the district of Abkhasia in the Caucasus Mountains of the Soviet Union.

Dr. Leaf's findings are from "Unusual Longevity: The Common Denominators," in *Hospital Practice*, October 1973.

Heredity:
1. Studies show that long-lived parents confer a significant but modest advantage. Could the entire advantage be mental—the parent serving as a model for longevity; the child confident that he also will be long lived because of his genetic inheritance?
2. There seems to be genetic purity in the Andes and Hunza people, but not in the Caucasus.
3. In the Caucasus, people expect to live to be 100.

Diet:
1. Vilcabamba: Calories—1200 daily
   Protein—35–38 grams, only 12 from animal
   Fat—12–19 grams
   Carbohydrates—200–250 grams
2. Hunzas: Calories—1923 daily
   Protein—50 grams, less than 1% from animal
   Fat—35 grams
   Carbohydrates—354 grams
3. Caucasus is different, a mixed agricultural/dairy economy. The Abkhasians eat animal products almost daily. They drink milk and eat cheese and yogurt three times a day. Leaf saw more than one fat centenarian.
   Calories—1800 daily
   Fat—60 grams
4. United States: Calories—2400 recommended daily
   Fat—120 grams

Physical activity:
1. Andes elevation—4500 feet
   Hunzas elevation—3500–7000 feet
   Caucasus elevation—3000–5000 feet
2. Key factor: "the incredible amount of physical exertion necessary just to attend to the daily business of living." Cardiovascular fitness results from a continuously high level of physical activity.
3. Given the choice, people will exert themselves minimally.

Psychological:
1. Leaf is now convinced that this area is very important to exceptional longevity.
2. Social status is positively age-dependent in the three locations: the older the age, the more prestige.
3. There is no retirement in agrarian societies. Aged people take part in work and social life.
4. The aged people have a sense of usefulness and purpose.

Habits:
1. Moderation.
2. Drinking: Centenarians in the three locales attribute their longevity to local alcoholic beverages. Drinking is a part of their way of life and they drink freely. But Leaf saw no drunkenness.
3. Sex: Libidinous attitude toward the opposite sex persists, but there are strong taboos against sex outside marriage. After death of spouse, remarriage occurs at an advanced age.
4. Marriage is the rule for the longevous.

APPENDIX 10
THE WILL TO LIVE

Arnold A. Hutschnecker, M.D., the author of *The Will to Live* (Englewood Cliffs, N.J.: Prentice-Hall, rev. ed. 1966), is a psychotherapist and pioneer in psychosomatic medicine. He makes the following observations:

• "Health is a state of balance maintained by perpetual adjustments to forces from within and without."

• Anxiety is a sign that the will to live is under attack; depression indicates a partial surrender to death.

• In a medical and psychological sense, life is always a matter of loss and replenishment of energy.

• "I believe we die only when we are ready to die, when we want to die." If we truly want to live and have something to live for, we do not die.

• The biological will to live is not enough to carry us through the complexities of our modern civilization. "The will to live in civilized man is a combined biological and psychological drive."

• Through the years, each human being strives toward some goal, whether explicit or not so clear. He continues until he achieves this aspiration or until he believes he has come to the point that he can never reach it and life loses its meaning. It is after the loss of goals that a person dies.

• People who die young and prematurely might be found to be those who set unrealistic, unobtainable goals. However, many people live contentedly with very little (by the world's standards).

• "To conform to others' standards is to surrender one's identity, and to resign oneself to the will of others is to surrender one's own will."

• Emotional health is our first line of defense. If we are emotionally sound, we will be physically well, for body and mind are one.

• Aging occurs according to events and our feelings toward them. One person suffers a reverse and ages overnight while another individual struggles to overcome adversity and goes on.

• Stress is the effect of external and/or internal disturbance on the body. Protracted stress doesn't give the body a chance to regenerate. Energy is constantly expended, organs relentlessly used—as in a state of mobilization. Stress sustains tension and burns up energy. It follows that we must learn ways to relieve tension, and to conserve and replenish energy.

293

• There is only one true adjustment for a human being. It lies in the choice between fight—an active adjustment to the situation—or flight—removing oneself from an unhealthy situation.

• "We keep our bodies young, not by putting intermittent violent strain on them, but by using them habitually in enjoyable physical activity." While muscles that are used can be preserved late in life before they deteriorate, the used mind need not age at all.

APPENDIX 11

THE STRESS OF LIFE

Hans Selye, M.D., Ph.D., D.Sc., first published about the stress syndrome in 1936. *The Stress of Life* (New York: McGraw-Hill, 1956) presented the findings of his research, his theory of the stress concept, and his philosophy for living successfully:

• Stress "is essentially the *wear and tear* in the body caused by life at any one time." Stress is caused by whatever we do and whatever is done to us; it is associated with all biological activities.

• The pituitary gland is a better judge of stress than the intellect is.

• More people are slaves of their stressful activities than of alcohol.

• Textbooks of psychosomatic medicine amply describe cases of gastric ulcers, hypertension, arthritis, and many other diseases caused by chronic worry. An effective way to remove worry is to displace it with other thoughts. A person who undertakes some strenuous task that needs all his attention accomplishes this displacement. Unpleasant thoughts can be erased by conscious concentration on pleasant ones.

• "Nature likes variety." It is important to remember this in planning one's life, particularly because our civilization tends to force people to do specialized tasks that become repetitive and monotonous.

• Aging is determined by the total amount of wear and tear to which the body has been subjected. When defined in this way, one can see the close relationship between stress and aging. We continually go through periods of stress and rest; just a little deficit of adaptation energy daily adds up and matters because each person only has the finite amount of adaptation energy he inherited.

• The human life span could be greatly lengthened by living in better harmony with natural laws. Selye does not believe that anyone has yet died from old age.

• Selye believes that of all the emotions, the feeling of gratitude is best suited for eliminating stress and that its negative counterpart, the need for revenge, is the emotion most calculated to produce stress. Awakening gratitude in another is perhaps the best way for assuring one's security, which Selye equates with homeostasis. The feeling of gratitude induces another person to want one's own well-being.

SUCCESSFUL AGING

Gerontologists, accustomed to concentrating on the problems of aging, held a conference at Duke University, June 7–9, 1973, devoted to aspects of aging successfully. These are the reports of four investigators associated with long-term studies.

Bernice Neugarten, Ph.D., professor, chairman of the Committee on Human Development, University of Chicago: There are many perspectives one could select in order to define a successful ager. Researchers at the University of Chicago have used the perspective of the individual himself and have constructed a measure of life-satisfaction based on five components:

1. The person takes pleasure from daily activities,
2. Regards his life as meaningful,
3. Feels he has achieved his major goals,
4. Holds a positive self-image and regards himself as worthwhile, and
5. Is optimistic.

These people tend to say the present is the best time of their lives. They hold high expectations.

George E. Vaillant, M.D., associate professor of psychiatry, Harvard Medical School, and Caroline O. Vaillant, M.S., social work: Mental health correlates with successful aging. The best-adapted people are characterized by:

1. More stable family life,
2. Regard their marriages as satisfying,
3. Rarely live alone,
4. Continue to grow in their careers,
5. Have no disabling mental illness,
6. No disabling alcoholism, and
7. Have less chronic illness.

Eric Pfeiffer, M.D., professor of psychiatry, project director of the Older Americans Resources and Services Program, Duke University: Successful agers are people who have decided to "stay in training" in three major areas of human functioning:

1. Physical activity,
2. Psychological and intellectual activities,

3. Their social relationships.
   Also:
4. They exhibit a pattern of active mastery of their lives, which maintains the quality of their lives and makes their old age enjoyable.

APPENDIX 13

A STUDY OF LONGEVOUS ELITE

Eric Pfeiffer, M.D., compared twenty males and seventeen females who were considered the most successful agers in the Duke Longitudinal Study with twenty men and seventeen women who were the first to die. "The present study seeks to discover physical, psychological, and social factors which differentiate short-term from long-term survivors among elderly persons *living in the community*. Simultaneously, this study becomes a comparison between elite and nonelite groups of aged individuals."

The study, published in the *Journal of the American Geriatrics Society* (8:4:273–85, 1970), used subjects all in their late sixties. The short-lived men survived an average of 2.42 years, the long-lived men had a life expectancy of 17.22 (the 10 years they had lived since the start of the Duke study plus their expected remaining years based on actuarial tables). The short-lived women survived an average of 5.5 years, the long-lived women had a life expectancy of 19.3 years.

The significant factors explaining the variance of the two groups, in the order of importance:

Men:
1. Financial status—70 percent of the long-lived men said they were comfortable; 80 percent of the short-lived men rated themselves poor.
2. Self-perception of health change—75 percent of the long-livers said their health was the same as or better than it was at age 55; 80 percent of the short-livers said their health was worse.
3. Physical functioning rating—63 percent of the long-livers had no pathology to mild disability; 60 percent of the short-livers had 20 percent to total disability.
4. Change in financial status—70 percent of the long-livers said their financial status was the same as or better than at age 55; 60 percent of the short-livers said it was worse than at age 55.
5. Marital status—95 percent of the long-livers were married, compared to 75 percent of the short-livers.

Women:
1. IQ—the long-lived women scored about 50 percent higher than the short-livers.

2. Self-perception of health change—47 percent of the long-livers said their health was better than it was at age 55; 53 percent of the short-livers saw their health as worse.
3. Marital status—71 percent of the long-livers were married; 71 percent of the short-livers were not married.
4. Physical functioning rating.
5. Change in financial status.

Pfeiffer concludes from the study that no single factor determines longevity "but rather a constellation of biological, psychological, and social factors, amounting to what may best be described as *elite status*." These elite are people with:

1. High intelligence,
2. Sound financial status,
3. Well-maintained health, and
4. Intact marriages.

APPENDIX 14

DUKE–CHAPEL HILL STUDY OF AGING

In 1958, Virginia Stone, Ph.D., interviewed more than nine hundred people older than 60 years in Chapel Hill and Carboro, North Carolina—virtually the entire aged population of the two sites. In 1971, Dr. Stone and Erdman B. Palmore, Ph.D., the director of the major Duke longitudinal study at Durham, made a follow-up study (reported in the *Gerontologist*, spring 1973: "Predictors of Longevity: A Follow-Up of the Aged in Chapel Hill"). They investigated 864 of the original group—388 were still living, 476 had died. In order of importance, the significant predictors of longevity were found to be:

1. Physical mobility—the unimpaired did best, those who had difficulty walking were in the middle, those in a wheelchair or bedbound were the poorest survivors.
2. Education—longevity corresponded positively with amount of education at every gradation.
3. Occupation—professors lived well beyond normal life expectancy and other white collar workers only slightly longer; blue collar workers slightly less, followed by housewives, with farmers faring the most poorly.
4. Employment—the employed fared best, housewives lived to the normal life expectancy, retired people somewhat under the normal expectancy.

Education and occupation together were more significant than the single health-measure of mobility. They are both considered indicators of the underlying dimensions of mental ability and socioeconomic status, factors that reinforce one another. Superior mental ability probably increases longevity directly by permitting better problem solving and adaptation to crisis and strain, and indirectly through effects on education and occupation. Higher-status occupations provide healthier and safer working conditions and more income for health care, nutrition, and housing.

APPENDIX 15
EXERCISE, HDL, AND HEART DISEASE

On November 28, 1977, Dr. Ralph S. Paffenbarger, Jr., professor of epidemiology at the Stanford University School of Medicine, reported to a meeting of the American Heart Association that a study of nearly seventeen thousand Harvard alumni found there were fewer heart attacks among men who engaged regularly in strenuous sports activities than among those who were less active.

Questionnaires were sent in 1962 and 1966 to more than thirty-six thousand alumni who had entered Harvard from 1916 through 1950. In 1972, follow-up questionnaires were sent to the 16,936 men who had returned the previous forms and who had said that as far as they knew they were free of any heart disease. Their ages ranged from 35 to 75 years. Among other things, the subjects were asked the daily amount of their walking, stair climbing, light sports play, and strenuous sports activities (such as jogging, swimming, tennis, and mountain climbing).

During the six- to ten-year interval, there had been 572 heart attacks. A steady decline in the incidence of heart attacks corresponded to the graduated increase of calories expended weekly in physical exercise—up to 2,000. After that, the protection against risk of heart attack did not improve, and actually showed a slight decrease with higher weekly expenditures of energy. Those men who expended less than 2,000 calories a week in physical exercise had a 64 percent greater chance of having a heart attack than the more energetic ones. The risk for the totally inactive subjects was about twice as great.

The protection against heart attack was provided no matter how the calories were expended—by walking as well as by jogging. Simple physical activity of any kind was beneficial. However, Dr. Paffenbarger found that at each level of caloric expenditure, the more strenuous physical activity provided greater protection than the more casual kind.

The study found that the protection given by physical activity was largely independent of other coronary risk factors, such as high blood pressure, cigarette smoking, obesity, and a family history of heart disease. The study also found against the argument that those people who are able to exercise strenuously are more fit to start with. Alumni who were varsity athletes were not protected against heart disease in their later years unless they continued to exercise, whereas non-athletes in college ran reduced risks of heart attacks when they were physically active later.

These findings were consistent with those of another study in which Dr. Paffenbarger was involved, but which did not receive as much attention as the Harvard study. Dr. Paffenbarger, Dr. Wayne E. Hale, Dr. Richard J. Brand, and Dr. Robert T. Hyde reported in the March 1977 *American Journal of Epidemiology* that a study of 3,686 San Francisco longshoremen showed that a regular pattern of hard physical work sharply reduces the risk of dying from heart attacks.

Using death records and work patterns collected over a twenty-two-year period, 1951 through 1972, the researchers found a correlation between the amount of energy expended and the numbers of heart attacks. The longshoremen were divided into three groups according to the energy required to do their work. The high-energy jobs required about 1,900 calories for an eight-hour workday. Low-energy jobs, comparable to office work, had only about half the caloric demands. The remainder were put into an intermediate category.

Three hundred ninety-five of the dockworkers died from heart attacks—49 of them in the hardest-working group, 71 in the intermediate group, 275 in the light-work group. Dr. Paffenbarger said it was not known if the high-energy output had led to a decreased risk of fatal heart attack or whether sedentary habits had led to an increased risk. A lack of hard physical work was found to be a risk factor equal to cigarette smoking or high blood pressure.

These were the first American studies showing a relationship between the incidence of heart disease and strenuous physical activity or inactivity. One earlier study among civil service workers in Great Britain revealed a lower rate of death from heart disease for those who either in their work or leisure-time exercise regularly expended more than 7½ calories a minute, the rate of expenditure for jogging 5 miles an hour, cycling 12 miles an hour, or downhill skiing.

Concomitantly, beginning in about 1975 and then rapidly gaining attention toward the very end of the decade, other research found an association between high-density lipoproteins (HDLs) and protection against heart disease, and also between HDLs and strenuous physical activity.

As early as 1951, David Barr at Cornell University Medical College found low concentrations of HDL in men with coronary heart disease. While Barr's findings were confirmed by other investigators, most clinicians focused on high concentration of total blood cholesterol as the culprit. Several studies had linked total cholesterol or low-density lipoproteins (LDLs), the major cholesterol carrier, to heightened risk of heart disease.

HDL was neglected until two researchers in Britain, Norman Miller and George Miller, reported an inverse relationship between HDL and total body cholesterol. Their explanation was that HDL might hold down the total amount of cholesterol in the body by taking part in its elimination. This suggestion was tested in five ongoing epidemiological studies, and confirmed. Furthermore, the studies found—once again—the same inverse correlation of HDL to atherosclerosis: the lower the HDL level, the higher the risk of heart attack. And this danger existed independently from other known risk factors, including high levels of LDLs.

At about this time, Peter Wood of the Stanford University Heart Disease Prevention Center was comparing the blood lipoproteins of forty-five male runners between the ages of 35 and 59 with sedentary men in the same age group. HDL concentrations in the inactive men averaged 45 milligrams per deciliter of blood, whereas men who ran at least 15 miles a week averaged 65 milligrams per deciliter. A later study by G. Harley Hartung et al. showed a very close relationship between HDL levels and distance run per week. Fifty-nine healthy, middle-aged marathon runners who averaged 40 miles a week had 65 milligrams of HDL per deciliter; eighty-five joggers who averaged 11 miles a week had HDL concentrations of 58 milligrams; seventy-four inactive men 43 milligrams.

These investigators took a close look at the food intake of the subjects and concluded: "Our data suggest it is primarily the jogging and running, rather than diet, that elevate HDL. . . ." The researchers said that several large epidemiological studies of diet "have shown no significant relations between dietary lipid intake and serum cholesterol of individuals. One of the factors contributing to this lack of relation, as our study suggests, is that the differences in activity levels may influence the lipid results."

In a study of women, Wood found the same 20-milligram increase of HDL in the blood of runners over nonrunners. Women average 55 milligrams per deciliter, 10 more than men; women, of course, have a lower risk of suffering heart disease.

In addition to being associated with exercise and being female, high HDL levels are associated with alcohol intake. One study (by Joseph Barboriak of Wood Veterans Administration Center and the Medical College of Wisconsin) showed that alcoholics have HDL concentrations of between 80 and 100 milligrams. If an alcoholic stops drinking, the level drops to normal in two weeks. Some epidemiological studies have found that moderate drinking, usually defined as one or two drinks a day, correlates with fewer fatal heart attacks. William J. Darby, a nutrition researcher and president of the Nutrition Foundation, defines moderate drinking as three drinks or less daily.

Lower than normal amounts of HDL in the blood are associated with lack of exercise, smoking, and obesity. Of course, people who exercise regularly and strenuously are not overweight and are un-likely to be smokers. William Castelli, director of the well-known Framingham study of cardiovascular disease says that for every 5 milligrams that the HDL level falls below the average value (45 for men, 55 for women), "your risk of heart attack increases by roughly 25 percent."

The studies have shown that the ratio of HDL to total cholesterol is an important indicator of protection against heart disease. The Framingham study found that for the average man, HDL constitutes 20 percent of the total cholesterol and LDL 80 percent. In the Hartung study, the HDL levels were 35 percent for the marathon runners, 29 percent for the joggers, 22 percent for the inactive men. The Framingham study found that the HDL percentage for most heart attack victims was just a few points below the average—17.5 percent.

These ratios of HDLs to LDLs may be so important because of their opposite roles. It is believed that LDLs carry cholesterol to the tissues and deposit it for the use of cells in making sex hormones, among other things. If more cholesterol is deposited than the cells require, then the cholesterol piles up. Accumulation of this fatty substance on the walls of arteries could produce atherosclerosis and coronary heart disease. HDLs, on the other hand, are believed to be the carriers that haul away excess cholesterol to the liver for disposal. This suggests that sufficient numbers of HDLs keep the arteries clear.

A Duke University study headed by cardiologist R. Sanders Williams found another benefit of regular, vigorous exercise: It improves a person's ability to dissolve blood clots.

APPENDIX 16

HEALTH PRACTICES STUDIES

In 1965, Nedra Belloc and Lester Breslow gathered questionnaires from 6,928 adults in Alameda County, California. The twenty-three-page questionnaire was designed to find out what relationship, if any, existed between health practices and health status. "Good practices are shown to be associated with positive health, and the relationship of these activities was cumulative: those who followed all of the good practices being in better health, even though older, than those who failed to do so. This association was found to be independent of age, sex, and economic status."

In a study five and a half years later, Belloc found that 371 people in the original sample had died, and she sought to find out the correlation of good health practices and/or their lack to mortality rates. The health practices are:

1. Sleeps seven or eight hours per night
2. Eats breakfast almost every day
3. Never eats between meals
4. Weight (between 5 percent under and 20 percent over desirable weight for men, not more than 10 percent over desirable weight for women)
5. Often or sometimes engages in active sports, swims, takes long walks, gardens, or does other physical exercise
6. Takes not more than four drinks of alcohol at one time
7. Never smoked cigarettes

Belloc found that mortality "was more strongly associated with poor health practices than it was with physical health status or with income level."

Belloc calculated that a 45-year-old man who observed fewer than four of these health practices had a life expectancy of 21.6 years whereas a man of the same age who followed six or seven had a life expectancy of 33 years—compared to the California average at the time of 27.6 years. For a 55-year-old man, the figures were 13.8, and 25, with 19.7 the California average. These ratios remained consistent until the age-85 category, where they inverted to 6.5, 5, and 4.9. Those who followed four or five of the good-health practices were always in the middle, even at age 85.

Women did not show as big a benefit in years as did the men, but the increases followed the same pattern and were consistent through all age brackets. A 45-year-old woman who observed three or fewer health practices had a life expectancy of 28.6 years, a woman of that age who followed six or seven practices had an expectancy of 35.8, with the average 33.1. At age 55, the figures were 20, 27.8, and 24.6. At age 85, 4.6, 7.6, and 5.5.

In this correlation, each of the seven health practices is given an equal value, but another table in the study shows that some practices were "more equal than others." The seven health practices were broken down into thirty subdivisions. This is the way they were associated with death.

Men

Rank	Highest Mortality		Lowest Mortality
1.	10 percent or more below weight	1.	Often participates in active sports
2.	No physical activity	2.	Never smoked
3.	2+ packs cigarettes daily	3.	10–20 percent above desired weight
4.	Rarely eats breakfast	4.	5–10 percent above desired weight
5.	6 hours of sleep or less	5.	20–30 percent above desired weight
6.	Snacks almost every day	6.	8 hours of sleep
7./8./9.	Smoking now/ smoking less than 1 pack a day/ being 30 percent or more over desired weight	7.	Eats breakfast almost every day
		8./9.	Smoked formerly/ also, sometimes takes part in active sports, swims
10.	5–10 percent below desired weight	10.	Has 1–2 drinks at a time
11.	Sometimes gardens or exercises	11.	Rarely snacks
12.	1–1½ packs cigarettes daily	12.	Often swims, gardens, exercises
13.	5 percent below– 5 percent above desired weight	13./14.	7 hours of sleep; doesn't drink
14.	3–4 drinks at one time		
15.	9 or more hours of sleep	15.	5 or more drinks at one time

Women

Rank	*Highest Mortality*		*Lowest Mortality*
1.	No physical activity	1.	Often swims, gardens, exercises
2./3.	Formerly smoked/ also, 9 hours of sleep or more	2.	5–10 percent above desired weight
		3.	5–10 percent below desired weight
4.	Now smokes	4./5./6.	Never smoked/ also,
5.	10 percent or more below desired weight		10–20 percent above desired weight/ also, 7 hours
6.	1–1½ packs cigarettes daily		of sleep
7.	Rarely eats breakfast	7.	6 hours or less of sleep
8.	Less than 1 pack cigarettes daily	8./9.	5 percent below–5 percent above desired weight/
9.	20–30 percent above weight		also, 1–2 drinks at one time
10.	Snacks almost every day	10./11./12.	Rarely snacks/ also,
11.	Does not drink		eats breakfast almost every day/ also, sometimes en-
12.	30 percent or more above weight		gages in active sports, swims
13.	8 hours sleep	13.	Sometimes gardens or exercises

There were only twenty-six categories for women because there were no significant data for them in four categories: smoking two or more packs of cigarettes a day, taking three to four drinks of alcohol at one time, taking five or more at one time, engaging in active sports.

mental disturbances. In
—stress and aggression—
ys, according to each per-

ressor. Stress, by his defi-
body to any demand." The
ed situation. Even the de-
new circumstance will pro-
stress—particularly, an in-
in endocrine products that
tant are:

hone of the pituitary gland;
ectly called epinephrine and
the inner core of the adre-
bove the kidneys;
hes produced by the adrenal
st known of these hormones

which is a neurohormone, a

he hypothalamus to transmit
ucts the pituitary to produce
odstream and stimulates the
er hypothalamic nerve stimuli
ome nerve endings to produce
phrine. These latter two hor-
ents in adaptation and defense.

When stress is put on a chain,
imilarly, different organs and
akness in different individuals.
thesis with laboratory animals
ns. Those rats placed on diets
ium were predisposed to have
ot peptic ulcers.
rmones: syntoxic (*syn* = "to-
lown, against"). The syntoxic
nical group of steroids to which
ones tranquilize tissues so that
armful substance instead of re-
o the person. With a mosquito
poison, that causes a problem.
st cases to seal off the point of

Influential Material Added during the Course of the Investigation

disease, high blood pressure, arthritis, an
different individuals, the nonspecific cause
might simply express itself in different wa
son's weakest part.

To Selye, the challenging event is the s
nition, "is the nonspecific response of the
body must adapt—adjust—to any chang
mands to adapt to a healthy or pleasant
duce telltale, and measurable, signs of
creased emission into the blood of certa
he calls stress hormones. The most impor

1. ACTH, the adrenocorticotrophic horr
2. Adrenalin and noradrenalin, more cor
   norepinephrine. They are secreted by
   nals, two small glands situated just a
3. Substances he calls *corticoids*, hormo
   cortex, the peripheral section. The be
   is cortisone;
4. CRF, corticotropin-releasing factor,
   hormone produced by nerve cells.

Nerve impulses in the brain cause t
CRF to the pituitary gland. CRF instr
ACTH, which is emitted into the blc
adrenal cortex to secrete corticoids. Oth
direct the adrenal medulla as well as s
and release epinephrine and norepine
mones, with the corticoids, are prime ag

• Selye uses the analogy of a chain.
it is the weakest link that breaks. S
organ systems are predisposed to we
Experiments have demonstrated this
exposed to the same stressful conditi
either of high sodium or low potass
heart attacks while those that fasted
• There are two kinds of stress h
gether") and catatoxic (*cata* = "
hormones generally belong to the che
the corticoids belong. Syntoxic horn
they will be able to coexist with a l
acting in a way potentially harmful
bite, it is the inflammation, not the
While inflammation is useful in mc

312

entry, the reaction to the mosquito bite is excessive. Cortisone and its derivatives in a sense say, "Cool it, we can live with this."

The syntoxic hormones have been well studied, but not so much is known about catatoxic substances, hormones that attack and destroy dangerous foreign substances directly, the way antibodies do. The existence of such hormones has only become known during the past few years. While the search to elucidate their composition and function continues, the type of actions they represent offers a model for dealing with the stress of life: that is, to learn to live with a stressful situation and not become upset by it, or else to deal actively with the cause of stress to remove, change, or avoid it.

• The stress of life has four basic variations, all depending upon the same central phenomenon. It might be shown this way:

```
                    Overstress
                   (hyperstress)
                        /
Good stress . . . . . . . . . . . . . STRESS . . . . . . . . . . . . . . Bad stress
 (eustress)                /                        (distress)
                    Understress
                   (hypostress)
```

The goal is to minimize distress, maximize eustress, and strike a balance between hyperstress and hypostress.

Different people have different suitable stress levels. One person may be happy at some passive activity while another may seek stress in the form of challenge or competition, even when playing. Some highly motivated people in pursuit of a goal find leisure activities disruptive and more stressful than their work. If these highly motivated people find no outlet for the kinds of work they consider eustressful, they may turn to drugs, violence, or other destructive activities.

Selye goes through a list of alternatives. Smoking, alcohol, tranquilizers, and eating all help to relieve the stress from excess of nervous excitation. (But the remedies cause problems of their own because they are habit forming.) He also is open minded about the potential ability of Eastern-style meditation, transcendental meditation, "relaxation response," and "progressive relaxation technique" to combat excessive stress.

Hyperstress may come from too much eustress (we are unable to tolerate prolonged ecstasy or orgies) or an excess of distress (neither can we stand intensely unpleasant events). Various relaxation techniques seem able to counter hyperstress from either cause but are ineffective against hypostress. Indeed, spending too much time on these methods may cause disturbances similar to sensory deprivation, a form of hypostress.

There are drugs to combat high blood pressure, peptic ulcers, headaches, and other ailments caused by stress in predisposed persons; there are tranquilizers to reduce anxiety and tension. But the effectiveness of these drugs is limited, and they all have undesirable additional effects.

Once stress is understood, then each person can be his own best physician, for he will know his mental needs better than anyone else. He must learn the stress level at which he functions best and then learn to stay within that level. This requires self-observation. Selye said, "I know when I have just 'had enough of it,' and then I stop." The best chemical tests and most refined machinery cannot do more. The individual must learn to balance the pleasure and stimulation of successful work and social engagements with needs for peace and solitude. Some people need danger signals—insomnia, irritability, indigestion, headaches, depression—to recognize the boundaries.

Selye follows this motto for living:

Fight for your highest attainable aim
But do not put up resistance in vain.

• Selye believes from five decades of research that the mechanisms of adapting to the stress of life are essentially the same on the cellular and molecular levels as they are in interpersonal and international relationships.

• Selye says that frustration and indecision are the most harmful psychogenic stressors, because nothing is as demanding upon the individual as the conflict of unresolved contradictory efforts.

• Selye does not believe it is possible to propose a code of behavior equally suitable for everyone. We are just too different in our inherited and acquired characteristics, our needs and desires. But one of the wisest and generally applicable behavioral laws is the Golden Rule and its variants. He does not believe that its extension "Love thy neighbor as thyself" can be carried out, because we are not biologically made that way. He proposes *altruistic egoism*: doing good things for others with one's own self-interest in mind—so that others will want to further one's welfare by doing good things in return. The principle behind altruistic egoism is "Be necessary."

• Selye sums up the main points of his study: Stress cannot be avoided. It is the body's response to any demand, necessary for continued life. We should strive for the most eustress and the least distress, find our own stress level and adhere to it. Thus we should have a goal that we, and not just society, consider worthwhile. It is disadvantageous to be a simple egoist, but absolute altruism is contrary to nature and encourages parasitism. We must earn our neighbor's love and at the same time protect our own interests by being necessary and useful to our fellow-men.

STRESS WITHOUT DISTRESS

SALIENT POINTS of Selye's *Stress without Distress* (Phila. and New York: J. B. Lippincott, 1974):
• The history of the stress syndrome suggests that the key to progress in stress studies was the discovery of objective indices, such as adrenal enlargement, thymus atrophy, and gastrointestinal ulcers. These conditions were observed clinically as early as 1842 and noted repeatedly in medical literature. But no one connected them to what Walter Cannon in 1932 called "emergency adrenalin secretion" in response to fear or rage. Cannon never discussed the roles of the pituitary gland or adrenal cortex, however, so that it would have been difficult for him to explore the syndrome as nonspecific adaptive reactions in coping with virtually any kind of demand.
• Selye calls the stress reaction the "general adaptation syndrome" (GAS) and says it occurs in three phases:
1. Alarm. There is a dip in resistance, and if the stressor is strong enough, the result may be death.
2. Stage of resistance. If the challenge is of less than lethal strength and if it continues, bodily signs of the alarm reaction disappear and resistance rises above normal.
3. Stage of exhaustion. Prolonged exposure to the same stressor, to which the body has become adjusted, eventually exhausts adaptation energy. Signs of the alarm reaction reappear, but now they are irreversible and the individual dies.

The three stages correspond to the stages of a person's life:

1. Childhood—low resistance and excessive responses to any kind of stimulus
2. Adulthood—adaptation to most common challenges; increased resistance
3. Old age—characterized by irreversible loss of adaptability and eventual exhaustion, ending in death

• There are two roads to survival: fight and adaptation. Usually adaptation is more successful.
The crudest form of adaptation is mutual indifference: Cells simply get out of one another's way. Mutual indifference allows coexistence but not cooperation. It prevents war but offers no positive gain for any one individual, such as acquiring neighbors who might actually

help. And it offers no safeguards against overcrowding, with the consequent exhaustion of living space and resources.

So during the course of evolution, colonies of cells combined. The loss of competition was more than compensated for by mutual assistance. Each member of the group could depend upon the others for help. Cells specialized differently. The development of this sophisticated system reduces internal stress: It cuts the demands made on the organism to avoid internal frictions and enables the constituent parts to live harmoniously. The opposite behavior of a part—reckless, egocentric development—is what we call cancer.

Still later came interdependence between individuals of different species in symbiosis and mutualism. Lichens are an example.

Most interesting is interdependence among human beings. Each of us has his own goals and needs. Interests often clash and become the major source of interpersonal stress. The human brain is better developed than the brain of any other species, and logic has helped us solve many problems of survival. Unfortunately, emotions tend to dominate interpersonal relations.

A century ago, Claude Bernard, who first called attention to the vital necessity for maintaining the stability of the body's internal environment, devoted the last section of his book *Introduction to the Study of Experimental Medicine* to the subject of collaboration among societies. Walter Cannon, who coined the term *homeostasis*, recognized the adaptive functions of adrenalin and of the sympathetic nervous system. The epilogue to his book *Wisdom of the Body* is entitled "Relations of Biological and Social Homeostasis."

• Among all the emotions, those that most account for the absence of harmful stress (distress) in human relations are the feelings of gratitude and goodwill. The emotion that most accounts for the presence of stress is their negative counterpart, hatred with the urge for revenge.

• On the cellular level, learning by experience depends mainly upon chemical conditioning—by the production of defensive substances, such as hormones and antibodies, and by the modification of their action by other chemical nutrients.

• Since there is a stereotyped physical pattern in the body's response to any challenge, the outcome of our interactions with the environment depend as much upon how we choose to react as upon the nature of the stressor. We must choose carefully between efforts to resist the challenge or to disregard it (by accepting it).

• There are large individual variations in the amount of stress a person needs for happiness. But those who are content to live a purely passive or vegetable life are exceptional. Most people have a number of things they want and are willing to strive to achieve them. At the

316

other end of the spectrum are people who are willing to give all their energy and time to accomplishing some extremely difficult goal, but these people are about as rare as the vegetative types. The average person would be just as bored living a purposeless existence as he would become fatigued from the compulsive pursuit of perfection. Most people dislike either a lack of stress or too much of it. That is why it is important to analyze oneself and decide upon one's most comfortable stress level.

- There are three types of feelings or attitudes toward events:
1. Positive feelings can be described as love, in the broadest sense. Gratitude, respect, trust, admiration for the excellence of important achievements—all of these amount to goodwill and friendship. Our homeostatic security in society is best ensured by the incitement of positive feelings toward us in as many people as possible; no one would be inclined to attack someone for whom he holds these positive feelings. As far as science can determine, the ultimate aim in life is the maintenance and enjoyment of life itself.
2. Negative feelings include hatred, distrust, disdain, hostility, jealousy, and the urge for revenge—the very attitudes that endanger one's security by encouraging aggressiveness in other people who fear they will be harmed.
3. Feelings of indifference can lead at best to an attitude of tolerance, making peaceful coexistence possible, but nothing more.

These positive, negative, and indifferent attitudes are built into the very substance of living matter. They regulate homeostatic adaptation on all levels of interaction—among cells, human beings, nations. Once this is fully understood and accepted, we will be better prepared to bring our behavior under voluntary control, on the interpersonal and the international levels.

The imperative biological laws of self-defense make it difficult to always make altruistic choices. But it is easy to pursue an altruistic egoism that helps others for the selfish reason of wanting to deserve their help in return.

It also is difficult to suppress the impulse for revenge when unjustly attacked, because we want to teach offenders that it does not pay to hurt us. But revenge and even the mildest forms of senseless vendetta should be avoided out of self-interest.

- How can the same work create both stress and distress? Nothing breeds success more than success, nothing blocks it more than frustration.

Selye believes that a major source of distress among people working in the middle and lower echelons of business, industry, agriculture, and public service is dissatisfaction with life—disrespect for their own accomplishments. They are frustrated by the conviction that they

317

could have done, and wanted to do, much more. They look for scapegoats and make excuses, refusing to accept that they were responsible. This is consistent with Selye's postulate that a finite amount of adaptation energy is genetically inherited; a person spends this vitality to complete whatever he considers his mission.

• "Man must work. I think we have to begin by realizing that work is a biological necessity." Muscles and mind degenerate unless used for some work we deem worthwhile. Most people believe they work for economic security or social status or a successful business career, only to find that when these are gained and there is nothing further to fight for, they become bored.

The best way to avoid harmful stress is to select an environment (spouse, boss, friends) that conforms to one's innate preference and to find work one likes and respects. For many old people, the most difficult part of retirement is the feeling of being useless.

To function normally, people need work as they need air, food, sleep, social contact, and sex. The question is not whether we should or should not work, but what kind of work suits us best. The Western world is being pressed by insatiable demands for less work and more pay. Stress is associated with every kind of work, but distress is not. The questions that should be asked are, Less work to get more time to do what? More pay to buy what?

• There exists a close relationship among work, stress, and aging. Aging results from the sum of all the stresses to which the body has ever been exposed and apparently corresponds to the exhaustion stage of the GAS. The main difference between aging and the GAS appears to be that the adaptation syndrome is more or less reversible with rest. But we must remember that although stress and aging may be closely related, they definitely are not identical.

STRESS AND AGING

SALIENT POINTS of "Stress and Aging," by Hans Selye, in the *Journal of the American Geriatric Society*, September 1970:

• "In a strictly medical sense, stress is the rate of wear and tear to which a living being is exposed at any one moment. By contrast, aging appears to reflect the sum of all the stresses which have acted upon the body during a life-span."

• Stress plays a major role in peptic ulcers, hypertension, certain forms of arthritis, and acute cardiac accidents. Not only is there some correlation between stress and aging, but between aging and a disturbance in calcium metabolism as well. In the aged, bones tend to lose calcium while certain soft tissues appear to develop an affinity for it. In the course of laboratory work, he noticed that the artificial interference with calcium metabolism in young animals produces changes characteristic of aging, including hair loss, wrinkled skin, loss of muscle protein, atrophy of sex organs.

• Acute cardiac arrests are seen more frequently in older people, especially after being exposed to stress. By pretreating laboratory animals with certain adrenal hormones and sodium salts, no cardiovascular damage is apparent, but if the animals are then exposed to stress (forced muscular exercise, cold baths, nervous tension, or physical trauma), the heart undergoes the same changes found after a coronary thrombosis.

APPENDIX 18
TYPE A BEHAVIOR

The following are excerpts from the article "Type A Behavior: A Progress Report" by Meyer Friedman, in the February 1980 issue of *The Sciences*, a publication of the New York Academy of Sciences.

Dr. Friedman is director of the Harold Brunn Institute at the Mount Zion Hospital and Medical Center in San Francisco, and a pioneer in the study of Type A behavior.

• "The Type A behavior pattern is an action-emotion complex exhibited by people who are unable—or unwilling—to evaluate their own competence. Such people prefer to judge themselves by the evaluations of those whom they believe to be their superiors. And to enhance themselves in other people's eyes, they attempt to increase the quantity (but rarely the quality) of their achievements. Their self-esteem becomes increasingly dependent on the status they believe they achieve."

But whatever self-esteem they gain in this way does not seem to be enough to overcome the insecurity and the subsequent agitation caused by their "surrender" to outside standards and authorities. Caught in a vicious cycle, they constantly strive to achieve a satisfactory level of self-esteem by trying to accomplish more and more in less time. The unending struggle "together with a free-floating, but covert, and usually well-rationalized, hostility" make up the Type A pattern. "The sense of urgency and hostility give rise to irritation, impatience, aggravations and anger: the four components which I believe comprise the pathogenic core of the behavior pattern."

Friedman suspects that the eventual arterial damage and heart attack are brought about by the high levels of corticotropin and norepinephrine usually observed in the blood.

APPENDIX 19
RELAXATION

Salient points from *Relaxation* (Philadelphia: Lea & Febiger, 1969), by Josephine L. Rathbone, Ph.D., a pioneering physical therapist.

• Rathbone defines *hypertonus* as " 'too much' (*hyper*) 'tension in the muscles' (*tonus*), although it may be persistent after effort has passed (residual)." It is not a pathologic condition (unless sustained for too long), but simply what happens after overusing muscles—particularly, holding the body in a still position, as is required, for instance, in desk work. "Hypertonus in the neuromuscular system always precedes exhaustion," but this state of breakdown can be avoided by alternating periods of effort with periods of release and by relieving excess tension in the nervous and muscular systems with relaxation.

• The muscular activity that goes with mental work is the tonic type, featuring postures of attention and arrested movement. The head is usually bent forward, breathing is constricted because of tension in the diaphragm and other respiratory muscles, and muscles in the shoulders, lower back, buttocks, and legs are tensed to keep the body alert.

Few tense people select forms of recreation that are relaxing. They don't take the time to learn the benefits that can come from unexciting diversions such as reading alone, making useful things with one's hands, or enjoying the out-of-doors.

• The most common sign of excessive tension is insomnia. When muscles become tense from overwork and the brain has been extremely active, it takes time for the body to slow down. Insomnia is induced by the noticeable degrees of tonus associated with mental work and worry: the tonus of attention and held positions.

It is not easy to find the proper proportions of work, recreational diversion, and cessation of activity. Inability to find and maintain the right balance of the three is the chief cause of chronic fatigue and neuromuscular hypertension.

• There are a number of physical factors in tension and distress. Just sitting or standing against the pull of gravity produces muscular contraction or tension. Physical activities as simple as reading and writing can cause fatigue if sustained for too long. "Organized thinking is a cumulative trauma that must be interrupted by rest."

The accretion of too many stimuli at one time—sights, noises, held positions, and especially pain—produce tension and fatigue.

"Lucky is the farmer, mason, or woodcutter whose employment takes him into many kinds of weather. Fortunate is the woman who has a garden. Fortunate is the man who has a boat. Fortunate, also, are the people who have a chance to walk back and forth to work every day. Sensible are the others who find a way, through outdoor sports or through camping and hiking, to get their share of physical activity in various kinds of weather."

"Recreation can be envisioned as a state of mind attained through all-absorbing activity in which one can lose oneself." The activity may be physical, but doesn't have to be.

Scientific investigators and physicians have recognized a relationship between symptoms of arthritis and "nervousness."

The neck and lower back are the places that show the most static strain in such workers as business and professional people, housewives, and students. These symptoms result from trying to keep heads and trunks erect or in other set positions too long.

"All fears arrest movement and cause residual muscular hypertonus. Fears set the individual against his environment physically as well as psychologically."

Muscles can contract temporarily in response to stimulation, or they can maintain contraction. The first action is called phasic or kinetic contraction; the second is called tonic, static, or postural contraction. The most demanding physical activity is powerful tonic contraction, as in weightlifting. There may not be enough tonic contraction in routine daily activities to cause discomfort, but if we deliberately try to hold one position for a great length of time, we realize that it is work. This is the type of muscular contraction from which most of us must learn to relax.

Mental work, especially, causes tension. We "think" with muscles because every thought is associated with muscular contraction and each contraction causes some feeling. Most muscular contraction associated with thinking is tonic. It results in arrested movement and in attention, which is also a muscular phenomenon.

• Laughter is important to good health in many ways. Rathbone suggests that laughter is interrelated with both physical and psychological health, and that laughter can contribute to physical health as well as to psychological well-being. It relaxes the entire body as well as the mind. "As any physician can testify, it is more effective than a drug, when a tonic is needed." Not only is laughter a sign of good health, but we laugh when we feel we are masters of a situation or safe from a problem. "Unfortunately, very few people feel superior in their work, so very few people laugh or sing at their work." They must find their laughs in other activities. Humor has great value as a diversion and refuge from fear.

APPENDICES, SECTION V
Data

APPENDIX 20

A. CENTENARIANS ON SOCIAL SECURITY ROLLS, JUNE 1979—BY AGE AND SEX

Age	Total	Male	Female	Percent Female
Total	13,216	3,679	9,537	72.2
100–104	11,621	3,082	8,539	73.5
100	4,548	1,165	3,383	74.4
101	3,053	844	2,209	72.4
102	1,898	511	1,387	73.1
103	1,292	338	954	73.8
104	830	224	606	73.0
105–109	1,367	512	855	62.6
105	540	195	345	63.9
106	353	130	223	63.2
107	210	78	132	62.9
108	153	62	91	59.5
109	111	47	64	57.7
110–114	228	85	143	62.7
110	50	17	33	66.0
111	56	26	30	53.6
112	54	17	37	68.5
113	45	16	29	64.4
114	23	9	14	60.9

B. CENTENARIANS ON SOCIAL SECURITY ROLLS, JUNE 1979—BY AGE AND RACE

Age	Total	White	Black	Other	Percent White
Total	13,216	11,566	1,433	217	87.5
100–104	11,621	10,332	1,115	174	88.9
100	4,548	4,134	357	57	90.9
101	3,053	2,735	273	45	89.6
102	1,898	1,668	201	29	87.9
103	1,292	1,105	168	19	85.5
104	830	690	116	24	83.1
105–109	1,367	1,064	271	32	77.8
105	540	430	96	14	79.6
106	353	280	67	6	79.3
107	210	161	46	3	76.7
108	153	118	30	5	77.1
109	111	75	32	4	67.6
110–114	228	170	47	11	74.6
110	50	34	13	3	68.0
111	56	45	8	3	80.4
112	54	38	15	1	70.4
113	45	37	5	3	82.2
114	23	16	6	1	69.6

C. CENTENARIAN SURVIVAL RATIO RE U.S. BIRTH COHORTS

Age	Total Centenarians	Adjusted*	Birth Year	Total U.S. Births	Ratio of Centenarian Survival
Total	13,216	10,771	1865–1879	18,233,000**	one in 1,692
100–104	11,621	9,471	1875–1879	7,118,000	one in 752
100	4,548	3,707	1879	1,524,000**	one in 411
101	3,053	2,488	1878	1,473,000	one in 592
102	1,898	1,547	1877	1,423,000	one in 920
103	1,292	1,053	1876	1,373,000	one in 1,304
104	830	676	1875	1,325,000	one in 1,960
105–109	1,367	1,114	1870–1874	5,940,000	one in 5,332
105	540	440	1874	1,278,000	one in 2,904
106	353	288	1873	1,232,000	one in 4,277
107	210	171	1872	1,187,000	one in 6,942
108	153	125	1871	1,143,000	one in 9,144
109	111	91	1870	1,100,000	one in 12,088
110–114	228	186	1865–1869	5,175,000	one in 27,823
110	50	41	1869	1,074,000	one in 26,195
111	56	46	1868	1,051,000	one in 22,848
112	54	44	1867	1,034,000	one in 23,500
113	45	37	1866	1,016,000	one in 27,460
114	23	19	1865	1,000,000	one in 52,632

* The adjusted figure represents an estimate of the native-born American centenarians, the number of survivors from the U.S. population born during the year one century earlier (or 101 years, 102 years earlier, etc.). This estimate is based on the proportion of native-born American centenarians in the 1,200-member cohort used for the inquiry: 81½ percent.

** The number of births per year are approximations extrapolated from the 1860, 1870, and 1880 censuses.

A. SOURCES OF INTERVIEWS, COMPOSITION OF COHORT FOR INQUIRY AMERICA'S CENTENARIANS, BY SOCIAL SECURITY ADMINISTRATION

Volume	Birth Year	Males	Fe-males	Whites M	Whites F	Blacks M	Blacks F	Hispanic M	Hispanic F	N.A. Indian M	N.A. Indian F	Asian M	Asian F
I–IV	1838–1863	189	88	143½	78	33½	7	7½	1	2½	2	2	1
V	1864	33	25	27	23	4	2	2					
VI	1865	56	37	48	32	5	4	2			1	1	
VII	1866	61	34	48	33	12	1	1					
VIII	1867	30	33	25	31	4	2					1	
IX–X	1868	84	132	78	128	4	2	2	1				
XI	1869	64	80	58½	73	5	7	½					
XII	1870	49	50	38½	48	7	2	1		1½		1	
XIII	1871	33	49	29	47	3	2					1	
SSA Totals		599	528	495½	493	77½	29	16	2	4	3	6	1
Added by Author-Press	1860–1880	38	35	34	31	2	2	½	1	1½	1		
Total Cohort		637	563	529½	524	79½	31	16½	3	5½	4	6	1

B. BIRTH YEARS OF COHORT

Year	Total Number	Native American	Foreign Born
1838	1	1	
1842	1	1	
1849	1	1	
1850	3	3	
1851	1	1	
1852	2	2	
1853	2	2	
1854	7	7	
1855	6	5	1
1856	15	12	3
1857	8	7	1
1858	16	13	3
1859	29	22	7
Subtotal:	92	77	15
1860	38	28	10
1861	33	30	3
1862	60	46	14
1863	60	47	13
1864	58	47	11
1865	92	74	18
1866	94	76	18
1867	64	52	12
1868	216	181	35
1869	144	125	19
Subtotal:	859	706	153
1870	98	77	21
1871	82	67	15
1872	3	3	
1873	10	6	4
1874	12	9	3
1875	7	7	
1876	17	11	6
1877	6	5	1
1878	6	5	1
1879	6	3	3
1880	2	2	
Subtotal:	249	195	54
Total:	1,200	978	222

C. ORIGINS OF FOREIGN-BORN CENTENARIANS
(30 Nations and the High Seas)

Country of Origin	Total Number	Males	Females
1. Germany	40	19	21
2. Italy	27	14	13
3. Canada	25	15	10
4. Sweden	19	13	6
5. England	17	6	11
6. Norway	12	6	6
7. Poland	9	5	4
Russia	9	8	1
9. Austria	7	3	4
Ireland	7	3	4
11. Denmark	6	2	4
Mexico	6	6	
13. Czechoslovakia	5	4	1
Scotland	5	3	2
15. Hungary	3	2	1
Lithuania	3	3	
17. China	2	2	
High Seas	2	2	
Holland	2	2	
Japan	2	1	1
Korea	2	2	
Switzerland	2		2
Turkey	2	2	
24. Azores	1	1	
Belgium	1		1
Bermuda	1	1	
France	1	1	
Greece	1	1	
India	1	1	
West Indies	1	1	
Yugoslavia	1	1	
Totals:	222	130	92

D. AGES OF CENTENARIANS IN COHORT*

Age	Total Number	Age	Total Number
99/100	1,022	110	1
101	84	111	1
102	38	112	1
103	13	113	1
104	12	118	1
105	8	121	1
106	7	122	1
107	4	137	1
108	2	Total:	1,200
109	2		

* If the date of death is known, the age at death is used; otherwise, the age used is the age at the time of the interview. Ages older than 113 years are scientifically questionable.

E. MARITAL HISTORY*

Years Married	Number of Centenarians		Times Remarried	Number
1–10	5		1	116
11–25	26		2	24
27	1		3	8
31–35	10		4	2
36–39	23		6	1
40–44	20		7	1
45–49	27		9	1
Total:		112 (32%)		
50–54	49			
55–59	43			
Total:		92 (27%)		
60	11			
61–65**	12			
61	3			
62	8			
63	2			
64	13			
65	12			
66	6			
67	10			
68	12			
69	3			
Total:		92 (27%)		
70	12			
71	6			
72	8			
73	5			
74	1			
75	11			
78	1			
79	2			
80	2			
Total:		48 (14%)		
Total for data known:	344			

* Of the more than 1,100 centenarians who had been or still were married (see page 340), further details are known only for the more limited numbers presented here.
** SSA reports are imprecise.

Age when Remarried	Number	Age when Remarried	Number
30–34	2	74	1
35–39	0	76	1
40–44	5	77	1
45–49	7	78	2
50–54	3	79	1
55–60	5	81	1
61	2	82	2
63	1	83	2
64	1	84	1
65	2	87	4
66	1	89	2
67	1	90	2
68	2	91	1
69	2	92	2
70	3	95	1
71	1	98	1
72	3	100	2

F. PROGENY

Number of Children		Number		
0		205		
	Total:		205	(18%)
1		151		
2		156		
3		119		
4		123		
	Total:		549	(48%)
5		92		
6		67		
7		57		
8		42		
9		34		
	Total:		292	(25%)
10		29		
11		21		
12		18		
13		9		
14		13		
	Total:		90	(8%)
15		2		
16		4		
17		1		
18		2		
19		1		
	Total:		10	(1%)
20		1		
21		1		
38		1		
40 or more		1		
	Total:		4	
Total for data known:		1,150		
No data:		50		

Number of Grandchildren	Number	Number of Grandchildren	Number
0	3	20	14
		21	8
1	45	22	3
2	69	23	6
3	55	24	4
4	51		
		25	6
5	54	26	3
6	35	27	4
7	34	28	2
8	34	29	2
9	37	30	6
		31	2
10	28	32	2
11	17	33	2
12	13	35	2
13	13	36 or more	20
14	17		

(highest numbers of grandchildren given: 70, 75, 82, 150, circa 200)

15	14		
16	12		
17	9		
18	7		
19	8		

F. PROGENY (continued)

Number of Great-Grandchildren	Number	Number of Great-Grandchildren	Number
1	21	31	5
2	20	32	5
3	42	33	3
4	33	34	4
5	28	35	3
6	35	36	4
7	24	37	1
8	24	38	4
9	24	39	5
10	22	40	4
11	10	41	2
12	13	42	1
13	20	43	1
14	12	44	2
15	16	45	2
16	11	46	1
17	7	47	4
18	9	48	1
19	8	49	5
20	6	50	4
21	6	52	3
22	6	53	2
23	6	54	2
24	12	55	1
25	6	56	1
26	4	57	3
27	9	59	1
28	7	62 or more	17
29	4		
30	9		

(highest numbers given: 91, 100, 103, 114, 125)

Number of Great-Great-Grandchildren	Number		Number of Great-Great-Great-Grandchildren	Number
1	36		1	1
2	30			
3	28		2	1
4	15		6	1
5	11			
			20	1
6	7			
7	9			
8	5			
9	8			
10	3			
11	5			
12	2			
13	8			
14	4			
15	6			
16	2			
17	1			
18	1			
19	4			
20	4			
21	2			
22	3			
25	1			
27	3			
33	1			
39	1			
41	1			
42	1			
50	1			
70	1			
100+	1			
150	1			

G. BIRTH MONTHS

Month	Males Number	Males Percent	Females Number	Females Percent	Total Number	Total Percent
January	64	10½	58	10½	122	10½
February	53	9	62	11	115	10
March	63	10	60	11	123	10½
April	39	6¼	41	7	80	7
May	39	6¼	54	10	93	8
June	43	7	35	6¼	78	6½
July	43	7	40	7	83	7
August	63	10	44	8	107	9
September	50	8	33	6	83	7
October	55	9	44	8	99	8½
November	47	7½	39	7	86	7½
December	54	9	46	8¼	100	8½
Totals:	613		556		1,169	

H. BORN UNDER ZODIAC SIGNS

Sign	Males Number	Percent	Females Number	Percent	Total Number	Percent
Capricorn	61	10¼	57	10½	118	10¼
Aquarius	57	9½	53	9¾	110	9½
Pisces	55	9¼	72	13¼	127	11
Aries	48	8	40	7¼	88	7¾
Taurus	42	7	57	10½	99	8¾
Gemini	37	6¼	33	6	70	6
Cancer	42	7	46	8¼	88	7¾
Leo	60	10	37	6¾	97	8½
Virgo	57	9½	37	6¾	94	8¼
Libra	53	9	38	7	91	8
Scorpio	36	6	39	7	75	6½
Sagittarius	48	8	38	7	86	7½
Totals:	596		547		1,143	

APPENDIX 22
QUESTIONNAIRE TOTALS

I. GENERAL

1. Number: 1,200
2. Name:
3. Address:
4. Born: See Appendix 21B
5. Date of interview:
6. Age: See Appendix 21D
7. Died: See Appendix 21D
8. Final Age: See Appendix 21D
9. Birth Month: See Appendix 21G
10. Zodiac Sign: See Appendix 21H
11. Sex: male 637, female 563
12. Photograph: 298
     Smiling 106 (31%)
     Smiling face 44 (13%)
     Pensive, interested 127 (37%)
     Unanimated 60 (17½%)
     Sour 5 (1½%)
13. Marital status:
     A. Married 118 (10%)
        Widowed 972 (82½%)
        Single 69 (6%)
        Divorced 10 (1%)
        Separated 8 (½%)
     B. How many times remarried_____ See Appendix 21E
        Remarried at age(s): See Appendix 21E
     C. No data 23 (2%)
14. Progeny: See Appendix 21F
     A. Number of children_____
     B. Number of grandchildren_____
     C. Number of great-grandchildren_____
     D. Number of great-great-grandchildren_____
     E. Number of great-great-great-grandchildren_____
15. Number of siblings: See Appendix 31A
16. Position among siblings: See Appendix 31B
17. Race: See also Appendix 21A
     White 1,053½

29. Work arrangement:
Alone 36 (3%)
Own boss 407 (32%)
For others 653 (52%)
Small outfit 10 (1%)
Company 157 (12%)

Hereditary

30. Influence of:
    A. Mother Insufficient data
    B. Father Insufficient data
    C. Siblings Insufficient data
31. Parents were hard workers: Insufficient data
32. Parents kept regular lives: Insufficient data

III. PSYCHOLOGICAL SPHERE

33. Attitudes:
    A. Happy with life, takes pleasure from daily activities 583 (53%)
       (Cheerful 24)
    B. Takes satisfaction from work 212 (19%)
    C. Loves life 89 (8%)
       Loves, likes people 173 (16%)
       Joie de vivre 200 (18%)
       Life has been exciting 109 (10%) No 400 (36%)
    D. Wants to live, will to live 208 (19%)
       Has something to live for 75 (7%)
       Positive view of life, people, world 204 (19%)
       Hopeful outlook 32 (3%)
    E. No regrets 77 (7%)
       Accomplished (all) (most) goals 214 (19%)
       Feels fortunate 73 (7%)
    F. Doesn't worry 108 (10%)
       Everything in God's hands, trust in God 204 (19%)
       At ease 188 (17%)
       Sense of humor 179 (16%)
    G. Lives one day at a time 65 (6%)
    H. Looks to future 135 (12%)
       Still has goals 170 (15%)
    I. Expected long life 39 (4%) No 3
    J. Ambition to be 100 32 (3%) No 2
    K. High self-esteem, positive self-image 213 (19%)

343

L. Believes in Golden Rule 116 (11%)
M. Takes responsibility for life, health 326 (30%)
N. Ethical 83 (7½%)
O. Religious 556 (50½%)
P. Reverent without narrow sectarianism 16 (1½%)
Q. Toward death
    Thinks about it constantly 10
    Never thinks about it 3
    Fears it 1
    Not afraid 22 (2%)
R. Longevity a matter of luck 8
S. Bitter 2
T. Complaining 4
U. Anxious 1
V. Depressed 2
W. No data 98 (8%)
34. Behavior/personality:
    A. Harmonious life 306 (26%)
    B. Does what he likes, likes what he does 88 (7½%)
    C. Does no chores 140 (12%)
    D. Escaped conflict with authority 20 (1½%)
    E. Doesn't hurry 25 (2%)
    F. Maintains autonomy, independence 681 (59%)
    G. Makes decisions about own life 505 (44%)
    H. Has control of life, life well organized 719 (62%)
    I. Daily activities well organized 374 (32%)
    J. Honest 47 (4%)
    K. Excels in something 151 (13%)
    L. Does useful work 364 (31%)
    M. Ability to accept change 1,081 (93%)
    N. Ability to deal with loss 1,041 (90%)
    O. Ability to vary schedule 374 (32%)
    P. Ability to modify role 292 (25%)
    Q. No data 39 (3%)
35. Intelligence/mental status:
    A. Curiosity, interest in life 961 (82%)
    B. Learning new things 66 (6%)
    C. Creating new things 132 (11%)
    D. Interest in politics, community, world 361 (31%)
    E. IQ achievements 156 (13%)
    F. High awareness 946 (81%)
    G. Useful activities 454 (39%)
    H. Orientation to himself, time, place 1,048 (90%)
    I. Memory: good 905 (77%) poor 94 (8%)
    J. Neurotic symptoms 1

K. Senile 1
L. No data 31 (3%)

IV. BIOLOGICAL SPHERE

36. Physical:
    A. Still performs physical activities 409 (36%)
    B. Exercises 18 (1½%)
    C. Looks younger 401
    D. Good personal care 297
    E. Erect posture 260
    F. Weight
       Obese 0
       Somewhat obese 26 (9%)
       Average 139 (48%)
       Lean 123 (43%)
       Gaunt 0
    G. Young skin, few wrinkles 231
    H. Good muscle tone 98
    I. Hair: Strong, dark, or young looking: 205 (males, 94; females, 111)
    J. Vision very good 32
    K. Still has teeth 27 (males, 22; females, 5)
    L. Signs of strength 35
    M. Hearing excellent 12
    N. Works at job 33
    O. Sexual activity 48
    P. Disabilities
       a. Hearing 296 (26%)
       b. Vision 338 (29%)
       c. Arthritis 54 (4.7%)
       d. Other 252 (22%)
    Q. Uses cane 59
    R. Needs walker 61
    S. Wheelchair 88
    T. Bedridden 54
    U. Does not wear glasses 104
    V. No data 48 (4%)

Health

37. Subjective evaluation:
    A. Excellent 112 (13%) (males, 80 [72%]; females, 32 [28%])
       Good 574 (69%)

345

Fair, good for my age 98 (12%)
Poor 52 (6%)
  B. Vitality/energy
     Strong 40 (5%)
     Moderate 10 (1%)
     Weak 36 (4%)
  C. No data 364 (30%)
38. Objective evaluation:
  A. Good physical functioning 958 (87%)
  B. Mobile 786 (75%)
     With cane, walker 120 (12%)
     Wheelchair 88 (8%)
     Bedridden 54 (5%)
  C. Vitality/energy:
     Strong 161 (15%) (males, 94; females, 68)
     Moderate 8 (1%)
     Weak 28 (3%)
  D. No data 101 (8½%)
39. History/profile:
  A. Disease
     a. At present: See Appendix 29A
     b. In middle age: See Appendix 29B
     c. In youth: See Appendix 29C
  B. Disability
     a. At present: See Appendix 29D
     b. In middle age: Insufficient data
     c. In youth: Insufficient data
  C. Eating habits
     Same as in past 42
     Changed from past 6
  D. Weight
     Same as in past Insufficient data
     Changed from past Insufficient data
  E. Reliance on health care
     a. Sees physician frequently 53 occasionally 45
        never 133
     b. In later years saw doctor frequently 14 occasionally
        8 never 127
     c. In middle years saw doctor frequently 4 occasion-
        ally 2 never 34
     d. In hospital in past year 56 never 168
        In later years 123 never 138
        In middle years 8 never 145
     e. Never takes drugs/medicine 130

Takes occasionally 3
Regularly 41
   f. In later years never took drugs/medicine 121
Took drugs/medicine 8
   g. In middle years never took drugs/medicine 113
Took drugs/medicine 6
   h. In youth never took drugs/medicine 109
Took drugs/medicine Insufficient data
   i. No data 867 (72%)

F. Sleep
   a. Hours of sleep Insufficient data
   b. Hours of sleep in later years Insufficient data
   c. Hours of sleep in middle years Insufficient data

G. Alcohol

	Present	Later Years	Middle Years	Youth
Never	165	155	153	147
Infrequent	8	8	8	7
Moderate	45	43	40	34
Liberal	12	19	28	31

H. Smoking

	Present	Later Years	Middle Years	Youth
Never	143	141	141	135
Occasionally	3	2	1	1
Less than 1 pack daily	1	1	1	1
1 pack daily	11	15	15	18
2 or more packs daily	3	4	6	8
Cigars	34	36	37	25
Pipe	28	33	27	18

40. Diet:
   A. Three meals a day 152
   B. No special diet, eat everything 59
Followed special diet 175
     a. No meat 3
     b. Vegetarian 4
     c. Moderation 40
     d. Ate carefully 19
     e. Other 109 (See Appendix 30B)
   C. Watched calories, low calories 0
   D. No/low salt 0
   E. No/low sugar 2

F. Coffee:
    Never 8
    Infrequently_____
    One cup a day 2
    Two cups a day 2
    Three or more 9
G. No data 937 (78%)

41. Habits:
A. Hard physical work: still 121 until recently 52
    most of life 691 in middle life 14 in youth 14
    Total 892 (77%)
B. Conscientious work: still 62 until recently 26
    most of life 170 in middle life 5 in youth 3
    Total 266 (23%)
C. Keeps active 662 (57%)
    Sedentary 341 (30%)
D. Exercises 29 (2½%)
E. Arises early 58 (5%)
    Arises late 9 (¾%)
F. Goes to bed early 50 (4%)
    Goes to bed late 8
G. Alcohol
    Never 165
    Occasionally 30
    Daily 35
H. Smoking
    Never 143 moderately 14 heavily 14
    Cigars 34
    Pipe 28
I. No data 42 (3½%)

42. Mental/emotional:
A. Healthy 1167 (98%)
B. Neurotic traits
    a. Sleeplessness 2
    b. Nervous 0
    c. Anxious 1
    d. Depressed 2
    e. Other 0
C. Sleeps well 43
D. Memory: good 946 (80%) failing 99 (8%)
E. Senile 1
F. No data 13 (1%)

43. Longevity runs in family: 77 (64 stated, 13 unstated); No: 11 (7 stated, 4 unstated)
    A. Mother's age: Long-lived, 49; short-lived, 53
    B. Father's age: Long-lived, 47; short-lived, 63
        Long-lived uncles, aunts, grandparents, etc.: 34
44. Sibling longevity:

Number

  *Centenarian
  Over 90:   Long-lived siblings: 80
  80–90:
  70–80:   Siblings all dead: 33
  Under 70:

45. Children's longevity:
    *A. Number of children   Children living: 745
        alive_____   Children all alive: 305
        Over 80_____   More than half of children
        70–80_____   alive: 226
        60–70_____   Half of or fewer children
        50–60_____   alive: 214
    *B. Number of children   Children dead: 530
        dead_____   Children all dead: 90
        Died over 80_____ One-half or more children
        70–80_____   dead: 214
        60–70_____   Fewer than half of children
        50–60_____   dead: 226
        Under 50_____
    C. No data 160 (13%)
46. Stock: Insufficient data (See Appendix 21C for foreign born)

V. ORDER/DISCIPLINE

47. Organization:
    A. Organized daily activities/routine 596 (52%)
    B. Organized lifetime activities/goals 1,097 (95%)
    C. Harmonious, integrated life 501 (44%)
    D. Managing life in own house 364 (32%)
    E. Three meals a day 152 (13%)
    F. Followed disciplined regimen 304 (26%)
    G. Realized all or most goals 331 (29%)
    H. Still has goals 170 (15%)

* Data for the specific age categories were not available.

I. Looks to future 135 (12%)
J. No data 49 (4%)
48. Regularity: 19 (2%)
   A. Still working 139 (13%) or regular routine of activities 529 (50%)
   B. Regular social visits, meetings, recreation, etc. 286 (27%)
   C. Arises, retires same hour every day 112 (11%)
   D. Three meals a day 152 (15%)
   E. No data 155 (13%)
49. *Moderation: 69 (11%)
   A. In eating 100 (16%)
   B. Moderate weight 221 (35%)
   C. Use of alcohol 203 (32%)
   D. No smoking 143 (23%) or cigars 34 (5%) or pipe 28 (4%)
   E. Use of coffee Insufficient data
   F. Drugs/medicine 133 (21%)
   G. No data 570 (48%)
50. Stability:
   A. Continuous place in family 835 (72%)
      a. Still married 118 (10%)
      b. Lives with child, grandchild or other relative 560 (48%)
      c. Sees children 373 (32%)
      d. Sees siblings, relatives 319 (28%)
   B. Continuous place in community 414 (36%)
   C. Continuity in work 809 (70%)
   D. Continuity in interests 714 (62%) (Church/religion: 430 [37%])
   E. Living in same house 88 (7½)
         town 406 (35%)   Total: 905 (78%);
         area 411 (35½%)   Lifetime: 401 (35%)
   F. Traveled extensively 42 (4%)
   G. Married very long time 456 (39%)
   H. No data 43 (4%)
51. Social:
   A. Strong family fabric 844 (75%)
   B. Structure of friends 297 (26%)
   C. Structure of neighbors 219 (19%)
   D. Scheduled meetings, regular get-togethers, etc. 221 (20%)
   E. No data 71 (6%)

---

* The figures for "Moderation" are not representative because often in the interviews the subjects of smoking, weight, etc., never came up, or the interviewer did not include any mention in his comments on the interview.

52. Usefulness:
    A. Still gainfully employed 99 (9%)
    B. Performs useful role(s) 485 (42%)
       In home 440 (38%) for community 84 (7%) for so-
       ciety 32 (3%)
    C. Important to one other person 99 (9%) many people 746
       (65%)
    D. No data 53 (4%)
53. Work:
    A. Worked hard 1,066 (89%)
    B. Worked long time 1,038 (87%)
    C. Has easy life now 935 (78%)
    D. Had easy life 10

VI. FREEDOM/INDEPENDENCE

54. Physical:
    A. Still does physical work, exercises 339 (30%)
    B. Takes walks 168 (15%)
    C. Good physical functioning 950 (83.6%)
    D. Still mobile 819 (72%)
    E. Mobile with cane, aids 101 (9%)
    F. Drives car 13 (1%)
    G. Travels 46 (4%)
    H. Sexual activity 74 (6½%)
    I. Freedom from disability 269 (24%)
    J. Freedom from disease 752 (66%)
    K. Freedom from health establishment 471 (42%)
    L. No data 64 (5%)
55. Intellectual:
    A. Still creates 186 (16%)
    B. Still learning 78 (7%)
    C. Curious, interested in immediate world about him/her 964
       (83.9%)
    D. Solves puzzles 46 (4%)
    E. Reads 344 (30%)
    F. Attends meetings 194 (17%)
    G. Watches TV 231 (20%)
    H. Listens to radio 121 (11%)
    I. No data 51 (4%)
56. Psychological:
    A. Makes decisions 526 (46%)
    B. Autonomous life—freedom from dependence (on medical,
       physician, nursing home, social services) 720 (63%)
    C. Freedom from stress, anxiety 869 (76%)

D. Flexible, adaptive 400 (35%)
E. No data 62 (5%)
F. Attitude toward Social Security: See Appendix 27
57. Personal life:
    A. Takes responsibility for life, health 568 (49%)
    B. Manages own home 257 (22%)
    C. Living in own place alone (including housekeeper) 148 (13%)
    D. Living at home with spouse 107 (9%)
    E. Living in home of relative 524 (45%)
    F. Nursing home 259 (23%)
    G. Sexual activity 62 (5%)
    H. Freedom of choice 10
    I. No data 45 (4%)
58. Economic:
    Wealthy 27 (2.4%)
    Comfortable 208 (18.6%)
    Independent, makes ends meet 837 (75%)
    Poor 43 (4%)
59. Work:
    A. Freedom of choice 16 (1.4%)
    B. Still works at chosen vocation 219 (19%)
    C. Works part time 18 (1.6%)
    D. Able to perform useful role(s) 489 (43%)
    E. No data 63 (5%)
60. Social:
    A. Freedom of choice 25 (2%)
    B. Still meets new people 108 (10%)
    C. Variety of friends 345 (30%)
    D. Takes part in group activities, meetings 245 (22%)
    E. Family 916 (81%)
    F. Sexual activity 56 (6½%)
    G. No data 65 (5%)

VII. INDIVIDUAL

61. Attributes longevity to: See Appendix 24
62. Philosophy of life:
63. Present goals:
64. Crises in life:
65. Most difficult time:
66. Most vivid memory:
67. Other pertinent characteristics:
68. Idiosyncracies/differences from others:
69. Comments (quotations, anecdotes, Americana):

APPENDIX 23

SALIENT CHARACTERISTICS ASSOCIATED WITH LONGEVITY

Trait	Number of Centenarians	Percent of 1,200 Cohort
1. Hard work on farm	312	26
Hard work, nonfarm	219	18
Hard work, partially on farm	133	11
Hard work, total:	664	55
2. Farm, hard work	312	26
Farm, partially	133	11
Farm, unassociated with work	26	2
Farm residence, total:	471	39
3. Quiet life	299	25
4. Religion	205	17
5. Belief in God	169	14
6. Enjoys life or some important activity, relationship, etc.	168	14
7. Family important	139	11½
8. Still sews, knits, etc.	133	11
9. Still gardens	119	10
10. No smoke and drink	83	7
No drink	27	2
No smoke	8	1
No smoke and/or drink, total:	118	10
11. Work, but not hard manual labor	111	9
12. Work satisfaction	106	9
13. Observes Golden Rule	103	8½
14. Genetic	90	7½
15. Diet	85	7
16. Music (singing, dancing, playing instrument)	81	6¾
17. Moderation	78	6½
No worry	78	6½
19. Sense of humor	77	6½
20. Happy	74	6
21. Good, clean life	70	6
22. Strong-willed	69	5¾
23. Kept busy, active	64	5½
24. Intellectual interest, mentally active	55	4½
25. Took care	53	4½
26. Independence	49	4
27. Regularity	37	3

Trait	Number of Centenarians	Percent of 1,200 Cohort
28. Will to live	35	3
29. Self-esteem, strong self-image	32	2½
30. One day at a time	31	2½
31. Content	28	2¼
32. Easy going, even-tempered	27	2¼
33. Cheerful	25	2
Likes, loves people	25	2
35. Never gets angry, upset; controls temper	24	2
36. Exercise	22	2
Sleep, rest	22	2

APPENDIX 24

CENTENARIANS' ATTRIBUTIONS FOR LONGEVITY

(Cohort—951 centenarians responded)

	Trait	Number of Centenarians	Percent of 951 Cohort
1.	Hard work	143	15
2.	No drink and smoke	92	9½
	No drink	37	4
	No smoke	9	1
	No drink and/or smoke, total	138	14½
3.	Eating habits	118	12½
4.	Kept busy, active	80	8½
5.	Doesn't know, but then gives attribution	70	7½
6.	God's will	67	7
7.	Doesn't know	57	6
	Doing or living right	57	6
9.	Living good, clean life	55	6
10.	Family long-lived	51	5½
11.	Took care of health	49	5
12.	Doesn't worry	45	4¾
13.	Had good health, constitution	44	4½
14.	Good Christian, church	43	4½
15.	Moderation	40	4
16.	Work	32	3¼
	Enjoyed life	32	3¼
18.	Trust in God	31	3¼
19.	Lord's blessing	30	3
20.	Exercise	29	3
21.	Serving God	26	2¾
	Never excited, upset, angry	26	2¾
23.	Drinking alcoholic beverages	25	2½
	Eating in moderation	25	2½
25.	Early to rise, to bed	24	2½
	Plenty of sleep, rest	24	2½
27.	Outdoors a lot	22	2¼
28.	No carousing, running around	21	2¼
29.	Happy	20	2
	Treating people right	20	2
31.	One day at a time	18	2
	Helping people	18	2
33.	Regularity	17	1¾
34.	Antimedicine, doctors	16	1¾

	Trait	Number of Centenarians	Percent of 951 Cohort
	Calm, easy-going, even disposition	16	1¾
	Quiet life	16	1¾
37.	Content, peace of mind	15	1½
	Honest	15	1½
	Lord's reward for goodness	15	1½
40.	Taking things as they come	14	1½
41.	Family	13	1½
	Good parents, upbringing	13	1½
	Interested in life, things	13	1½
44.	Minds own business	12	1¼
	Three meals a day	12	1¼
	Will	12	1¼
47.	Golden Rule	11	1¼
	Honored parents	11	1¼
49.	Doctors, medicine	10	1
	Plain, simple life	10	1
	Thankful	10	1
	Walking	10	1
53.	Enjoyed work	9	1
	Friends	9	1
	Had good care	9	1
	Has had good life	9	1
57.	Being obedient	8	
	Loves neighbors, everybody	8	
	Luck	8	
	No fighting, never in trouble	8	
61.	Doesn't drink coffee/tea/soda	7	
	Laughing	7	
63.	Fate, ordained, predestination	6	
	Kindness of family, friends	6	
	No hurry	6	
	Sense of humor	6	
	Wife or husband	6	
68.	Accepts/no complaints	5	
	Active mentally	5	
	No laborious work	5	
	Positive, optimistic outlook	5	
72.	Ambition to be 100	4	
	Ate slowly	4	
	Chewing tobacco	4	
	Tried her/his best	4	
76.	Ambitions, common sense, country/ fresh air, dancing, gets along with people, good children, no ambitions, normal life, with God's help	3	
85.	Cheerful, did not expect to reach 100, did what he/she wanted to, good appe-		

Trait	Number of Centenarians	Percent of 951 Cohort

tite, likes people, loves to live, full life, nature, no ambition to live long, never owned auto, abstaining from drink and smoke has nothing to do with it, singing, Christian Science — 2

98. Adjusts to times, breathing deeply, coffee, courageous, cautious, devilish, energetic, escaped disease, kept kidneys clean, kept same weight, kept warm, independence, ground and water (environment), looked ahead, love, never ashamed, no borrowing, no gossiping, no meanness, no regrets, no two women at the same time, expected to reach 100, necessity/ duty, orderly life, stoutness, snuff, self-sufficient, small man, to be useful, took responsibility for life and health, working with young people — 1

Total number of different attributions = 128

ODD ATTRIBUTIONS

He doesn't believe in germs

"Head to sunset and feet to sunrise. If you sleep in this position, not many celestial bodies can go over your body."

Eating a big bowl of oatmeal every morning

Sleeping with his head to the north

He proclaims, "I am not going to die."

Keeping kidneys clean with a special springtime herb that he used as a youth in Poland

An olive oil and turpentine elixir

Honey

Two raw eggs with a little vermouth every morning

Goat's milk

Ash cakes

Sunflower seeds

Fat pork

Rye bread

Black coffee with lots of sugar

Regular gargling and sleeping with window open

Root beer

Cod-liver oil

Spaghetti and good Italian food

Smoking water pipe

Salt

APPENDIX 25

OCCUPATIONS*

Vocation	Number of Centenarians	Percent of 1,200 Cohort	Percent of 2,800 Jobs
1. Farmer (includes 33 females)	229	19	8
Farmer entire career	105	8¾	3¾
Field worker	68	5½	2½
Subtotal:	402	33½	14¼
Farm wife	108	9	3¾
Farm boy or girl	236	19½	8½
Total farm:	746	62	26½
2. Housewife	234	19½	8¼
Solely housewife	126	10½	4½
Subtotal:	360	30	13
Farm wife	108	9	3¾
Total:	468	39	16¾
3. Factory/mill worker	104	8½	3¾
4. Schoolteacher	79	6½	3
5. Domestic, housework	77	6½	3
6. Sawmill, logging	74	6	2½
7. Laborer, railroad-track worker	72	6	2½
8. Store clerk, salesman	52	4¼	2
9. Seamstress, dressmaker	50	4	1¾
10. Ran grocery, general, or other store	44	3½	1½
11. Carpenter	41	3½	1½
12. Public-office holder	38	3	1¼
13. Rancher, cowboy	32	2½	1¼
14. Worked for company	28	2¼	1
15. Cook	25	2	1
U.S. Army or Navy (7 others served in foreign armies)	25	2	1
17. Miner	24	2	1
Handy man, did odd jobs	24	2	1
19. Janitor	22	2	¾
President of company	22	2	¾
21. Banker	21	1¾	¾
22. Construction work	20	1¾	¾
23. Salesman	18	1½	

* Because the great majority of centenarians worked at several vocations during their lives, about 2,800 job descriptions were given for the 1,200 subjects.

Vocation	Number of Centenarians	Percent of 1,200 Cohort	Percent of 2,800 Jobs
Teamster	18	1½	
25. Sailor, seaman	16	1¼	
Bookkeeper, accountant	16	1¼	
Practical nurse	16	1¼	
28. Minister	15	1¼	
Watchman	15	1¼	
30. Salesman	14	1¼	
Writer	14	1¼	
32. Sheriff, policeman	13	1	
Real estate	13	1	
34. Fireman (boiler, railroad, ship)	12	1	
35. Laundry	11	1	
36. Fisherman	10	¾	
Physician	10	¾	
Stenographer	10	¾	
39. Cabinetmaker	9	¾	
Office worker	9	¾	
41. Educator	8	¾	
Merchant	8	¾	
Postmaster	8	¾	
44. Blacksmith, butcher, engineer, gardener, lawyer, post-office worker, ran dress shop, ran hotel, ran lumberyard, preacher, school principal	7	½	
55. Auto agency, baby sitter/nurse-maid, druggist, greenhouse operator, machinist, loader, longshoreman, matron, plumber, printer, prospector, painter, oil-field worker, railroad conductor or engineer, taught piano or music, waitress, woodworker	6		
72. Cashier, cobbler/shoemaker, mailman, musician, photographer, shipyard worker, singer, telegrapher, treasurer, undertaker, water carrier	5		
83. Actress/actor, coachman, church leader, dentist, hotel maid, messenger, milliner, porter, newspaper publisher, professor, ran gas station, ran restaurant, repairman, shepherd, stable boy, upholsterer, waiter	4		

359

Vocation	Number of Centenarians	Percent of 1,200 Cohort	Percent of 2,800 Jobs
100. Barber, bought-repaired-sold houses, apartment superintendent, charity/philanthropist, chauffeur, circus performer, builder, icehouse worker, insurance agency, electrician, jeweler, leather cutter, librarian, maintenance man, midwife, minister's wife, newsman, artist, mechanic in factory, making brick, plasterer, pro baseball player, Pullman porter, groom, raised horses, secretary, storekeeper's wife, streetcar conductor/motorman, telephone operator, thresher, weaver	3		
130. Antiques, architect, bandmaster, brewer, built boats, china painter, coal operator, dress designer, debt collector, interior decorator, lecturer, lavatory/bathhouse attendant, music/song writer, nun, orange-grove owner, Salvation Army officer, public relations, selling coal, ship captain, taught singing, taxi driver, WPA	2		
152. National sorority president, authority on bridge, founder of women's society, forest-fire fighter, conductor, piano tuner, muralist-decorator, stock speculator, landscaper, inventor, violin maker, cinematographer, director of student center, manager of sugar plantation, builder/designer, ran trailer park, organized second Girl Scouts troop, trader in Indian relics, missionary, rabbi, hospital superintendent, chamber of commerce leader, trapper, optioned coal land, sign hanger, baker, contractor, bus driver, cigar maker, partner in tourist agency, dining hostess, bootblack, property owner, nursery supervisor, housemother, ran sandwich stand, hospital worker, elevator	1		

Vocation	Number of Centenarians	Percent of 1,200 Cohort	Percent of 2,800 Jobs

operator, telephone lineman, kiln
worker, Red Cross, bee producer,
tile setter, coppersmith, well
digger, loading railroad ties, inter-
preter, speculator, mason, pro
athlete, basket maker, companion,
cafe operator, milkman, master
mariner, masseuse, dental worker,
ran garage, dental technician,
newsboy, surgical fitter, motorcycle
rider, auctioneer, religious organization, hod carrier, brick-
layer, prison guard, hide evaluator,
sharpshooter, boat rigger, mill-
wright, fish cleaner, veterinarian,
mule tender, mule skinner, drape
maker, dancer, taught dress
design, maker of quality shoes,
tinsmith, ran woodworking business, altar boy, surveyor, building
manager, ran stage line, watch-
maker, jewelry designer, insurance
representative, kosher meat in-
spector, soda jerk, owned luggage
firm, furrier, judge, rooming
house packer for army, book
editor

Total job types: 248

APPENDIX 26

WORK AND ORDER

A. LENGTH OF WORK LIVES

Number of Work Years	Number of Centenarians	Percent of 640 Cohort*	Number of Centenarians	Percent of 775 Cohort*
49 or less	15	2¼	15	2
50–55	20	3	20	2½
56–60	25	4	25	3
61–65	52	8	52	7
66–70	83	13	110	14
71–75	88	13¾	115	15
76–80	105	16½	132	17
81–85	133	20¾	160	20½
86–90**	101	15¾	128	16½
91–95	13	2	13	1½
96 or more	5	¾	5	½
Subtotal:	640		775	
Worked long time	126			
Worked most of life	9			
Total:	775			

* The length of the work lives of 640 centenarians was known exactly. In addition, another 135 centenarians worked a long time or for most of their lives. These lengthy but inexactly measured work lives were distributed equally over the five most common work groups, from 66 to 90. It can be seen that the additions change the percentages only slightly.

** Thirty-six of the 101 centenarians worked 90 years. A total of 54 centenarians worked 90 or more years, about 8½ percent of the 640 cohort.

B. RETIREMENT AGES

Retirement Age	Number of Centenarians	Percent of Cohort of 701 (Including Those Still Working)	Percent of 482 Retirees
59 or younger	4	½	¾
60–65	20	3	4
66–70	22	3	4½
71–75	34	5	7
76–80	57	8	12
81–85	77	11	16
86–90	83	12	17
91–95	97	14	20
96+*	88	12½	18¼
Total retirees:	482	69	
Still working	219	31	
Total:	701		

* Includes three centenarians who retired at age 101 and one centenarian who retired at 102.

C. CENTENARIANS STILL WORKING

Job	Number of Centenarians	Number of Centenarians Earning Money
1. Housework/cooking	87	3
2. Gardening	27	3
3. Housework/gardening	11	1
4. Farming/yardwork	10	8
5. Sewing	7	4
6. Farmland management	5	3
7. Janitor	4	4
8. Housework/sewing	3	1
Insurance broker	3	1
Runs store	3	3
Works for company	3	3
Preacher	3	
13. Artist	2	2
Banker	2	2
Company president	2	2
Farming/housework	2	1
Sewing/gardening	2	1
Shoemaker	2	2
19. Farming/wire baskets	1	1
Basket weaving	1	1
Housework/produce stand	1	1
Bank/farming	1	1

Job	Number of Centenarians	Number of Centenarians Earning Money
Bank/real estate	1	1
Bank/property	1	1
Works at store	1	1
Takes in washing	1	1
Physician	1	1
Lawyer	1	1
Writing	1	1
Writing newspaper column	1	1
Judge	1	1
Runs correspondence school	1	1
Songwriter	1	1
Minister	1	1
Priest	1	1
Rabbi	1	1
Lecturer	1	1
Public relations representative	1	1
Works on electric motors	1	1
Fisherman	1	1
Longshoreman	1	1
Surveyor	1	1
Funeral director	1	1
Salesman	1	1
Selling antiques	1	1
Partner in clothing/hotel business	1	1
Housework/makes bandages	1	
Literary work	1	
Writing/sewing	1	
Assists at church	1	
Reading	1	
Dowager	1	
Stock speculator	1	
Medicine man	1	
Plays piano	1	
Antiques/gardening/housework	1	
Works in daughter's business/gardens	1	
Runs rooming house	1	1
Church patriarch	1	
Total:	219	70

D. IMPORTANT ITEMS IN "ORDER" CATEGORY

Item	Percent of Centenarians
1. Organized lifetime activities/goals	95
2. Worked hard	89
3. Worked long time	87
4. Lived in same place long time	78
5. Has easy life now	78
6. Strong family fabric	75
7. Important to one or many people	74
8. Continuous place in family	72
9. Continuity in work	70
10. Still working or regular routine	63
11. Continuity in interests	62
12. Organized daily activities	52
13. Lives with child, grandchild, or other relative	48
14. Harmonious, integrated life	44
15. Performs useful roles	42
16. Married very long time	39
17. Church/religion	37
18. Continuous place in community	36
19. Moderate weight	35
20. Managing life in own house	32
Use of alcohol	32
Sees children	32

APPENDIX 27

ATTITUDES TOWARD SOCIAL SECURITY
(Question 56F)

Attitude	Number of Centenarians
1. Thankful/happy/welcomes it	63
2. Never thought about it or expected it	55
Never thought about it or expected it, but now important	55
4. Surprised	44
5. Useful/it helps/important	30
6. Thought it was a good thing	29
7. Feels independent because of it	28
8. Thought it was a good thing, didn't expect to get it, now happy	26
9. Thought it was a good thing, thought would get it	23
10. Thought it was a good thing, didn't think would get it	22
11. Surprised/didn't expect to get it, now happy/main income	20
12. Didn't like the idea, but taking it	15
Never thought about it, now of minor importance	15
14. It's a necessity	14
15. Didn't like the idea, now loves it	10
Just extra money	10
17. Didn't think it would work, now respects it	9
Never thought would get it/surprised, now main income/gives sense of security/feels independent because of it	9
19. Thought it was a good thing, now it is unimportant	8
20. Thought would get it, now happy	7
One of reasons he retired	7
22. Thought would get it, now important	6
23. Thought would get it	5
It gives a sense of security	5
Didn't want it	5
Good, but not enough	5
27. Unimportant	4
28. Didn't like it, never thought about it, now only income	3
29. Thought it was a good thing, now gives feeling of independence	2
30. Likes Medicare	1
Total:	535

APPENDIX 28

IMPORTANT ITEMS IN "FREEDOM/INDEPENDENCE" CATEGORY

Item	Percent of Centenarians
1. Curious, interested in immediate world about him/her	83.9
2. Good physical functioning	83.6
3. Family	81
4. Freedom from stress, anxiety	76
5. Independent, makes ends meet	75
6. Still mobile	72
7. Freedom from disease	66
8. Autonomous life	63
9. Takes responsibility for life, health	49
10. Makes decisions	46
11. Living in home of relative	45
12. Able to perform useful roles	43
13. Freedom from health establishment	42
14. Flexible, adaptive	35
15. Reads	30
Still does physical work, exercises	30
Variety of friends	30

HEALTH

A. DISEASE REPORTED AT PRESENT OR IN LATER YEARS

Disease	Number of Centenarians	Males	Females
Absence of disease/never been sick	80	43	37
Cardiovascular	61	44	17
Heart disease	26	20	6
Stroke	18	12	6
Vascular	14	12	2
Dizzy spells	9	8	1
Hardening of arteries	3	2	1
Poor circulation	2	2	
High blood pressure	3		3
Cancer	6	4	2
Diabetes	3	2	1
Pulmonary	21	14	7
Pneumonia	8	5	3
Asthma	4	2	2
Influenza	4	3	1
Shortness of breath	3	2	1
Black lung	1	1	
Coughing spells	1	1	
Gastrointestinal	20	18	2
Gallbladder	4	2	2
Kidneys	4	4	
Indigestion	3	3	
Appendix	2	2	
Stomach pains	2	2	
Bladder	1	1	
Bowel	1	1	
Colic	1	1	
Eating difficulty	1	1	
Intestines	1	1	
Nervous	14	7	7
Sciatica	4	2	2
Headaches	2	2	
Shingles	2		2
Skin disorder	2	1	1
Trouble sleeping	2	2	
Diverticulosis	1		1
Neuritis	1		1

Disease	Number of Centenarians	Males	Females
Arthritis	54	28	26
Unspecified illness	13	6	7
Unspecified surgery	11	9	2
Rheumatism	7	6	1
Glaucoma	4	3	1
Hernia	4	3	1
Health failing	3	1	2
Spells	1	1	
Virulent fever	1	1	

B. DISEASE REPORTED IN MIDDLE AGE

Disease	Number of Centenarians
Unspecified illness	9
Appendectomy	5
Pneumonia	3
Asthma	2
Influenza	2
Gallstone operation	1
Surgery	1
Ulcers	1

C. DISEASE REPORTED IN YOUTH

Disease	Number of Centenarians
Measles	4
Typhoid	4
Tuberculosis	3
Diphtheria	2
Scarlet fever	2
Asthma	1
Croup	1
Lung infection	1
Mumps	1
Near death as baby	1
Smallpox	1
Typhoid pneumonia	1
Unspecified illness	1

D. DISABILITY REPORTED AT PRESENT OR IN LATER YEARS

Disability	Number of Centenarians	Males	Females
Broken hip	82	26	56
Broken leg	6	1	5
Broken arm	9	7	2
Fell and broke other bones	23	11	12
Total broken bones:	120	45	75
Blind	49	26	23
Cataracts	37	22	15
Leg troubles	56		
Amputations	3		
Artificial leg	1		
Weak, feeble	6		
Back troubles	3		
Speech impaired	3		
Aches and pains	2		
Stiffness	2		
Trouble with balance	2		
Arm shakes	1		
Teeth trouble	1		

APPENDIX 30
DIET

A. ATTRIBUTIONS OF LONGEVITY TO EATING HABITS*

Attribution	Number of Centenarians
1. Good, simple food	19
2. Eating carefully	14
3. Eating in moderation	11
4. Eating properly	10
5. Eating right	8
Eating only what is agreeable	8
No coffee, tea, or soda	8
No coffee and tea 2	
No coffee and soda 1	
No soda 5	
8. Eating well	6
9. Plain food	5
10. Lots of milk	4
Plenty of vegetables	4
Regular meals	4
Eating slowly	4
14. Balanced diet	3
Eating everything	3
Fresh foods	3
Good appetite	3
Meat	3
Vitamin pills	3
20. Enjoys food	2
Few sweets	2
Fresh fruit and vegetables	2
Good nutrition	2
Killed own meat	2
25. Plenty to eat; afternoon snack; liking most food;	1

small bites; nothing fried except eggs; home cooking;
good breakfast; ate to live; peas, greens, corn bread;
fatback, collards, turnips, cabbage; Adventist
vegetarian diet; homegrown food; fresh vegetables;
fruit; raw egg and fruits; berries; no meat; no rich
food; goat's milk; soup for supper; boiled cabbage;
Swedish cooking; good Italian food; spaghetti;
lots of chili; no starch; pork chops and potatoes; fat
pork; lots of ham; lots of coffee with lots of sugar;
tonics; lots of salt; big bowl of oatmeal every

* Cited by 118 centenarians, some making multiple attributions.

morning; two raw eggs with a little vermouth every morning; eight glasses of water a day; rye bread; honey; sunflower seeds; ash cakes

Total number of attributions: 172

B. SPECIAL DIETS FOLLOWED
(Question 40B,e)

Diet		Number of Centenarians
1. Breakfast		17
Hearty	3	
Best meal	1	
Most important—eggs and toast	1	
Heaviest—scrambled eggs and grits	1	
Bacon, eggs, coffee	1	
3 eggs, toast, bacon	1	
2 eggs, bacon, toast, 1 cup coffee	1	
2 eggs, toast, fried potatoes, coffee	1	
1 egg, 1 slice bread, coffee	1	
2 fried eggs, bacon, toast, cooked cereal, juice, milk	1	
2 raw eggs and whiskey	1	
Pancakes, bacon, coffee	1	
Oatmeal, coffee, apple sauce, sometimes egg	1	
Teaspoon of honey with butter and rolled oats	1	
Corn bread and tap gravy (lard, flour, and water)	1	
2. Lots of milk		10
3. Dinner		7
Big meal	1	
Coffee and doughnuts	1	
Cornbread and vegetables	1	
Fruit or something light	1	
Grapefruit	1	
Lettuce, vinegar, and peppers	1	
Soup	1	
4. No soda		6
5. Fresh fruits and vegetables		4
Lunch		4
Bowl of oatmeal	1	
Corn bread and vegetables	1	
Soup, cake, and coffee	1	
Very little—fruit, something light	1	
No coffee		4
Plenty of vegetables		4
9. Fresh vegetables		3
Lots of salt		3

Diet	Number of Centenarians
No tea	3
Vitamin pills	3
13. As much fruit as possible	2
Killed own meat	2
Little meat	2
Plenty of water	2
No sweets	2
18. Peas-greens-corn bread; carrots every day; no rich food; buttermilk; goat's milk; 2 spoons cod-liver oil; nothing fried except eggs; lots of boiled cabbage; no cake; vinegar on everything; honey; no extreme hot or cold food; no roughages or spices; peppermint candy to combat indigestion; bacon, veal, lamb, chicken the only meats eaten; lots of coffee; hogmeat only; plenty of corn; one meal a day; two meals a day; hot peppers; no heavy meals; no ice-cold food or drink; 2 glasses of hot water every morning; tonic with every meal; ice cream, bland foods; seafood; juices; cornmeal rolls; lots of rice; salads	1
Total number of special diets:	109

C. FAVORITE FOODS MENTIONED

Food	Number of Centenarians
1. Late afternoon snack	7
Cakes 3	
Bananas 2	
Ice cream 2	
2. Coffee	5
3. Bread, butter, and jelly	3
Ham	3
5. Apples	2
Chicken	2
Sauerkraut	2
8. Boiled roots; breakfast; candy; cookies; corn; collard greens, corned beef, and cabbage; doughnuts; evening meal; hot biscuits and syrup; lutefisk and lefse (Swedish) dinners; heavy sweet soups; corn bread; meat with chili; Norwegian sardines; peanuts; popcorn; potatoes; pork with lots of fat; rare steak; rice soup with can of tomatoes; rolls; sweet potatoes; tea in glass; Tootsie Rolls; turkey cakes; welsh rarebit	1
Total favorites:	51

APPENDIX 31
SIBLINGS

A. NUMBER OF SIBLINGS

Number of Siblings	Number of Centenarians	Number of Siblings	Number of Centenarians
None	1	7	20
1	7	8	19
1+*	5	9	21
2	6	10	16
2+*	13	11	9
3	13	12	6
3+	3	13	4
4	18	14	1
4+*	2	15	2
5	18	Many	2
5+*	1	63 (Mormon)	1
6	18	Uncertain	3
Several	7	Total:	216

* Plus signs indicate that the centenarians had at least that many siblings indicated, but it was impossible to determine how many more siblings they had.

B. POSITION AMONG SIBLINGS
(Question 16)

Position Among Siblings	Number of Centenarians
Oldest	35
Older of two children	2
Second oldest	8
Third oldest	10
Fourth oldest	7
Middle child	5
Fifth oldest	3
Sixth oldest	3
Seventh oldest	2
Ninth oldest	1
Younger of two children	3
Youngest	24
Total:	103

Number of Siblings	Number of Centenarians	Number of Siblings	Number of Centenarians
Oldest		**Youngest**	
2+	1	1+	1
3	5	2	1
4	2	2+	1
5	4	3	1
6	5	4	2
7	1	5	1
8	5	6	3
9	3	7	2
10	1	8	1
11	3	9	3
Several	2	10	2
Uncertain	3	11	3
Total:	35	Several	1
Second Oldest		Many	1
4	3	Uncertain	1
5	1	Total:	24
9	2	**Middle**	
11	1	2	1
12	1	4	1
Third Oldest		8	1
3*	1	10	1
4	1	14	1
5	1	**Fifth Oldest**	
7	1	7	1
8	1	8	1
9**	1	11	1
10	1	**Sixth Oldest**	
11	1	9	1
12	1	10	1
13	1	12	1
Fourth Oldest		**Seventh Oldest**	
5	1	8	1
6	1	10	1
7	1	**Ninth Oldest**	
9	2	10	1
10	1		
13	1		

* The only second youngest in group.
** The oldest girl.

APPENDIX 32

ATTRIBUTIONS OF LONGEVITY BY CATEGORY

A. NUMBER OF REASONS GIVEN

Attributions		Number of Centenarians
Single		351
Multiple		504
2	263	
3	140	
4	65	
5	25	
6	8	
7	2	
8	1	
Total:		855

B. ATTRIBUTIONS BY SPHERES

Attributions		Number of Centenarians
Single		540
Biological		346
Physical	282	
Genetic	40	
Physical-genetic	24	
Psychological		174
Social		20
Multiple		315
Psychobiological		171
Psycho-physical	149	
Psycho-physical-genetic	12	
Psycho-genetic	10	
Psychosocial		71
Sociobiological		42
Socio-physical	40	
Socio-physical-genetic	2	
Sociopsychobiological (S/P/B)		31
Sociopsycho-physical	28	
Sociopsycho-genetic	3	
Total:		855

APPENDIX 33
DEATHS, SELF-RATING, PREDICTORS

A. OCCURRENCE OF CENTENARIAN DEATHS*

Months after interview	6	9	12	15	18	32
Number whose death dates are ambiguous**	24	27	24	25	21	10
Pool: number whose death dates are known	133	130	133	132	136	147
Centenarians dead	29	45	72	98	114	137
Centenarians alive	104	85	61	34	22	10
Percentage dead	22	35	54	74	84	93
Percentage alive	78	65	46	26	16	7

* Total number of known dead = 157.
** See text (pages 131–132 and 187).

B. COMPARISON: OBJECTIVE RATING AND SELF-HEALTH RATING

Months after interview	6	9	12	15	18	32
Pool	133	130	133	132	136	147
Number of centenarians for whom predictor is applicable						
Self-rating (S/R)	101 (76%)	94 (72%)	98 (74%)	93 (71%)	98 (72%)	108 (74%)
Objective	129 (97%)	126 (97%)	128 (96%)	131 (99%)	135 (99%)	145 (99%)

(Continued)

Months after interview	6	9	12	15	18	32
Number of accurate predictions						
S/R	61	60	65	56	54	54
Objective	85	80	75	65	54	52
Percent accurate						
S/R	60.4	64	66.3	60	55	50
Objective	66	63.5	59	50	40	36
Percent accurate for pool						
S/R	46	46	49	42	40	37
Objective	64	62	56	49	40	35

C. COMPARISON: THE FIVE PREDICTORS

Months after interview	6	9	12	15	18	32
Pool	133	130	133	132	136	147
Usefulness						
Number applicable	130 (98%)	127 (98%)	130 (98%)	129 (98%)	133 (98%)	146 (99%)
Number of accurate predictions	68	74	86	79	79	86
Percent accurate	54	58	66.2	61	59	59
Percent accurate for pool	50	56	65	60	58	59
Percent of predictors	21	24	25	25	26	26
Work						
Number applicable	133(100%)	130(100%)	133(100%)	132(100%)	136(100%)	147(100%)
Number of accurate predictions	68	72	82	79	80	87
Percent accurate	51	55	62	60	58	59
Percent accurate for pool	51	55	62	60	58	59
Percent of predictors	21	23	24	25	26	27

Self-rating health (S/R)	6	9	12	15	18	32
Number applicable	101 (76%)	94 (72%)	98 (74%)	93 (71%)	98 (72%)	108 (74%)
Number of accurate predictions	61	60	65	56	54	54
Percent accurate	60.4	64	66.3	60	55	50
Percent accurate for pool	46	46	49	42	40	37
Percent of predictors	19	19	19	18	17.5	17
Memory						
Number applicable	111 (83%)	110 (85%)	106 (80%)	106 (80%)	107 (79%)	115 (78%)
Number of accurate predictions	94	74	60	42	36	31
Percent accurate	85	67	57	40	34	27
Percent accurate for pool	71	56	45	32	26	21
Percent of predictors	30	24	18	13	11.5	9
Goals						
Number applicable	75 (56%)	74 (57%)	74 (56%)	76 (58%)	77 (57%)	82 (56%)
Number of accurate predictions	25	33	46	57	59	67
Percent accurate	33	45	62	75	77	82
Percent accurate for pool	22	25	35	43	43	46
Percent of predictors	9	11	14	18	19	21

D. ACCURACY OF MULTIPLE PREDICTORS

Months after interview	6	9	12	15	18	32
Pool	133	130	133	132	136	147
Number of accurate predictions (percent of accuracy)						
Usefulness	67 (50%)	74 (56%)	86 (65%)	79 (60%)	79 (58%)	86 (59%)
Use.-work	70 (53%)	77 (59%)	88 (66%)	84 (64%)	85 (63%)	92 (63%)

Months after interview	6	9	12	15	18	32
Use.-work-goals	78 (59%)	86 (66%)	102 (77%)	104 (79%)	106 (80%)	116 (79%)
Use.-work-memory	109 (82%)	106 (81%)	106 (80%)	96 (73%)	93 (68%)	99 (67%)
Use.-work-S/R	93 (70%)	97 (74%)	106 (80%)	102 (77%)	100 (74%)	109 (74%)
Use.-work-goals-memory	117 (88%)	114 (87%)	116 (87%)	113 (86%)	112 (82%)	121 (82%)
Use.-work-S/R-goals	100 (75%)	104 (80%)	116 (89%)	115 (87%)	117 (86%)	127 (86%)
Use.-work-S/R-memory	120 (90%)	117 (90%)	118 (89%)	108 (82%)	107 (79%)	114 (78%)
Use.-work-S/R-goals-memory	122 (92%)	119 (91%)	122 (92%)	119 (90%)	119 (88%)	128 (87%)
Total predictions possible (5 per centenarian)	665	650	665	660	680	735
Total accurate predictions	316 (48%)	313 (48%)	339 (51%)	313 (47%)	308 (45%)	325 (44%)
Average correct predictions per centenarian	2.36	2.41	2.54	2.37	2.26	2.12

E. ACCURACY OF PREDICTION

Months after interview	6	9	12	15	18	32
Pool	133	130	133	132	136	147
5 out of 5	5	5	5	4	3	3
4 out of 4	13	13	12	9	7	9
3 out of 3	11	7	9	9	8	6
2 out of 2	1	1	3	3	4	6
1 out of 1				1	1	
Total all predictors correct:	30 (23%)	26 (19%)	29 (22%)	26 (20%)	23 (17%)	24 (16%)
4 out of 5	11	13	19	19	19	19
3 out of 4	17	17	18	14	15	14
2 out of 3	1	2	3	4	4	6

3 out of 5	$\frac{11}{40}$	$\frac{12}{44}$	$\frac{9}{49}$	$\frac{8}{45}$	$\frac{10}{48}$	$\frac{10}{49}$
Total, more than half predictors correct:	70 (53%)	70 (54%)	78 (59%)	71 (54%)	71 (52%)	73 (50%)
2 out of 4	11	11	13	12	14	17
1 out of 2	1	1	1	1		
	12	12	14	13	14	17
Total, half or more predictors correct:	82 (62%)	82 (63%)	92 (69%)	84 (64%)	85 (63%)	90 (61%)
2 out of 5	10	12	13	13	11	12
1 out of 3	8	5	3	3	2	3
1 out of 4	10	9	7	11	10	11
1 out of 5	13	9	7	8	11	12
Total:	41	35	30	35	34	38
Total, one or more predictors correct:	123 (92%)	117 (90%)	122 (92%)	119 (90%)	119 (88%)	128 (87%)
0 out of 1	1	1	1		2	1
0 out of 2	3	3	2	2	7	8
0 out of 3	2	7	5	6	7	8
0 out of 4	3	2	3	5	1	2
0 out of 5	1					
Total, no predictors correct:	10 (8%)	13 (10%)	11 (8%)	13 (10%)	17 (12%)	19 (13%)
Predictions made	558	538	549	543	555	597
Predictions correct	316	313	339	313	308	325
Percent correct	57	58	62	58	56	54

F. COMPARISON: ACCURACY OF THE FIVE PREDICTORS AND OBJECTIVE HEALTH RATING FOR VERY SHORT AND VERY LONG LIVERS

Months after interview	Less than 6	18–32	32+
Pool	29	10	12
Usefulness			
Number applicable	28 (97%)	10(100%)	12(100%)
Number of accurate predictions	19	7	9
Percent accurate	68	70	75
Percent accurate for pool	66	70	75
Percent of predictors	27	23	22.5
Work			
Number applicable	29(100%)	10(100%)	12(100%)
Number of accurate predictions	18	7	9
Percent accurate	62	70	75
Percent accurate for pool	62	70	75
Percent of predictors	25	23	22.5
Memory			
Number applicable	20 (69%)	10(100%)	10 (83%)
Number of accurate predictions	6	9	10
Percent accurate	30	90	100
Percent accurate for pool	21	90	83
Percent of predictors	8	30	25
Goals			
Number applicable	20 (69%)	6 (60%)	5 (42%)
Number of accurate predictions	17	1	2
Percent accurate	85	17	40
Percent accurate for pool	59	10	17
Percent of predictors	24	3	5
Self-rating health (S/R)			
Number of applicable	18 (62%)	8 (80%)	10 (83%)
Number of accurate predictions	11	6	10
Percent accurate	61	75	100
Percent accurate for pool	38	60	83
Percent of predictors	16	20	25
Objective health rating			
Number applicable	25 (86%)	10(100%)	12(100%)
Number of accurate predictions	10	9	12
Percent accurate	40	90	100
Percent accurate for pool	35	90	100

G. ACCURACY OF PREDICTION FOR VERY SHORT AND VERY LONG LIVERS

Months after interview	Less than 6	18–32	32+
Pool	29	10	12
5 out of 5			2
4 out of 4	2	2	3
3 out of 3	3	1	2
2 out of 2	1		
Total, all predictors correct:	6 (21%)	3 (30%)	7 (58%)
4 out of 5	4	1	2
3 out of 4	7	1	
2 out of 3	1		
3 out of 5	1	2	
	13	4	2
Total, more than half predictors correct:	19 (66%)	7 (70%)	9 (75%)
2 out of 4		1	1
Total, half or more predictors correct:	19 (66%)	8 (80%)	10 (83%)
2 out of 5	1	2	1
1 out of 3	2		
1 out of 4	3		
1 out of 5	1		
	7	2	1
Total, one or more predictors correct:	26 (90%)	10(100%)	11 (92%)
0 out of 2			1
0 out of 3	2		
0 out of 4	1		
Total, no predictors correct:	3 (10%)	0	1 (8%)
Predictions made	115	44	49
Predictions correct	69	30	40
Percent correct	60	68	82

APPENDIX 34
RELIGION AND ACTIVITIES

A. DENOMINATIONS OF CHURCH MEMBERSHIP REPORTED
(Question 25C)

Denomination	Number of Centenarians
1. Catholic	60
2. Methodist	54
3. Baptist	36
4. Presbyterian	27
5. Lutheran	21
6. Episcopal	12
7. Congregational	6
(First) Christian	6
9. Christian Scientist	5
Seventh Day Adventist	5
11. Church of Christ	4
Jewish	4
Unitarian	4
14. Friends	3
Mennonite	3
Mormon	3
17. Buddhist	2
Greek Orthodox	2
Nazarene	2
Reformed	2
United Brethren Evangelical	2
22. African Methodist Episcopal	1
African Orthodox	1
Amish	1
Church of God	1
First Brethren	1
House of God	1
Overcoming Church of God and Christ	1
Temple of Unity Truth	1
Yoga	1
Total:	272

Total denominations: 30

B. OTHER DAILY ACTIVITIES
(Question 25D)

Activity	Number of Centenarians
1. Reads (newspaper only: 102)	286
2. Watches TV	258
3. Housework	237
4. Goes for walks	150
5. Sews, knits, etc.	133
6. Listens to radio	128
7. Just sits	121
8. Gardens	119
9. Cooks	114
10. Visits	92
11. Does dishes	69
12. Talks (on telephone, with neighbors)	63
13. Has visitors	51
14. Plays games/does puzzles	50
Writes letters	50
16. Does yard work	47
17. Follows baseball	46
18. Shops	29
19. Does handicrafts	28
20. Fished/fishing	26
Prays	26
22. Goes for rides	25
23. Writes	17
24. Paints, draws	14
25. Follows sports (other than baseball)	13
26. Still travels	11
27. Goes out to eat	8
28. Travels on public transportation	6
29. Works on family genealogy	4
30. Goes to school	3

APPENDIX 35

RELATIONSHIPS

Living with	Total Number of Centenarians	Percent of Cohort	Living at Home	Living Elsewhere
Spouse	107	10	100	In nursing home, 3; in hospital, 1; plus daughter, 1; plus son, 1; plus child and grandchild, 1
Daughter	230	21		
Son	83	7½		In hotel: 1
Child (sex unspecified)	148	13½	19	
Subtotal:	461	42	19	
Grandchild (sex unspecified)	19	1½	1	
Granddaughter	12	1	1	
Grandson	5	½	1	
Subtotal:	36	3	3	
Sister	14	1	3	In nursing home: 2
Brother	1	*		
Niece	16	1½		
Nephew	4	*		
Great-niece	3	*		
Great-nephew	2	*		
Great-great-grandchild	1	*		
Relatives	7	½	1	
Daughter-in-law	11	1	7	
Son-in-law	1	*		
Subtotal:	60	4	11	
Total living with relatives:	664	59	133	

* Less than ½ percent.

Living with	Total Number of Centenarians	Percent of Cohort	Living at Home	Living Elsewhere
Friends	7	¾	7	
Others	13	1¼	13	
Total:	20	2	20	
Alone	154	14	148	In boarding house, 6; with housekeeper, 10; with nurse, 3
Nursing home	260	24		In hospital: 5
Lodge, convent	6	½		
Total:	1,104	100	301	

APPENDIX 36

PROFILES/TRAITS

NUMBERS (AND PERCENTAGES) OF TRAITS

Category of traits	Order/ Freedom	Socio-psycho-biological	Both Profiles	Neither Profile
Total (1,200)	628 (52%)	8 (⅔%)	501 (42%)	63 (5%)
Very many	1		9 (2%)	
Many	19 (3%)	1 (12½%)	50 (10%)	1 (1½%)
Moderate-to-many	26 (4%)		73 (15%)	
Moderate	110 (18%)	1 (12½%)	123 (25%)	3 (4¾%)
Few-to-moderate	115 (18%)		127 (25%)	2 (3%)
Few	230 (37%)	4 (50%)	65 (13%)	17 (27%)
Many-incomplete			4	
Moderate-incomplete	19 (3%)		10 (2%)	3 (4¾%)
Few-incomplete	60 (9½%)	1 (12½%)	28 (6%)	8 (13%)
Incomplete	48 (7½%)	1 (12½%)	12 (2%)	29 (46%)
Elite (total = 240)	28 (12%)	2	204 (85%)	6 (2½%)
Superelite (total = 9)			9 (100%)	

Bibliography of Selected Readings

CHAPTER 1

Schema

Segerberg, Osborn, Jr. *The Immortality Factor.* New York: Dutton, 1974.

Palmore, Erdman B. *Social Patterns of Normal Aging.* Durham, N.C.: Duke University Press, 1981. A final report on the social and longevity aspects of the Duke longitudinal studies.

———. "The Relative Importance of Social Factors in Predicting Longevity." In *Prediction of Lifespan,* edited by Erdman B. Palmore and Francis C. Jeffers. Lexington, Mass.: Heath Lexington Books, 1971. Highlights of findings.

———. *Normal Aging.* Durham, N.C.: Duke University Press, 1970. Reports from the Duke Longitudinal Study, 1955–69.

———. *Normal Aging II.* Durham, N.C.: Duke University Press, 1974. Reports from the Duke longitudinal studies, 1970–73.

Three-Sphere

Granick, Samuel, and Patterson, Robert D., eds. *Human Aging II: An Eleven-Year Followup Biomedical and Behavioral Study.* Rockville, Md.: National Institute of Mental Health, 1971.

Dubos, René. *Mirage of Health.* New York: Harper & Brothers, 1959.

Hutschnecker, Arnold A. *The Will to Live.* New York: Cornerstone Library, 1975 (paperback); Englewood Cliffs, N.J.: Prentice-Hall, 3d ed., 1966.

Holmes, Thomas, and Rahe, Richard. "The Social Readjustment Rating Scale." *Journal of Psychosomatic Research* 11 (1967): 216.

Segerberg, Osborn, Jr. *Where Have All the Flowers, Fishes, Birds, Trees, Water and Air Gone? What Ecology Is All About.* New York: David McKay, 1971.

Rathbone, Josephine L. *Relaxation.* Philadelphia: Lea & Febiger, 1969.

Reynolds, Vernon. *The Biology of Human Action.* San Francisco: W. H. Freeman, 1976.

Engel, George L. "The Need for a New Medical Model: A Challenge for Biomedicine." *Science,* 8 April 1977, 129–136. "Medicine's crisis stems from the logical inference that since 'disease' is defined in terms of somatic parameters, physicians need not be concerned with psychosocial issues, which lie outside medicine's responsibility and authority."

World Health Organization and UNICEF. *The Declaration of Alma Ata* at the conclusion of the International Conference on Primary Health Care, 12 September 1978, includes: "The Conference strongly reaffirms that health, which is a state of complete physical, mental and social well-being, and not merely the absence of disease or infirmity, is a fundamental human right. . . ."

Order-Freedom

Schrödinger, Erwin. *What Is Life?* Cambridge: Cambridge University Press, 1944.

Dubos, René. "The Mysteries of Life." In *Encyclopaedia Britannica,* 15th ed. (1974), Propaedia, p. 127.

Rose, Steven. *The Conscious Brain.* New York: Knopf, 1975.

Social Security Administration. *America's Centenarians: Reports of Interviews with Social Security Beneficiaries Who Have Lived to 100.* 13 vols. Baltimore: Social Security Administration, December 1963–1972.

Rose, Charles L. "Critique of Longevity Studies." In *Prediction of Lifespan,* edited by Erdman B. Palmore and Francis C. Jeffers. Lexington, Mass.: Heath Lexington Books, 1971.

McWhirter, Norris, ed. *Guinness Book of World Records.* New York: Bantam, 1980.

Comfort, Alex. *The Process of Ageing.* 2d ed. New York: New American Library, 1964.

Holden, Constance. "Centenarians and Representatives." *Science,* 30 November 1979.

Siegel, Jacob S., and Passel, Jeffrey S. "New Estimates of the Number of Centenarians in the United States." *Journal of the American Statistical Association,* September 1976.

Timiras, P. S. *Developmental Physiology and Aging.* New York: Macmillan, 1972.

"Method for Poll." *New York Times,* 15 January 1980.

Tavris, Carol, and Sadd, Susan. *The Redbook Report on Female Sexuality.* 2d ed. New York: Dell, 1977.

Pfeiffer, Eric. "Physical, Psychological and Social Correlates of Survival in Old Age." In *Prediction of Lifespan,* edited by Erdman B. Palmore and Francis C. Jeffers. Lexington, Mass.: Heath Lexington Books, 1971.

CHAPTER 3

Hard Work

In the opening paragraph "Aging, Natural Death, and the Compression of Morbidity," in the *New England Journal of Medicine,* 17 July 1980, James F. Fries, M.D., of the Stanford University Medical Center gives advice using exactly the same words used by two of the centenarians herein interviewed. Dr. James writes: "An important shift is occurring in the conceptualization of chronic disease and of aging. Premature organ dysfunction, whether of muscle, heart, lung or joint is beginning to be conceived as stemming from disuse of the faculty, not overuse. At the Stanford Arthritis Clinic I tell patients to exercise and 'to use it or lose it'; 'Run, not rest' is the new advice of the cardiologist. The body, to an increasing degree, is now felt to rust out rather than wear out."

Exercise, HDL

Leaf, Alexander. "Unusual Longevity: The Common Denominators." *Hospital Practice,* October 1973.

National Heart, Lung, and Blood Institute. *Arteriosclerosis: The Report of the 1977 Working Group to Review the 1971 Report by the National Heart and Lung Institute Task Force on Arteriosclerosis.* Washington, D.C.: DHEW Publication No. (NIH) 78-1526.

Brody, Jane E. "Study of 17,000 Men Indicates Vigorous Sports Protect Heart." *New York Times,* 28 November 1977. Dr. Ralph S. Paffenbarger's study of Harvard alumni.

Altman, Lawrence K. "Exertion Found to Ease Heart Risk." *New York Times,* 24 March 1977. The study of Dr. Ralph S. Paffenbarger et al. on San Francisco longshoremen.

Brody, Jane E. "Chemical Carriers of Cholesterol Casting Light on Coronaries Puzzle." *New York Times,* 18 January 1977.
"Hard Work Makes the Heart Grow Safer." *New York Times,* 4 December 1977. On caloric expenditures of various exercises.
" 'Good' v. 'Bad' Cholesterol." *Time,* 21 November 1977.
Brody, Jane E. "Latest Data Suggest Exercise Helps Curb Heart Attacks." *New York Times,* 27 March 1979.
Marx, Jean L. "The HDL: The Good Cholesterol Carriers?" *Science,* 17 August 1979.
Hartung, G. Harley, et al. "Relation of Diet to High-Density Lipoprotein Cholesterol in Middle-Aged Marathon Runners, Joggers and Inactive Men." *New England Journal of Medicine,* 14 February 1980.
Brody, Jane E. "Protein That Lowers Heart Risk Tied to Moderate Drinking and Exercise." *New York Times,* 13 November 1980.

CHAPTER 5

The Invisible People

Beard, Belle Boone. *Social Competence of Centenarians.* Athens, Ga.: University of Georgia Printing Department, 1967.
Moses, Anna Mary Robertson. *My Life's History.* New York: Harper & Brothers, 1948.

CHAPTER 6

Declarations of Independence

Dunbar, Flanders. "Immunity to the Afflictions of Old Age." *Journal of the American Geriatrics Society,* December 1957.
Jewett, Stephen P. "Longevity and the Longevity Syndrome." *The Gerontologist,* spring 1973.

Placebos

Benson, Herbert. *The Mind/Body Effect.* New York: Simon & Schuster, 1979. Contains an excellent discussion of the placebo effect.
Brody, Jane E. "Placebos Work, but Survey Shows Widespread Misuse." *New York Times,* 3 April 1979.
"Puzzling Pills; Are Placebos Magic or Real." *Time,* 30 July 1979.

Loftus, Elizabeth F., and Fries, James F. "Informed Consent May Be Hazardous to Health." *Science,* 6 April 1979.

Type A Behavior

Friedman, Meyer. "Type A Behavior: A Progress Report." *The Sciences,* February 1980.
Brody, Jane E. "Study Suggests Changing Behavior May Prevent Heart Attack; Controversial 'Type A' Pattern Gains Acceptance as Cardiac Risk." *New York Times,* 16 September 1980.

CHAPTER 7

Health

Reichel, William. "Editorial Comment: Senile Dementia—A New Frontier." *Newsletter,* American Geriatrics Society, August 1978.
Gruenberg, Ernest M. "Epidemiology of Senile Dementia." In *Second Conference on the Epidemiology of Aging,* edited by Suzanne G. Haynes and Manning Feinleib. U.S. Department of Health and Human Services, NIH Publication No. 80-969, July 1980.
National Institute on Aging. "NIA Studies Causes of Alzheimer's Disease." In *Special Report on Aging: 1980.* Washington, D.C.: NIH Publication No. 80-2135, August 1980.
———. "Senility: Myth or Madness?" In *AGE Page* (NIA fact sheet), October 1980.
Schmeck, Harold M., Jr. "Research Attempts to Fight Senility." *New York Times,* 28 August 1979.
Lancaster, Jane B., and Whitten, Phillip. "Family Matters." *The Sciences,* January 1980.
Gould, Stephen Jay. "Mankind Stood Up First and Got Smart Later." *New York Times,* 22 April 1979.
National Institute on Aging. "Osteoporosis and Vitamin K." In *Special Report on Aging: 1979.* Washington, D.C.: NIH Publication No. 79-1907, September 1979.
Brody, Jane E. "Personal Health: Bone Loss Is Not Inevitable with Age." *New York Times,* 1 October 1980.
Tortora, Gerard J., and Anagnostakos, Nicholas P. *Principles of Anatomy & Physiology.* 2nd ed. New York: Harper & Row, 1978.
American Council of Life Insurance. *Life Insurance Fact Book: 1978.* Washington, D.C.: American Council of Life Insurance, 1978.

CHAPTER 8

Diet, Sex, and Genes

Eating Habits

Belloc, Nedra B., and Breslow, Lester. "Relationship of Physical Health Status and Health Practices." *Preventive Medicine* 1 (1972): 409–421.

Belloc, Nedra B. "Relationship of Health Practices and Mortality." *Preventive Medicine* 2 (1973): 67–81.

Schoenborn, Charlotte A., and Danchik, Kathleen M. "Health Practices Among Adults: United States, 1977." For The National Center for Health Statistics, U.S. Department of Health and Human Services. H.H.S. Publication No. (PHS) 81–1250, 4 November 1980. Survey of 110,000 persons found that one-quarter of Americans do not eat breakfast, 38 percent snack between meals, 58 percent were overweight, and only 24 percent were within desirable weight.

Sheraton, Mimi. "Conflicting Nutrition Advice Bewilders U.S. Consumers." *New York Times,* 20 March 1979.

Drinking

Associated Press. "Doctors Say Moderate Drinking May Be Healthy in Some Cases." *New York Times,* 21 June 1978. A report on the annual meeting of the American Medical Association.

Darby, William J. "The Benefits of Drink." *Human Nature,* November 1978.

Brody, Jane E. "A Few Drinks May Help Curb Heart Attacks." *New York Times,* 20 March 1979.

———. "Protein That Lowers Heart Risk Tied to Moderate Drinking and Exercise." *New York Times,* 13 November 1980.

Marx, Jean L. "The HDL: The Good Cholesterol Carriers?" *Science,* 17 August 1979.

Sex

Brody, Jane E. "Survey of Aged Reveals Liberal Views on Sex." *New York Times,* 22 April 1980. Report on the Starr-Weiner study.

National Institute on Aging. *Special Report on Aging: 1978.* Washington, D.C.: NIH Publication No. 78-1538.

Frank, Ellen, and Anderson, Carol. "Sex and the Happily Married." *The Sciences,* July/August 1979.

Masters, William H., and Johnson, Virginia E. "Human Sexual Response: The Aging Female and the Aging Male." In *Middle Age and Aging,* edited by Bernice L. Neugarten. Chicago: University of Chicago Press, 1968.

Genetic

Rose, Charles L. "Critique of Longevity Studies." In *Prediction of Lifespan,* edited by Erdman B. Palmore and Francis C. Jeffers. Lexington, Mass.: Heath Lexington Books, 1971.

Sacher, George A. "The Role of Physiological Fluctuations in the Aging Process and the Relation of Longevity to the Size of the Central Nervous System." In *Aging and Levels of Biological Organization,* edited by Austin M. Brues and George A. Sacher. Chicago: University of Chicago Press, 1965.

Brody, Jane E. "Genetic Explanation Offered for Women's Health Superiority." *New York Times,* 29 January 1980.

CHAPTER 9

Profiles

Palmore, Erdman B., and Stone, Virginia. "Predictors of Longevity: A Follow-Up of the Aged in Chapel Hill." *The Gerontologist,* spring 1973.

CHAPTER 10

Chance

Bolitho, William. *Twelve against the Gods.* 2d ed. New York: Viking Press, 1957.

CHAPTER 12

Character Facets: The Road Taken

Erikson, Erik H. *Childhood and Society.* 2d ed. New York: W. W. Norton, 1963.

CHAPTER 13

In Absentia

Carr, Arthur C., and Schoenberg, Bernard. "Object-Loss and Somatic Symptom Formation." In *Loss and Grief: Psychological Management in Medical Practice,* edited by Bernard Schoenberg, Arthur C. Carr, David Peretz, and Austin H. Kutscher. New York: Columbia University Press, 1970. The study cited for the greater mortality of widows and widowers is "Mortality of Bereavement," by W. D. Rees and S. G. Lutkins, in *British Medical Journal,* 4 (1967): 13.

CHAPTER 14

Rosetta Stones

Wren, Christopher S. "Soviet Centenarians Say It's Diet, Work and Family—Not Yogurt." *New York Times,* 9 September 1977. Dr. Nikita B. Mankovsky, deputy director of the Kiev Institute of Gerontology is quoted as saying: "We should note that physical activity that began at ten years old was connected with positive emotions. The person made things and he was happy."

CHAPTER 15

Will

Taylor, Richard, ed. *The Will to Live: Selected Writings of Arthur Schopenhauer.* New York: Ungar, 1962.
Hutschnecker, Arnold A. *The Will To Live.* New York: Cornerstone Library, 1975 (paperback); Englewood Cliffs, N.J.: Prentice-Hall, 3d ed., 1966.

CHAPTER 16

Conclusion

Cousins, Norman. Interview with Dick Cavett on PBS (WMHT-TV, Albany, N.Y.), 14 January 1980.

————. *Anatomy of an Illness as Perceived by the Patient.* New York: W. W. Norton, 1979.

Selye, Hans. *The Stress of Life.* New York: McGraw-Hill, 1956.

————. "Stress and Aging." *Journal of the American Geriatrics Society,* September 1970.

————. *Stress without Distress.* Philadelphia: J. B. Lippincott, 1974.

————. *The Stress of My Life.* New York. Van Nostrand Reinhold, 1979.

Friedman, Meyer. "Type A Behavior: A Progress Report." *The Sciences,* February 1980.

Mind-Body Research or Brain/Nerve Chemistry

Cannon, Walter B. " 'Voodoo' Death." *American Anthropologist,* April-June 1942. Death is brought about by hyperactivity of the sympathetic nervous system.

Richter, Curt P. "On the Phenomenon of Sudden Death in Animals and Man." *Psychosomatic Medicine* 19 (1957): 191–98. Death is brought about by overstimulation of the parasympathetic nervous system.

Lex, Barbara W. "Voodoo Death: New Thoughts on an Old Explanation." *American Anthropologist* 76 (1974): 818–23. Death occurs after the breakdown of the reciprocal relationship of the sympathetic and parasympathetic nervous systems and simultaneous excitations in both systems.

Guillemin, Roger, and Burgus, Roger. "The Hormones of the Hypothalamus." *Scientific American,* November 1972.

Axelrod, Julius. "The Pineal Gland: A Neurochemical Transducer." *Science,* 28 June 1974.

Edelson, Edward. "Discovery of Brain Hormones a Giant Step for Doctors." *New York News,* 22 June 1975.

Strand, Fleur L. "The Influence of Hormones on the Nervous System." *Bioscience,* September 1975.

Finch, Caleb E. "Neuroendocrinology of Aging: A View of an Emerging Area." *Bioscience,* October 1975.

Schmeck, Harold M., Jr. "Opiate-Like Substances in Brain May Hold Clue to Pain and Mood." *New York Times,* 2 October 1977.

Edson, Lee. "4,000 Scientists in California Find the Universe in the Brain. They Confirmed the Notion at Last Week's Meeting That the Brain Can Only Be Understood Through Chemistry." *New York Times,* 13 November 1977.

Gutstein, William H., et al. "Neural Factors Contribute to Atherogenesis." *Science,* 27 January 1978.

Goldstein, Avram. "Endorphins." *The Sciences,* March 1978.

Wade, Nicholas. "Guillemin and Schally: The Years in the Wilderness (The first of three articles describing the history of the pursuit of the brain's hormones by Roger Guillemin and Andrew Schally)." *Science,* 21 April 1978.

————. "Guillemin and Schally: The Three-Lap Race to Stockholm." *Science,* 28 April 1978.

————. "Guillemin and Shally: A Race Spurred by Rivalry." *Science,* 5 May 1978.

Guillemin, Roger. "Peptides in the Brain: The Endocrinology of the Neuron." *Science,* 27 October 1978. The text of his Nobel-Prize lecture, delivered 8 December 1977.

Landfield, P. W.; Waymire, J. C.; Lynch, G. "Hippocampal Aging and Adrenocorticoids: Quantitative Correlations." *Science,* 8 December 1978.

Schmeck, Harold M., Jr. "Chemical Links Found between Body Functions and Behavior." *New York Times,* 29 May 1979.

Krieger, Dorothy T., and Liotta, Anthony S. "Pituitary Hormones in Brain: Where, How, and Why?" *Science,* 27 July 1979.

Benson, Herbert. *The Mind/Body Effect.* New York: Simon & Schuster, 1979.

Marx, Jean L. "Brain Peptides: Is Substance P a Transmitter of Pain Signals?" *Science,* 31 August 1979.

Sobel, Dava. "In Pursuit of Love: Three Current Studies." *New York Times,* 22 January 1980. The loving brain pours out its own chemical correlate to amphetamine—phenylethylamine.

Cherry, Laurence. "How the Mind Affects Our Health." *New York Times Magazine,* 23 November 1980.

Stress

Benson, Herbert. "Your Innate Asset for Combating Stress." *Harvard Business Review,* July-August 1974. A concise presentation of the "relaxation response."

————. *The Relaxation Response.* New York: William Morrow, 1975.

Timiras, P. S. *Developmental Physiology and Aging.* New York: Macmillan, 1972. Discussion of stress, pages 543–47, 605.

Dohrenwend, Barbara Snell, and Dohrenwend, Bruce P., eds. *Stressful Life Events.* New York: Wiley-Interscience, 1974. Papers from a conference in New York in June 1973.

Gunderson, Eric, and Rahe, Richard H., eds. *Life Stress and Illness.* Springfield, Ill.: Charles C. Thomas, 1974. Papers from a symposium held in Beito, Norway, in June 1972.

Hicks, Nancy. "Family Stress Called a Menace to Health." *New York Times,* 19 October 1976. Harvard public-health researcher Robert J. Haggerty says that "accidents and abuse have been shown to be two to three times as common in families with frequent moves, recent deaths, and evidence of social dysfunction, such as unmarried mothers, marital problems, unemployment."

Rabkin, Judith G., and Struening, Elmer L. "Life Events, Stress, and Illness." *Science,* 3 December 1976. Presents the history and interrelationships of research into stress, life events and psychosomatic medicine, and their relationship to illness.

Antelman, Seymour M., and Caggiula, Anthony R. "Norepinephrine-Dopamine Interactions and Behavior: A New Hypothesis of Stress-related Interactions between Brain Norepinephrine and Dopamine Proposed." *Science,* 18 February 1977.

Peters, Michael. "Hypertension and the Nature of Stress." *Science,* 7 October 1977.

Friedman, Richard, and Iwai, Junichi. *Science,* 7 October 1977. Comment on Peters's article, above.

"Brain vs. Heart." *New York Times,* 12 December 1978. Dr. James Kinner of the Baylor College of Medicine reports several recent investigations indicate that fatal heart attacks where there is no evidence of physical impairment may be caused by stress recognized by the brain and communicated to the heart. Some of the most common causes of stress he cited: marital strife, job insecurity, and bereavement.

"Tender Loving Care." *New York Times,* 18 September 1979. Researchers at Ohio State University found that rabbits given ordinary care had twice as much atherosclerosis as rabbits given tender loving care. "The researchers said they could offer no immediate explanation. However, the result was consistent with other studies that have shown stress to be a factor accelerating heart disease. The rabbits that received tender care presumably felt less stress than those that did not."

"Study Explains Tears of Sorrow." *New York Times,* 15 January 1980. William H. Frey II, a biochemist in the department of psychiatry at St. Paul-Ramsey Medical Center in Minnesota is studying the hypothesis that tears of anguish help rid the body of chemicals produced by stress.

"Death by Fright." *Time,* 24 March 1980. Pathologists Marilyn Cebe-

lin and Charles Hirsch reviewed autopsies of fifteen assault victims
whose deaths could not be attributed to their physical injuries. The
researchers reported in *Human Pathology* that eleven of the people
had lesions in the heart similar to the ones that develop in experimental animals subjected to great stress. The pathologists concluded that the victims died of fright.

Holden, Constance. "Behavioral Medicine: An Emergent Field."
Science, 25 July 1980. A new approach to health and illness, syn-
thesizing the findings of stress theory, psychosomatic medicine,
neuroendocrinology, and behavioral medicine—the holistic approach advocated by Dr. Herbert Benson in *The Mind/Body Effect.*
A fundamental tenet of behavioral medicine is that the patient is
responsible for his own well-being and must be an active participant
in his treatment.

National Institutes of Health. *To Understand the Aging Process: The
Baltimore Longitudinal Study of the National Institute on Aging.*
Washington, D.C.: DHEW Publication No. NIH 78-134, 1978.
Among other information about the longitudinal study, this publi-
cation reports on the research that found a decline with age in the
number of hormone receptors.

Index